THE
FIGHT
FOR
INFLUENCE

**ALEXEY
MALASHENKO**

THE
FIGHT
FOR
INFLUENCE
RUSSIA IN CENTRAL ASIA

CARNEGIE
ENDOWMENT FOR
INTERNATIONAL PEACE

Carnegie Endowment for International Peace
1779 Massachusetts Avenue NW
Washington, DC 20036
P+ 202 483 7600
F+ 202 483 1840
CarnegieEndowment.org

The Carnegie Endowment does not take institutional positions on public policy issues; the views represented here are the author's own and do not necessarily reflect the views of Carnegie, its staff, or its trustees.

To order, contact:
Hopkins Fulfillment Service
P.O. Box 50370
Baltimore, MD 21211-4370
P+ 1 800 537 5487 or 1 410 516 6956
F+ 1 410 516 6998

Cover design by Jocelyn Soly
Composition by Cutting Edge Design
Printed by United Book Press

Library of Congress Cataloging-in-Publication Data

Malashenko, A. V. (Aleksei Vsevolodovich), author.
  [TSentral'naia Aziia. English]
  The fight for influence : Russia in Central Asia / Alexey Malashenko.
    pages cm
  Translation of: TSentral'naia Aziia : na chto rasschityvaet Rossiia? / Aleksei Malashenko. Moskva : ROSSPEN (Rossiiskaia politicheskaia entsiklopediia) : Moskovskii tsentr Karnegi, 2012.
  ISBN 978-0-87003-411-4 (pbk.) -- ISBN 978-0-87003-412-1 (cloth) -- ISBN 978-0-87003-413-8 (electronic) 1. Russia (Federation)--Foreign relations--Asia, Central. 2. Asia, Central--Foreign relations--Russia (Federation) 3. Asia, Central--Strategic aspects. 4. Security, International--Asia, Central. 5. Muslims--Asia, Central. I. Title.

  DK857.75.R8M358 2013
  327.47058--dc23

                    2013025266

CONTENTS

FOREWORD

Russia has lost much of the power and influence that the Soviet Union once enjoyed. Moscow's efforts to position itself as a leader among its neighboring states and to hold on to the remnants of the post-Soviet space have largely failed. Central Asia, once firmly in the Soviet Union's sphere, is increasingly out of the Kremlin's reach, and the United States and China have filled the void as Russian influence has faded.

Yet, Central Asia remains integral to Russia's national interests, and Moscow wants to strengthen its position there. For the Kremlin, the region is the last best hope for restoring Russia's status as a global political actor. Moscow agrees with many of the Central Asian regimes' policies, and the region provides important transit routes for Russia's energy resources. And by elevating its position in Central Asia, the Kremlin aims to contain the influence of outsiders and to strive for balance between the East and the West.

Will Russia be able to establish itself as the dominant power in Central Asia? Alexey Malashenko, a seasoned Central Asia expert, offers some answers. *The Fight for Influence: Russia in Central Asia*, the culmination of years of research, offers unique insights into Russia's interests and actions in the region.

Malashenko argues that Russia has sufficient economic and political potential to maintain some influence. But it cannot bring the entire region under its umbrella and will have to accept the fact that its power in Central Asia is declining. Instead of attempting to rebuild the vestiges of Soviet power, it must focus on solving real problems and crafting a cohesive strategic approach to the region.

According to Malashenko's analysis, it is clear that this adjustment will require Moscow to recognize that it is dealing not with post-Soviet republics but with new and independent states. That means Moscow will have to build partnerships based on mutual interests with each individual country rather than relying on common ideology.

Russia needs to develop a modern, dynamic Central Asia policy. This is a qualitatively new age of politics in the former Soviet space. It will soon be clear whether Russia's ruling establishment is capable of understanding this new landscape and acting accordingly.

— Dmitri Trenin
Director
Carnegie Moscow Center

INTRODUCTION

Central Asia can hardly be called one of Russia's greater foreign policy priorities, all the more so with Russian influence in the region on the decline. Russia still faces its old strategic dilemma of choosing between West and East, but if what constitutes the "West" is clear enough, "East" seems a rather vague concept. "East" could perhaps better be defined in Russian strategic terms as "non-West," a notion that at once embraces China, the Asia-Pacific region and India, and even to some extent the entire BRIC group.[1] This sort of choice between two global political, economic, and cultural directions is always relative rather than absolute in nature, and it is never a clear-cut and unconditional choice of strictly one or the other. At the same time, however, one cannot clearly define one's place in regional politics without first settling on one's role globally.

The post-Soviet space has been drawn into this "bipolar choice": it is not "the East" in the fullest sense of the term, but it is also definitely not "the West." This accounts for Central Asia's auxiliary and even secondary status as part of both "the East" and the post-Soviet space, which applies throughout the entire post-Soviet territory. Russia's activities in the region have centered on ways to integrate relations with it into Russian-European, Russian-Chinese, or Russian-Muslim relations. Economically, the region is of importance only in terms of providing energy transit routes. At the psychological level, however, the region is the last remaining part of an ecumenical sphere where the Kremlin still enjoys the feeling of being a political leader, albeit ever more rarely and with ever greater reservations. Moscow seriously believes the view that a "suite" of satellites elevates its status as a global political actor in the eyes of both East and West.

Kazakhstan has its own privileged position. Unlike the rest of the Central Asian region, it is self-sufficient, even prosperous. Its stability was shaken after deadly riots in Zhanaozen in 2011, which became emblematic of the country's overall social and economic deterioration and failures of its political system. Still, while not immune from the general Islamization trend, Kazakhstan has managed to escape social and religious turmoil and avoid internal religious conflicts. Moreover, it enjoys particularly close relations with Russia. The two countries have similar economic and political systems, and the Kazakh president's friendly attitude toward Vladimir Putin, initially the prime minister and then once again (since 2012) the Russian president, has strengthened the ties. In fact, Putin's efforts to establish the Eurasian Union and the Common Economic Area (CEA) were based primarily on relations between Russia and Kazakhstan. Belarus, being totally financially dependent upon Moscow, has had little choice but to go along with and participate in these organizations; the same could be said of Kyrgyzstan. However, the establishment of these two institutions will not likely radically change Russia's standing in Central Asia.

As Zbigniew Brzezinski wrote at the end of the last century, although Russia is too weak politically to completely close the region to outside forces, it is too poor economically to develop the region on its own.[2] The start of the twenty-first century has brought nothing new to this: Russia still lacks the strength and the means to establish an economic or political monopoly in the region.

What has defined and shaped Russian interests in Central Asia? Or, to put it more simply, what does Russia want from the region?

First, Russia wants to retain its influence as part of its plan to strive to keep the remnants of the post-Soviet space under its own supervision.

Second, it wants to protect the authoritarian regimes in the region, which are similar in outlook and perception to the regime in Russia itself.

Third, it wants to minimize potential losses from the shift of energy resource transit routes away from its own territory.

Fourth, it wants to stem the trafficking of narcotics, insofar as this is possible.

Fifth, it wants to contain outsiders in the region (above all China and the United States) and to strive for balance between competition and partnership with them, while simultaneously doing what it can to keep them out of the region.

This list does not mention stability, since that is *not* one of Russia's unwavering strategic demands for the region. Although the Kremlin has repeatedly stressed its commitment to stability, Russia nevertheless finds shaky situations more in its interests, as the inherent potential for local or regional conflict creates a highly convenient excuse for persuading the governments of the region to seek help from Russia in order to survive. In Afghanistan, for instance, it is clear that Moscow's best option for preserving its influence in the region is for the country to remain unstable. That is why while expressing support for the U.S.-led coalition there, Russia is not involved in resolving the Afghan crisis.

There is also no mention in the list of any concern for the almost 6 million Russians in Central Asia whom Russia has left to their fates. In the Kremlin's eyes, by ignoring this group's interests and displaying the inability (or rather the unwillingness) to guarantee them decent security and living conditions, Russia gains something of a political card that it can play in its game with the local elites. Russia has almost never used the "Russian issue" as a means for exerting political pressure on its southern neighbors. Although it would be difficult to imagine a sovereign country such as Britain, France, or Portugal, say, ignoring the plight of its ethnic kin abroad, Russia's model for politics in the Central Asian region leaves no room for the interests of Russians living there. Indeed, Moscow has been unable to protect the interests of ethnic Russians even on its own soil in the North Caucasus. However, the defenselessness of the Russians in these countries could turn tragic in the aftermath of social and political upheavals, especially those of a religious political nature.

What can Russia do in Central Asia? Will it be able to pursue and protect its national interests in the region? Since Russia has not yet managed to clearly and rationally express its national interests, they are often interpreted emotionally and hearken back to some recent historic memory. In their statements on the actions of their Central Asian partners, Russian politicians have expressed not only outrage, but sometimes even aggressive anger directed at the outside forces operating in the region.

So what can Russia hope to achieve in the region? First, even though in its new and weakened form, Russia cannot be a presence in Central Asia, it wants to be able to maintain its influence there—and it has the economic and political capability to do so. However, it must be recognized that such influence would remain concentrated primarily in just two or three countries; Russia will not be able to bring the entire region under its umbrella. And as its influence grows in one country, it could diminish in another. It will be forced to accept an overall decrease in its influence in the Central Asian region and to concentrate on realistic tasks and objectives.

In order to reassert itself in Central Asia, Russia will need to recognize that it is now dealing not with post-Soviet republics, but with new and independent countries, each with its own aspirations and each setting priorities based on its own national interests and foreign policy. Russia will need to determine just what sort of countries these are. This will be possible only if a non-biased approach is taken that combines recent political experience with centuries of accumulated academic and human knowledge about the region (for which there is currently precious little demand).

Russia must also understand that Central Asian leaders sometimes worry about its intentions in the region. And rather than look toward Moscow for a model, these leaders can look to the West, with its prosperity, quality of life, and advanced technology, and to the Muslim world, with its principles of social justice, morality, ethics, and an ideal state and social order. Where does Russia fit into these models?

Second, Russia can continue to support the authoritarian model of rule that will persist in Central Asia in any case, even without Moscow's help. The experience of four of the region's five countries demonstrates that authoritarianism in the region is becoming more rigid in nature and is showing little inclination of transforming into the kind of semi-authoritarian regimes that "allow little real competition for power" but "leave enough political space for political parties and organizations of civil society."[3] The past decade has brought no transition toward a semi-authoritarian government.

However, the region's regimes are certainly grateful to Moscow for not having meddled in their internal affairs—it has studiously avoided interacting with opposition groups and figures in neighboring countries—and for having supported them at critical moments. (Of course, such sensitive issues as civil society, democracy, and human rights are not on the agenda in discussions between Russia and the Central Asian countries.) The main goal for Russia has long since ceased being to support local authoritarian regimes merely because they are similar to Moscow's own model. The task has now become being an important ally and partner of each individual country. The extent of Moscow's cooperation is determined by each country's specific interests, specifically drawing up common economic and political goals, and establishing contacts with the region's new rulers (and, more broadly, with the groups now on their way into power).

Third, since it will not be possible to continue with the status quo in the energy transit sector, Russia should participate to the greatest possible extent in projects to build new pipeline routes that bypass its territory. In Tajikistan, for example, Russia hopes to take part in large-scale energy projects, which incidentally would help keep Tajikistan within its sphere of influence. In Kyrgyzstan, there is Russian participation in all of the major projects under way. However, in Turkmenistan, a falling-out over gas sales created an opening for China, which is becoming the main purchaser of gas from Turkmenistan. One pipeline to China was opened in 2009, and work has begun on a second one.

Although this is a very complicated and sensitive area, if Russia does not take part in large-scale energy projects, it could end up being isolated due to energy transit route diversification. Much here will depend not merely on economic interests, but also on political trustworthiness, which Russia has gradually been losing.

Fourth, Russia does have the capability to restrict the import and transit of narcotics through its territory. This problem has continued to grow, with Russia being both a main link in the transit of drugs to markets in the West and, gradually, a market in its own right. Although the desire to interdict trafficking in drugs has been a prime motivator for cooperation between the Central Asian countries and outside actors, such cooperation continues to be largely formal in nature. Many people depend upon the cultivation of narcotic plants for their livelihood, which complicates the situation.

Fifth, at the level of long-term strategy, Russia can and should optimize its relations with the main outside actors. China and the United States have moved to fill the void resulting from Russia's waning influence in Central Asia and are happy with their common divided responsibility for the situation in the region.

Tajikistan is an example of their increased involvement in Central Asia. With investments in Tajikistan including 63 projects that total $2.3 billion, China has become Tajikistan's largest investor. The United States, meanwhile, plans to double the amount of military aid that it gives to Tajikistan, and the coming withdrawal of coalition troops from Afghanistan makes U.S.-Tajik strategic military and political cooperation increasingly important.

For politics in Central Asia to be "modernized," Moscow will need to improve its political capabilities and strike a reasonable balance between maintaining bilateral relations (which should remain a priority) and using existing or new organizations both within the region and beyond. All such international organizations eventually get put to the test (never an easy process), and by no means will all of them turn out to be effective or even viable.

A relatively new factor in relations between Russia and Central Asia is migration, which binds both sides together—Russia's economy is dependent on migrant workers, and the money these workers send home makes up a large share of their countries' GDP—but at the same time creates reciprocal problems by contributing to feelings of irritation and rejection on both sides of the border. Local crises, unemployment, and the lack of land and water are the primary reasons for migration from the Central Asian countries to Russia.

Precise data are not available on how many Central Asian migrants are working in Russia, because most enter the country illegally. The number of Kyrgyz citizens working in Russia is variously estimated in the hundreds of thousands, and these workers' remittances total $2 billion a year—a figure that, if correct, is larger than the entire $1.8 billion national budget. According to the Tajikistan Migration Control Directorate, more than 1 million Tajiks were working in Russia at the end of 2011; they sent nearly $3 billion home, which amounts to nearly half of Tajikistan's GDP. Up to a third of the Uzbek working population travels abroad to work (mostly to Russia); together these workers send back what has been estimated as 15 to 59 percent of the Uzbek GDP.

No discussion of Russia's relations with its former republics in Central Asia would be complete without a mention of the Islamic factor. It was assumed in the 1990s that ties to the Soviet past would be sufficient for former Soviet republics to withstand a rising influence on the state by Islam. However, that turned out not to be the case. The revival of Islam across Central Asia began almost immediately after the dissolution of the Soviet Union and has only gained momentum as totalitarian regimes have faltered. Over the past two decades, the Islamic renaissance has been to various degees intense and politicized, depending on the country. Re-Islamization has particularly taken hold in Tajikistan, both as an important factor of socialization and an instrument of state policy, and its influence is growing in Uzbekistan. In the process, both states have abandoned the Soviet legacy. Elsewhere in Central Asia, identifying with Russia has also become problematic. In Kyrgyzstan, politicians are increasingly appealing to Islam. Kazakhstan has avoided the organized Islamic activities that have occurred elsewhere, but it, too, is being drawn into the Islamization trend. In Turkmenistan, Islam has not become politicized but the country can hardly ignore changes occurring in the rest of the Muslim world.

The Central Asian countries are both subjects and objects in intra-regional politics. In the view of Evan Feigenbaum, deputy aide to the U.S. secretary of state for Southern and Central Asia, the Central Asian countries today face a strategic choice.[4] In reality, however, they have already made their choice, and it is not to link their futures to a single partner. Their choice is one of pursuing a multivectoral policy that involves maintaining and developing relations with several centers of economic, political, and military gravity, including China, Russia, the United States, and also Europe and the Muslim world. None of these centers will acquire absolute priority, and the main strategic task for each of the Central Asian governments will be to maintain a convenient balance among the various foreign partners. Since the breakup of the Soviet Union, its former republics have sought new partners outside Russian dominance, while not forfeiting its economic and political support.

Strategic partnership with the Central Asian countries will depend on the internal political and regional situations, which, as the last decade has shown, can change substantially.

Russian policy in the former Soviet region has entered a fundamentally new stage. Time will soon tell if the Russian establishment has realized this and will be able to respond appropriately.

CHAPTER 1

WASTED OPPORTUNITIES

RUSSIAN PRESENCE AND IDEOLOGY

The main priority for Russia's policies in Central Asia has been to preserve and strengthen the Russian presence and influence in the region. The same is true for its policies toward certain other parts of the former Soviet Union—Belarus, Moldova, Ukraine, and perhaps Armenia, although the remaining former Soviet republics have gone their own way so irreversibly that even the most ardent would-be restorers of the Soviet Union realize that there is little they would be able to do now. These ideas of "presence" and "influence" should be considered as being distinct from each other. "Presence" reflects Russia's desire to remain involved in Central Asia and take part in the affairs of the Central Asian region. This could be called an attempt to reconstruct history, that is to say, to restore a former common space and pursue neo-imperialist plans. However, recapturing the past will not be possible, if only because none of the former republics would now be willing to give up its independence. Furthermore, Russia has neither the strength nor the means to incorporate any of them into its own fold, which would imply, apart from anything else, that the already very fragile system of international relations would again need to be reorganized.

Russia has long since abandoned any real imperialist ideology, and its sporadic aggressive outbursts are intended to express disapproval of the behavior of its now foreign neighbors rather than claims on their territory. Still, Central Asian leaders at times worry about Russia's intentions in the region. Commenting on the Russian and Belarusian plans to form a union state in the late 1990s, Uzbek President Islam Karimov said that "establishing a union of this sort is the strategic objective of strong-state communists and national patriots, who want to then use the Russia-Belarus union to make Ukraine join as well, and then use this so-called 'Slavic union' as a base for dictating their will to the other sovereign states in the post-Soviet space."[1]

Influence and presence are not the same thing. Presence exists or does not exist. Influence is mobile. It can strengthen and weaken. Russia's policy toward its former Soviet neighbors can be seen only in the context of influence. Thus, Moscow and the other outside actors in the region are all on a level playing field.

It is common in Russia to use the term "near abroad" to refer to the country's neighbors. The "near abroad" in modern Russian parlance means the same thing as the post-Soviet space, a term that would perhaps best be abandoned as a description of Russia's nearest neighbors, especially because Finland and Mongolia, for example, are not covered by the term, although, in contrast to Kyrgyzstan, Moldova, and Uzbekistan, they share a border with Russia. "The post-Soviet space, for all the contradictions in the processes under way there, does not meet the criteria that would make it possible to define it as transnational political space."[2] A good example of the arbitrary nature of the post-Soviet space concept is the Commonwealth of Independent States. The CIS was created for the purpose of achieving a "civilized divorce" and cannot be used as an instrument for integrating the former Soviet republics. As a political institution, the CIS has become an "optional" presidents' club, which each is free to leave for any reason whatsoever, most commonly to pursue a multivectored foreign policy and establish alternative foreign ties. It could be said that the CIS continues to exist only because it really does not bother anyone. Its existence depends entirely on Russia, which is not in a position now to be either leader or even arbitrator in the post-Soviet space. Moscow does not issue orders; more often, it tries to persuade its neighbors.

At the same time, however, "the examples of military intervention in Abkhazia, Chechnya, Tajikistan, and Transnistria have made some Central Asians fear that Russia may provoke conflict in order to put pressure on the newly independent states."³ Fear of Russian intervention became especially strong after the five-day Russian-Georgian war in 2008. Rumors of impending conflict between Russia and Ukraine over the Black Sea Fleet's base spread in late 2008. For a brief time, there was even talk that Russia and Kazakhstan could potentially clash over discrimination against the Russian population in Kazakhstan. Kazakhstan's president, Nursultan Nazarbayev, made a statement shortly after the Russian-Georgian war in which he declared that the principle of territorial integrity is recognized by the entire international community. The conflict over Nagorno-Karabakh has damaged Russia's influence. Both parties in the conflict are members of the CIS and continue military technical cooperation with Russia. Russia is faced with the same situation in Central Asia, where it has ceased to be the leader in resolving key issues such as water resource distribution and, as the events in Kyrgyzstan in 2010 showed, it cannot act alone to ensure security and stability in the region.

Central Asia, like the other former Soviet republics, is a new space made up of previously unknown states with which the Russian Federation, also new in its existence as a separate state, is in the process of building relations. In terms of economic, diplomatic, and demographic weight, Russia is the successor to the Soviet Union only in an increasingly formal sense. A new Russian identity is starting to take shape and is still in a state of crisis. In its new and weakened form, Russia cannot be a presence in Central Asia, although it still has enough potential to have an influence in the region.

As throughout the former Soviet area, Russia has been fighting in Central Asia not only to protect its influence, but also for this influence to be recognized, which is equally important for building relations with the rest of the world, especially China and the United States. Most political theorists acknowledge, in particular, that Russia has "a key political role to play."⁴ This is just as important for Russia as its economic and political interests. Recognition of Russia's interests and the legitimacy of its claims are directly connected to the country's image abroad. Russia has gone from being a superpower to becoming no more than an oil and gas appendage for Europe, and soon for China as well; it has dropped to the rank of a second-rate science and technology power, and it has lost its influence in Europe, the Middle East, South Asia, and other places, all of which makes a positive international image all the more valuable for the country. Russia's elite may lose influence at home unless the country can maintain an image of strength and authority abroad. It is not by chance that when Vladimir Putin came to power, he became so attentive to the issue of Russia's image abroad. Speaking on the topic of Russia's negative post-Soviet image, Sergei Yastrzhembsky, then Putin's special representative in relations with the European Union, said, "The national image is a serious undertaking that will require a lot more than just one-off services from information agencies to fix."[5]

Important as it is, image needs to be based upon a solid foundation and material support of some kind. A negative economic, social, and political climate cannot form the basis for building a respectable international image. Out of 178 countries, Russia is currently ranked 65 on the human development index, 136 in the peacefulness ranking (the war against Georgia had an impact there), 75 on the social development index, 71 for attractiveness of life, 111 for the quality of its roads, and, finally, 172 on the "happiness index."[6]

Most people in Central Asia probably have little idea of these rankings, and in any case, their own countries' rankings are probably no higher than Russia's, and indeed are more likely even lower. Whatever the case, Russia is not seen in the region as a success story, all the more so as migrant workers returning home have little flattering to say about life there. The Eurasian Monitor project, however, offers some interesting figures: 49 percent of the Russian population say they are happy with their lives and 45 percent are not happy, while in Kazakhstan the figures are 72 percent happy and 27 percent not happy.[7]

NEW ROLE MODELS

Russia today cannot fulfill the civilizing mission it played in the mid-nineteenth century. Today's models for Central Asia are the West on the one hand and the Muslim world on the other, but even their influence and attractiveness are only relative and cannot be imitated to the letter. The attractiveness of the West derives from its prosperity, quality of life, and advanced technology, while Islamic tradition offers a chance to form an identity as part of a great civilization based upon principles of social justice, morality, ethics, and an ideal state and social order. Belonging to the Islamic civilization is compensation for Western superiority and helps to overcome the "little brother" complex that developed in Central Asia with regard to the Russians over the decades of Soviet rule and was transferred to its relations with the United States and Europe after the Soviet collapse.

Russia has no place in this dichotomy. It cannot position itself as a great power, and it has ceased to be the West's equal in the global political arena. Unlike the Islamic world, it cannot challenge the West (or take up the West's challenge), and it has not been able to propose an original alternative development path. True, Russia retains a relatively central place in the policies of the Central Asian countries. But it does not represent an ideal for these countries and is not the model they would choose to emulate as they strive to achieve success in everything from economic reform to developing civil and cultural value systems.

Like the other players in the region, Russia is faced with the question of whether to treat all of Central Asia as a single region. The very notion of "Central Asia" increasingly appears as a relic of the past, which, although certainly rooted in history and geography, is far from homogeneous and covers very different cultural and political environments: "There is no 'Central Asia' or other common territorial entity."[8] The culture and way of life of nomadic peoples, for example, differed greatly from that of the settled peoples of the Ferghana Valley; independent states have emerged and vanished. The only thing that really unites today's Central Asia is its almost continuous "colonial past" as a region that was repeatedly invaded by powerful neighbors who tried to keep its lands under their control. It became part of the Russian Empire in the nineteenth century and remained a part of the Soviet Union after the Russian Empire fell. Since Soviet political terminology was unable to find a suitable common definition for the whole region, Soviet textbooks and historical works referred to "Central Asia and Kazakhstan."

More than twenty years after the Soviet collapse, Central Asia can be spoken of only as a conglomerate of independent countries, each in the process of forming its own national interests and foreign policy priorities. There are practically no consolidated regional interests. Instead, there is talk of restoring the "Silk Road"; the need to resolve the water resource issue, which is important for all countries in the region; and the common threats that each country is essentially fighting on its own. Relations among the countries remain tense and periodically worsen as problems occur.

Since the borders between the countries are neither stable nor clearly defined, local conflicts flare up from time to time. A section of Uzbekistan's border with Tajikistan and Kazakhstan has been sown with land mines for many years. In 2000, Turkmenistan opened 21 new border checkpoints in the Tashauz and Lebap districts on its border with Uzbekistan and increased the number of border guards by 500.[9] At about the same time, Kazakhstan and Uzbekistan deployed new border guard units along their common border. The situation has been exacerbated by the interethnic tension that erupted in a bloody conflict in 2010 between the Uzbeks and Kyrgyz of southern Kyrgyzstan, after which Uzbekistan closed its side of the border for eighteen months.

The latent instability in Central Asia, the conflict in Nagorno-Karabakh, the secession of Abkhazia and South Ossetia from Georgia, and the unresolved Transnistria issue can all be seen as part of the aftermath of the Soviet collapse.

COMMON INTERESTS

Of course, some circumstances bring the Central Asian countries together whether they like it or not, for example, the "threat from the south" (growing Islamic radicalism). Nevertheless, these circumstances have not contributed to political integration despite the numerous official declarations and international conferences and seminars devoted to such threats. Turkmenistan, for example, had been prepared to cooperate with Afghanistan no matter who was in power there. Without waiting for the situation there to stabilize, Ashgabat (with the support of foreign businesses) initiated construction of the Turkmenistan-Afghanistan-Pakistan-India (TAPI) gas pipeline. Incidentally, this project could be seen as providing indirect evidence that Turkmenistan had considered this a more reliable route than transit via Russia. In Tajikistan, one hears ever more frequently that the Afghan threat will not last forever, and that sooner or later the time will come to develop economic relations with Afghanistan.[10] The situation in Afghanistan has had no noticeable impact on Kazakhstan, where the talk of the foreign threat from the south has been essentially rhetorical in nature. Tashkent is probably most wary about developments in Afghanistan, considering the links that exist between local radicals from the Islamic Movement of Uzbekistan and the Taliban. At the regional level, there have been no appreciable independent efforts to counter Islamic radicalism. Most of the activity in this area has relied upon outside actors, chiefly Russia and the United States.

This lack of common regional interests has been reflected in the inability of the Central Asian countries to form regional organizations without needing to rely on outside participation. "Dependence on the center [that is, on Moscow] has given way to independence from both the center and from each other."[11] The Central Asian countries "clearly lack the strength to establish regional organizations that would fully meet their interests."[12] In the absence of mutual interests, selfishness has prevailed, and the countries hesitate to sacrifice their national interests for the sake of the common regional good. "It does not seem possible that between the Central Asian Republics a full integration will form in the near future," said Turkish analyst Esra Hatipoglu.[13] Tajik researcher Rashid Abdullo noted that the Central Asian countries "are only at the start of the road toward becoming national states" and pessimistically concluded that "it will be a good many years yet before they reach the point of carrying out any European-style integration."[14]

Over the past twenty years, any attempt to establish a new organization has always resulted in internal disagreements being brought out into the open and in leadership battles being set off. In 1998, Kazakh scholar Sanat Kushkumbayev wrote that "integration in Central Asia would depend, above all, on the positions of Kazakhstan and Uzbekistan."[15]

In August 1991, just before the Soviet Union collapsed, the leaders of the then Soviet Central Asian republics and Kazakhstan signed an agreement to establish a regional consultative council, and in 1993, based on the Uzbek-Kazakh agreement on measures to intensify economic integration over the period 1994–2000, made an attempt to organize interregional cooperation. These efforts gave rise to the Central Asian Union, which lasted until 1998. In 1997, Kazakhstan, Kyrgyzstan, and Uzbekistan signed a trilateral Agreement on Eternal Friendship, and in 2002, they signed an agreement setting up the Central Asian Cooperation Organization, which fell apart after the 2005 revolution in Kyrgyzstan without anyone really even noticing.

One would think that Moscow would have found it easier to preserve its influence in the region by playing on the contradictions among the former Soviet republics. However, the likelihood that they could be united under the aegis of Russia or that regional organizations could be established under Russian leadership has been steadily diminishing.

BILATERAL TIES

It would be a mistake to regard Russian policy in Central Asia as a unified whole. It is based primarily on bilateral ties, and although on the whole relations with Kazakhstan and Kyrgyzstan have been good enough, Russia has had its differences and even periodic conflict in its relations with the other countries and is therefore forced to approach each country individually.

According to Anna Matveeva, the Kremlin's Central Asian policy is more a reflection of "pragmatic opportunism" than "an attempt to revive the shared space."[16] This opinion is only partially valid, since this "pragmatic opportunism" is interlaced with ideological considerations. Another view has it that "Russia's policy toward the members of the CIS did not really evolve. It was characterized by bluster and a lack of realism. Russia came up with one harebrained scheme after another."[17]

Be that as it may, Russia will not be able to completely turn its back on the ideological residue of its Central Asia policy anytime soon, even though that complicates relations with the countries of the region. The main ideological precept here is a more or less veiled notion of the specific nature of the post-Soviet space and hence the privileged role that Russia has been called upon to play there. This view has two components: a veiled "post-Sovietism" and a Eurasian vision. In a presidential

decree of September 14, 1995, then president Boris Yeltsin called reintegration of the post-Soviet space around Russia "a top foreign policy
priority."[18] This was clearly a sincere statement from the Kremlin on the
future of the former Soviet territories. This view was never again formulated in such direct terms, especially after outside players became more
active and Russia simply did not have the strength to form the core of
any newly reintegrated parts of the former Soviet Union.

The stratagem, however, continued as a policy vector and ideological
component, albeit in truncated form. It was ultimately modified and
became part of a more neutral neo-Eurasian vision, which sought princi-
pally to provide the cultural and philosophical justification for Russia to
take the lead in Eurasia. Marlene Laruelle called it "a new pragmatic for-
mulation of 'Sovietism,' a substitute for the global explanatory schemes
of Marxism-Leninism."[19]

Neo-Eurasian ideologue Alexander Dugin put more pathos into his
words: "Russia is in the process of giving birth to a new Eurasian vision,
clearly destined to become the 'new Marxism' and new geopolitical
gospel."[20] By likening this Eurasian vision to a "new Marxism," Dugin
dismayed his potential partners, especially Muslims in Central Asia.
Appeals to a Eurasian vision in Russian policy have been instrumental in
nature, and to some extent not even a matter of choice, as policymakers
have not yet managed to come up with a more attractive ideology for
cooperation in the post-Soviet space.

Apart from Russia, neo-Eurasianism has spread in Kazakhstan and
to a lesser extent in Kyrgyzstan as well. From the perspective of the
Kazakh ruling class, Eurasianism would not be the same as recognizing a dominant role for Russia at all but would primarily provide a
foundation for the country's own identity and self-sufficiency. Kazakh
President Nazarbayev, who had begun to reflect on the new ideology
even before the Soviet Union had collapsed (which in his words "had
to happen sooner or later"[21]), remains Eurasianism's main proponent.
Speaking at Moscow State University in 1994, he proposed the idea of
establishing a Eurasian Union, and in 2011, addressing an audience at
the Lev Gumilyov Eurasian National University in Astana, he defined
Eurasianism as the "idea of the future and the jewel in the integration
crown."[22] Eurasianism is the most convenient ideology for Kazakhstan

and can also serve as a basis for the country's multivector policy. Nazarbayev's successors seem prepared to continue the Eurasian line, although without quite the same passion.

The ruling elites of the other Central Asian countries have been largely indifferent to Eurasianism and tend to perceive it as a tool of Russian policy. As for the common people, most have scarcely heard of the idea.

Eurasia is a geographical concept rather than a common cultural space, and, what is more, does not exist in the political sense. Proponents of Eurasianism argue that "within the context of Eurasian integration, the military strategic deterrent as a key part of geopolitical maneuvering could be reflected in intensified military cooperation and subsequent development of common military building and command mechanisms," and that "uniting the military capabilities of the CIS countries and other interested Eurasian countries would guarantee respect in the international arena for the rights of Russia and its partners and make it possible for them to ensure an adequate military response to any threats."[23] However, such ideas could not be implemented in practice and simply amount to so many harmful illusions.

In general, it would not be possible to establish any kind of common integrating ideology throughout Eurasia, and indeed, such an ideology is not even needed, especially with Russia basing its policy on pragmatism. This does not stop people from trying, however, and the ideas they propose sometimes take quite unexpected forms. Dugin was already mentioned. Abdul-Vakhed Niyazov, leader of the Muslim Refah Party (which had emerged in Russia in the late 1990s), declared his support for Eurasianism and in 2001 registered the Eurasian Party of Russia. The majority of the Muslim clergy in Russia lent their support to spreading Eurasianism. Damir Mukhetdinov, rector of the Faizkhanov Islamic Institute in Nizhny Novgorod, said that integration should be built on the Islamic foundation provided by Tatarstan and Bashkortostan in Russia's North Caucasus region, as well as by Azerbaijan and all of the Central Asian countries.[24] Unrealistic though it might be, this approach could certainly win the support of some Muslim politicians.

In the words of historian and political analyst Igor Yakovenko, "Russia has always tried to become the center of gravity for countries lagging behind in their modernization, so as to establish a second power center, which it can then play to its advantage."[25] However, such a center of gravity cannot be created in the absence of the necessary institutions (including political institutions), and the existing institutions are often far from being up to the challenge.

AUTHORITARIAN REGIMES

The strong side of Russian-Central Asian relations lies in the similar authoritarian nature of their political regimes. Russian and Central Asian leaders feel an almost genetic closeness and share an understanding of what constitutes the best kind of political model: a hardline regime based on unquestioned leadership for life and rejection of any alternative. None of these countries has any real (as opposed to "on-paper") systemic opposition. As for the nonsystemic opposition, it has been the target of persecution and repression. The nonsystemic opposition in Russia is largely composed of secular liberals and, of late, increasingly of nationalists as well, while in Central Asia it is dominated by Islamic radicals.

Relations between Russia and the Central Asian countries rarely touch on mutually sensitive issues such as civil society, democracy, and human rights. Moscow, Tashkent, and other capitals in the region constantly stress that democracy and human rights issues have been artificially blown out of proportion by outside forces seeking to change the local political situation in their own interests. This has been an important issue for Russia and the Central Asian regimes in connection with their "suspicions over 'sponsors' of the 'color revolutions' in Georgia, Ukraine, and Kyrgyzstan...."[26] Added to this now is the mutual fear of a repeat of events in the Middle East and North Africa, where popular Arab Spring protests in early 2011 toppled the regimes of authoritarian presidents who had been in office for many years. Little effort is required to see the similarities.

Russian and Central Asian leaders also share the view that their countries have their own individual development roads to follow that suit their traditions and history. Announcements of specific homegrown development models centered on a strong state and the priority of the collective over the individual are met with feelings of mutual understanding. The advocates of authoritarianism express their love for tradition above all else by affirming the decisive role of the state (that is to say, their own decisive roles) in all spheres of life and by maintaining loyalty to their immediate and extended families and clans. There is also a practical dimension in appealing to tradition, in that it can be used by authoritarian regimes as a means to ensure their own self-preservation. As Russian liberal politician Boris Nemtsov put it, "following one's own development road" means "violation of civil freedoms, censorship, absence of justice, arbitrariness of state officials, unprecedented corruption and total power of state monopolies."[27] Nemtsov is absolutely correct (though perhaps a bit simplistic) in his assessment, as can be seen by looking at any of the authoritarian regimes that are busy defending their "own development road," whether in Central Asia or in Russia.

In the Central Asian countries, the search for a national idea has been based upon real or mythical historical figures and harkens back to a glorious past when the various dynasties were at the heights of their power. In Uzbekistan, it was Khan Timur (1336–1405); in Tajikistan, it was the Samanid dynasty that ruled in the ninth and tenth centuries; in Kyrgyzstan, it was the legendary hero Manas, the main figure of the eponymous epoch; and in Kazakhstan, it was the eighteenth-century Khan Ablai, the founder of the Kazakh proto-state. Typical in this respect are the words of one official Uzbek scholar: "Like the great Timur, we are all seized with the desire to build a country with a brilliant future."[28]

In Turkmenistan, where the search through history would reveal neither stable statehood nor any great leaders, the return to its roots has taken a different tack. Independent Turkmenistan's first president, Saparmurat Niyazov, came up with the brilliantly simple solution of incarnating the glory and greatness of the Turkmen people in his own person by assuming the title of Turkmenbashi ("Father of all Turkmens") and wrote a post-modernist Turkmen "epos," the *Ruhnama* (it is symbolic that a good quality translation of this work into Russian was done by famous poets Yevgeny Rein, Igor Shklyarevsky, and Mikhail Sinelnikov). The basis of Turkmenistan's national idea was as simple as possible: Niyazov was both its founder and its one and only demiurge.

By the end of the 2000s, the similar views on domestic political organization that had given Moscow a certain advantage had lost some of
their significance. In any case, the similar authoritarian political models
and ideology had never engendered unconditional mutual trust and
certainly had never guaranteed that the Central Asian countries would
continue to remain within Russia's orbit. The Western partners of the
Central Asian governments agreed, essentially, to recognize the "unique"
development roads of these countries, while raising complaints about
antidemocratic practices and human rights issues less frequently and
reducing discussion for the most part to pure formality. This approach
was most clearly evident in the response to the events in Uzbekistan in
2005, when Islam Karimov put on a brutal show of force to suppress
an uprising in Andijan. The initial outcry against Karimov's actions
gradually subsided, and although the assessments of the Andijan tragedy did not change, the subject eventually faded from political and
diplomatic view. Although it is true that in 2011 the European Union
decided not to issue visas to individuals who had been involved in the
use of force in Andijan and imposed a ban on arms sales to Uzbekistan
for refusing to allow an independent international investigation into the
events in Andijan, the withdrawal of American troops from Afghanistan
that was taking place at the same time opened up new opportunities
for Uzbekistan to receive arms for free from the United States. In this
respect, it is noteworthy that Secretary of State Hillary Clinton did not
raise the Andijan issue during her visit to Uzbekistan at the end of 2011,
and the commentary on her visit on the State Department website says
that Karimov had forgiven the United States for the criticism it had
levied in 2005.[29]

The Central Asian regimes have taken some steps to make a show
of liberalization. In 2009, for example, 5,000 nongovernmental organizations (NGOs) were operating in Uzbekistan. Although pressure
continues to be exerted against the nonsystemic opposition, Uzbek
authorities have begun to exhibit a more tolerant attitude toward some
"dissidents" by reducing prison sentences and even releasing some
prisoners. True, these were people who had effectively abandoned their
struggle and become domesticated members of a "pocket opposition."
Tashkent "played along with the West, hoping through individual

pardons to give the country a more positive image abroad."[30] There has been some change even in Turkmenistan, where since 2009, President Gurbanguly Berdimuhamedov has been incorporating human rights issues into his political vocabulary and authorities have been cooperating with some NGOs and Western institutions.[31] According to Tajik analyst A. Akhmedov, who, as a member of the country's administrative and intellectual elite, is close to the authorities there, "although all of the Central Asian political systems have some authoritarian characteristics, multiparty systems exist de jure in practically every country in the region, and governments affirm respect for democratic principles."[32] In reality, "political modernization ... is taking place in the context of the clan, local and family ties that shape identity, loyalty and the organization of social and power hierarchies."[33]

On the one hand, there is a formal "democratization" process under way; on the other hand, the screws continue to tighten as the governments stamp out even the slightest signs of dissent. In this respect, Uzbekistan has begun to look more like Turkmenistan; Kazakhstan, where the 2011 parliamentary election left only the ruling Nur Otan Party in parliament, looks more like Uzbekistan. Significantly, after President Nazarbayev concluded in January 2012 that having a one-party parliament would compromise Kazakhstan's political system in the eyes of the West and undermine his government's legitimacy, he decided to hold an extraordinary parliamentary election, which brought the two opposition parties (more accurately, imitations of opposition parties) Ak Zhol and the Communist People's Party into the parliament. Independent experts contend, however, that the election had been marred by widespread violations and fraud, which only further served to highlight Kazakhstan's authoritarian bent.

The regime in Tajikistan has also become more authoritarian, although the position of President Emomali Rahmon (who dropped the Russian "ov" ending from his last name in 2007) is not as secure as that of his colleagues in the region.

Since the 2011 parliamentary election in Russia, the Central Asian regimes stopped seeing Moscow as the benchmark for maintaining order and preserving government authority. The protests against election fraud that had brought tens of thousands of people onto the streets of Moscow, St. Petersburg, and other large Russian cities have had an impact on the opposition forces in Central Asia as well, especially in Kazakhstan, although it is difficult to say how great their influence will end up being.

The paradox is that just as the Russian authorities, and particularly the president and prime minister, were coming under fire for the mass public protests in Moscow, Nazarbayev took decisive action and sent in the military to quell protests by miners demanding wage increases in the Kazakh town of Zhanaozen, where an estimated fifteen to seventy people were killed during the suppression. This was Nazarbayev's practical lesson for his neighbors and allies in the way a ruler wanting to keep a firm hold on power should behave in critical situations, and at the same time a demonstration that Central Asian authoritarianism can be every bit as unbending as the Russian version.

Europe and the United States have been firmer in their condemnation of Russian authoritarianism, and Moscow has been held to a higher standard of respect for human rights and democratic norms than has Nazarbayev or his colleagues. The West has been willing to show lenience toward the Central Asian countries for ethnic and historical reasons, but it has not taken such a "forgiving" approach toward Russia, which it considers to be closer to the West in terms of its culture and sense of civic values. This might have been flattering to Russia's ruling class and society, but in Central Asian eyes it has made Russia appear alien and belonging to a different, Euro-Christian world. Seen in this context, the assertion by Vladislav Surkov, the former head of the Russian Presidential Administration and chief Kremlin ideologue, that "Russia has done far more to democratize Eastern Europe and Central Asia than have Washington and London"[34] appears quite ambiguous. If this is indeed the case, then the Central Asian authoritarian rulers would be well advised to treat Russia with greater caution.

PERSONALITIES AND PERSONAL RELATIONSHIPS

Another important factor for Russia and the other former Soviet republics since the beginning of their existence as independent countries has been personal relations among the leaders. As a group, all of the post-Soviet presidents had grown up and been educated in the Soviet Union, had been in informal contact with each other, shared a circle of acquaintances, and used a common political and everyday vocabulary. In the company of each other, they were among their own.

The collapse of the Soviet Union had left them all in the same psychological position as leaders of newly independent countries, and personal contact was one way for them to become accustomed to each other in their new capacity as presidents. Before signing an agreement or treaty, they would first discuss it "within the family circle," so to speak. Symbolically, this was precisely the same situation as in Belovezhskaya Pushcha in Belarus in December 1991 when the agreement that sealed the Soviet Union's fate was signed.

Mairam Akayeva, wife of former Kyrgyz President Askar Akayev, in recalling her close family ties with the Nazarbayev family in Kazakhstan (the Akayevs' son Aidar had been married to Nazarbayev's younger daughter Aliya from 1998 to 2001), described "heart-to-heart talks, short hikes, skiing together, sailing, attending performances at the tops of mountains up in the clouds."[35]

Although Nazarbayev and Akayev both had good personal relations with Russian leaders, this was not always the case. The second president of Kyrgyzstan, Kurmanbek Bakiyev, for example, had failed to establish any such good personal rapport, and he was not alone. "It might be that Uzbekistan's president did not establish friendly relations with Putin," wrote analyst Alexander Karavayev, "but Nursultan Nazarbayev was clearly won over to some extent by Putin's charisma and determination to deepen regional integration."[36]

For his part, Putin is by nature inclined to attempt to build personal relationships of trust with his counterparts. This has been particularly evident in his contacts with German Chancellor Angela Merkel, former French president Nicolas Sarkozy, and former Italian prime minister Silvio Berlusconi. Putin even had a personal affinity for George W. Bush, former president of the "hostile" United States. This factor of personal relationships may be seen in interactions between Putin and some Russian politicians as well (his close bond with Chechen leader

Ramzan Kadyrov being the most striking example) and between the Russian federal government and Chechen authorities in general. Boris Yeltsin's approach had been similar in this respect, making much of his friendship with German Chancellor Helmut Kohl and his warm feelings for Bill Clinton. In Soviet times, Leonid Brezhnev had also been known for having his personal "favorites."

This personal factor has been lacking in Putin's (not to mention Dmitry Medvedev's) relations with Tajik President Emomali Rahmon. Meanwhile, Saparmurat Niyazov of Turkmenistan was quick to dispense with informal contacts with his counterparts and even—if what politicians close to him say is true—tried to set the Central Asian presidents against each other. Putin and Niyazov personally disliked each other from the very beginning, as evidenced by Putin's visit to Turkmenistan in 2000, when Niyazov (who was already convinced of his own greatness) treated Putin, who had only recently become president, like an immature child. When Putin addressed Turkmenistan's political elite, Niyazov asked the audience to forgive their guest from Moscow "if he is a bit clumsy in his words," adding after Putin spoke, "Don't pay attention to the way he spoke ... he was just nervous."[37] Putin was understandably offended, and the episode cast a negative pall on the personal relations between the two leaders, and, inevitably, on bilateral relations between the two countries.

Medvedev's election as president in 2007 and the formation of the "Putin-Medvedev tandem" put the Central Asian leaders in a difficult position. There had been rumors in Moscow of differences between the views of Medvedev and Putin, with Medvedev being portrayed as more liberal leaning and inclined to use Western values as a reference. The Central Asian leaders, who were used to dealing with clear and undisputed national leaders, were forced to adapt to the new situation and to try to identify exactly who had the last word in Russia. They sized up Medvedev at their meetings, trying to ascertain the extent of his psychological independence and the limits of his ambitions. Gradually their doubts faded, however, and Putin remained the one and only real leader in their eyes, which meant that they could continue their old, familiar approach.

ERASING THE PAST

As events of the past decade have shown, none of the Central Asian countries (with the exception of Kyrgyzstan) has developed a clearly structured pro-Russian lobby willing to follow in Moscow's wake no matter what. What is more, power has been gradually passing into the hands of a new generation, which is less attached to the past in its sentiments than the current leaders. The real change in perceptions of Russia will occur when those who had been ten to fifteen years of age when the Soviet Union collapsed and did not undergo Soviet indoctrination take the helm. Reflecting on the situation in Kazakhstan, Martha Brill Olcott wrote of "differences in values between generations, not just among elite but within the population,"[38] and this is even more true for the other Central Asian countries. "Future relations between the countries, a positive image of Russia in the region, and the emergence of a pro-Russian segment among these countries' elites still rest upon the old Soviet foundation,"[39] but this common Soviet past's reserves have dwindled fast over the past twenty years and will continue to do so.

To a great extent, Central Asia's Soviet past had been more of a Soviet-Russian past, considering that the process of sovietization had involved spreading the use of the Russian language, Russifying the local elites, and spreading Russian culture, which was simultaneously part of European culture. Leaving aside the impact that Russian culture has had in the region, it is telling that the de-sovietization process there goes hand in hand with the process of de-Russification. Uzbek writer Alexander Dzhumayev rightly noted the "unclear fate in Central Asia of a Soviet cultural heritage that grew out of a synthesis of Russo-European and local traditions."[40] There is another circumstance that also stands out: in the minds of the people of the region, the Soviet era equated to the feeling of belonging to a great country based on social justice and a collective spirit, both of which are also associated with Islamic tradition. This has created a strange symbiosis: although Islam and "Sovietness" had been in confrontation with each other, underlying similarities between them make substituting an Islamic outlook for the Soviet one somewhat understandable.

The main goal of the de-sovietization process has not been to erad-icate the Soviet era's social values, which had quickly been organically integrated into local traditions, but rather to eliminate all attachment to the previous nation and replace it with their own "empire" that had a glorious past of its own, thereby overcoming the "younger brother" complex. One country that has been making efforts to eradicate any trace of the Soviet state is Uzbekistan. In 2011, for example, the memo-rial to the Tashselmash plant workers who had left their factory for the front during the "Great Patriotic War" (World War II) was demolished, and the monument to blacksmith Shaakhmed Shamakhmudov, who together with his wife Bakhri Akramova had adopted fifteen children of various nationalities during the war, was dismantled. A monument in Samarkand to the first cosmonaut Yury Gagarin was demolished in 2008, a monument to freedom was destroyed in 2009, and a park that had boasted 150-year-old poplar trees dating from old Russian Tashkent was torn up, along with a nineteenth-century church designed by Alexander Benois. Over the past nineteen years, 90–95 percent of town and village streets that had previously borne Russian, Korean, Kazakh, or European names have been renamed.[41] In 2007, Islam Karimov announced that two memorials to the victims of the "Russian colonial regime" would be erected. The Soviet regime is now associated with the pre-revolutionary imperial regime and is recognized as its successor. In Kyrgyzstan's parliament, for example, the 1916 uprising by Kyrgyz during World War I was characterized as being in reaction to oppres-sion by the czarist army. The Basmachi movement of the 1920s is now described as having been a movement for liberation. The "monument wars" in the Baltic republics and Georgia addressed old and more recent grievances, while in Central Asian countries it has been about trying to free themselves from a past associated with Russia and to erase the now unneeded and even dangerous Russia from their history.

THE LANGUAGE ISSUE

De-Russification, both overt and latent, has been proceeding in all of the Central Asian countries. One of its main objectives has been to eliminate the Russian language as a rival to the national languages. This is an objective process, given that during the Soviet period the use of the national languages had been restricted, and without a good knowledge of Russian it had been impossible to pursue a successful career, even in one's own republic. Unless a fully fledged national language has been preserved or developed (which was necessary in some cases), the task of forming a national state would be nearly impossible. At the same time, however, the sidelining of the Russian language also reflects a desire to cast aside everything that had not originally been indigenous to the national cultural heritage. Moreover, it was emphasized that Russian had been the language of the colonialists. A similar situation developed in other former colonies, such as Algeria, which announced a policy of encouraging the use of Arabic in the 1960s, although the French language remained as a sign of belonging to the educated class (knowledge of Arabic among the first generation of independent Algerian politicians was inadequate). The fate of the Russian language in Central Asia will be sadder than that of French or English in their former colonies, partly because Russian cannot compare to English or even French in terms of its global reach. As the ties with Russia weaken, English, albeit on a limited scale, could eventually replace Russian as the main foreign language in the region.

The Russian language has been in decline in all of the Central Asian countries. Of the Turkic language countries, only Kyrgyzstan still uses the Cyrillic alphabet, and this will continue for no more than a limited time. Nursultan Nazarbayev explained that Kazakhstan's decision to use the Roman alphabet had been motivated by the fact that "the Roman alphabet dominates today in communication."[42] Tajikistan is adopting an Arabic alphabet, which will ultimately make not only Russian literature but also world literature less accessible, since the works of the likes of Shakespeare or Victor Hugo are available only in Russian translation, while translations into any of the national languages have used the Cyrillic alphabet. It could be argued that the Russian language has served as a kind of intermediary link between the regional national cultures and the outside world and that this link can now be made directly, without having to resort to the use of Russian. This is true, but it will be some time before even the most progressive segments of society will be able to learn a new foreign language (there are very few language teachers), and in the meantime at least two to three generations could end up culturally isolated.

The use of Russian remains widespread at the youth subculture level. Pop songs in Russian can be heard in all of the larger cities throughout the region, in markets and in taxis. Russian detective novels are popular, as are Russian glossy magazines. As far as the Russian press goes, the weekly *Argumenty i Fakty* has a visible presence, and, to a lesser extent, so does *Komsomolskaya Pravda*. A handful of other magazines are read in their online versions. Sometimes, issues of such Russian newspapers as *Nezavisimaya Gazeta* are tacitly removed from distribution if they contain articles critical of the local leadership. In 2002, Saparmurat Niyazov prohibited subscribing to or importing any foreign print media into Turkmenistan. In particular, the delivery of Russian print media into Turkmenistan was pronounced "not economically profitable." True, Niyazov's successor, Berdimuhamedov, reversed this decision in 2011 and even allocated 5 million rubles to pay for subscriptions to Russian print media,[43] although with the passage of time its readership had already become accustomed to living without it.

There are now fewer Russian television channels broadcast than in the 1990s, and local programs in Russian draw relatively large audiences only in Kazakhstan and Kyrgyzstan. How broad the Russian presence is on the Internet remains an open question, but the Internet alone will not be able to preserve the Russian language, all the more so since all of the Central Asian governments (with the exception of Kyrgyzstan) have been working to block the free flow of views and information. In 2010, the international organization Reporters Without Borders added Turkmenistan and Uzbekistan to its list of the "Enemies of the Internet."

The shrinking use of the Russian language in general has gone hand in hand with a decline in the number of schools that teach in Russian, which fell by more than two-thirds in Turkmenistan over the 1990s and by half in Kazakhstan and Uzbekistan. The number of Russian-language schools in Tajikistan dropped from 90 to 30, and the number of mixed-language schools dropped by a third. In 2001, all of the Russian-language schools in Turkmenistan were converted into mixed-language schools and shifted to the nine-year school system

borrowed from Turkey. By the early 2000s, the number of students
in Russian-language classes and schools in Uzbekistan had fallen by
half (from 668,000 students to 327,000), although during that period
(according to official statistics) the number of Russians in the country
had decreased by no more than a quarter. During the same time frame,
only 1 percent of students in Tajikistan were receiving an education in
Russian. The situation was somewhat better in Kazakhstan, where 50
percent of the students were studying in Russian, and Kyrgyzstan, where
the figure was 20 percent.[44]

The status of the Russian language has declined throughout the
region. It remains an official language in Kyrgyzstan, is considered
a "language of inter-regional communication" in Tajikistan, and
simply a foreign language in Uzbekistan. Even in Kazakhstan, where
Russians account for up to a quarter of the population, a group of
local activists and politicians sent Nazarbayev a letter in September
2011 requesting that the provision allowing Russian to be used on an
equal basis with Kazakh be removed from the constitution. Russian-
language broadcasting over the state television channel in Kazakhstan
ended at the same time.

Russia cannot be accused of having done nothing to try to protect
the Russian language. The Russian World Foundation, established in
2007, organizes seminars and conferences and all manner of exhibi-
tions and presentations. It has opened nine Russian Centers, three each
in Kazakhstan, Kyrgyzstan, and Tajikistan,[45] but these have all been
nothing more than palliative measures that will not be enough to halt
the continuing decline of the use of Russian. The main reason for this
decline has been the departure of the region's Russian-speaking population. Since 1991, 80 percent of the Russians in Tajikistan have left,
while 50 percent have left Uzbekistan and more than two-thirds have
left Turkmenistan.[46] In 2007, the Russian population of Central Asia
was estimated at 5.5–5.7 million, compared with nearly 9 million at
the time the Soviet Union collapsed. About 1 million Russians were
in Uzbekistan in 2007, about 470,000 in Kyrgyzstan, no more than
90,000 in Turkmenistan, and 45,000–50,000 in Tajikistan.[47] Since
then, the number of Russians has continued to fall. Fewer than 400,000
Russians remain in Kyrgyzstan today. Although newspaper reports on

the regulation concerning the exchange of foreign passports in 2011 had mentioned that 120,000 Russians were living in Turkmenistan, this number was clearly exaggerated.[48]

The Russian communities in Central Asia have always been passive in their political behavior. However, it is true that in some countries in the early 1990s the Russian communities had attempted to organize their own movements. The best known among these, the Republican Slavic Movement (known by the abbreviation LAD), was formed in Kazakhstan in 1992 but failed to establish a niche for itself in the political process, and many of its activists ended up moving permanently to Russia. The Russian communities were rapidly (although not without pain) transformed from a group that had played a dominant role during the Soviet period into a depressed ethnic minority that was incapable of exerting any real influence on important political decisions. In Kazakhstan, more than 90 percent of government positions are held by Kazakhs (the country's main ethnic group),[49] while the corresponding figures for the other countries in the region are even higher.

Russia has not provided any sort of substantial support to the Russian communities. The "Russian issue" is seldom raised at CIS summits or other CIS events. Moscow has not wanted to sour relations with the Central Asian countries and thus has taken a line that fundamentally differs from its policy in the Baltic countries, where it has consistently portrayed itself as protecting the interests of the local Russian population. Although demonstrations have frequently taken place in front of the Latvian and Estonian embassies in Moscow, no such demonstrations have occurred in front of the embassies of Turkmenistan or Uzbekistan. The Congress of Russian Communities, which was established in 1992 and has portrayed itself as an international and national Russian social and political union of compatriots and patriotic organizations, has used the problems that face the Russian minorities living abroad as an instrument to win influence within Russia itself.

In the eyes of the Central Asian countries, by abandoning the battle for the rights of ethnic Russians, Moscow had provided yet more evidence that it was seeking to keep relations on an even keel and to avoid conflict and meddling in their internal affairs.

RUSSIA'S INFLUENCE

Can Russia have any real influence on the political situation in Central Asia, change it, or shape it to serve its own interests? The answer is a clear "no." Although Russia can influence some of the more important decisions in the region, nowhere, aside from Kyrgyzstan, does it now play any decisive role (and even in Kyrgyzstan it does not enjoy sole or absolute influence).

Russia does not have the means at its disposal to influence who will succeed Nazarbayev in Kazakhstan or Karimov in Uzbekistan. These are purely internal matters for the ruling classes of those countries to decide. The next leaders in Kazakhstan and Uzbekistan will be chosen based upon the power balances between the ruling elites. Outside factors will play a role, of course, but like the policies of these Central Asian countries in general, they will be multivectoral in nature; in other words, they will depend upon the system of checks and balances of the China-Russia-United States triangle. Russia might show interest in or even support particular candidates, but no candidate would probably risk demonstratively relying on Russia's support alone.

In any case, the Kremlin had learned a lesson from its experience in Ukraine, when seemingly loyal ally Viktor Yanukovych had become president and began to pursue a line of his own that was far less than always in agreement with Moscow's. A similar situation could await in any of the Central Asian countries.

Illustrative in this respect was the power handover in Turkmenistan in 2005. Moscow had refrained from intervening at all in the choice of a new leader there. Indeed, Moscow may not have had any clear idea of exactly who might become the next president. Well-known Russian politician Alexei Mitrofanov, who attended Niyazov's funeral, said that the Russian delegation headed by then prime minister Mikhail Fradkov had left for home immediately after the funeral, and only Mitrofanov stayed behind for the closed part of the ceremony, where he had the opportunity to talk with local politicians.[50] From that point on, Moscow lacked the means to influence the internal situation in Turkmenistan and never attempted to do so.

Russia's influence in Tajikistan has been more visible but is also far from absolute. There are several nuances here to consider. First, Russia (together with Iran) had played a very active part in finding a settlement to the civil conflict in Tajikistan, which resulted in the signing of the 1997 agreement between the United Tajik Opposition and Emomali Rahmon's People's Front. This was probably one of Russia's greatest political achievements in the CIS. By supporting Rahmon, Moscow had influenced the balance of political power in Tajikistan and the composition of the country's ruling elite. "Characterizing Russia as a 'third party,' therefore, must not obscure the fact that from the beginning of its involvement it has been partial, supporting one party in the conflict,"[51] wrote Swedish researcher Lena Jonson, who described the civil war in Tajikistan as a "challenge to Russian policy."

The Tajik civil war and the conflicts relating to Nagorno-Karabakh, Transnistria, and Georgia-Abkhazia were crisis situations to which Russia responded by apparently attempting to manage them. These were not just chance sporadic crises, but symptoms of the inevitable processes that were under way in the post-Soviet space as the former Soviet Union was coming apart. The civil war in Tajikistan was something of an exception to this list, in that it was the only case where Russia actually succeeded in resolving the situation. The other conflicts remain unresolved to this day, and Moscow has not managed to find the key to their settlement.

The settlement in Tajikistan opened the way for Moscow to maintain a military presence in the country and have an indirect influence on the domestic political situation there. It is possible that the Russian troops of the 201st Division, which had been stationed in Tajikistan since 1993 and had been based in the country since 2005, had saved Rahmon's regime at a time when the country was going through a severe economic crisis, people were freezing in the winter cold, and growing discontent was threatening to erupt into mass antigovernment demonstrations. The Kremlin's choice to support Rahmon at that moment brought stability to the country; some within Rahmon's entourage at the time have asserted that he had asked Moscow to provide military support if the circumstances called for it.

Russian intervention in Kyrgyzstan, when it occurred, was moderate in nature. Although Moscow had not welcomed the local Orange Revolution (Kyrgyzstan's first revolution in 2005 was dubbed the Tulip Revolution, after the flowers that the women from the opposition had handed out to demonstrators), it became clear overall that no matter who among the revolutionaries came to power, they would not try to sour relations with Russia. In this, the Kyrgyz revolutions differed noticeably from those that had taken place in 2003–2004 in Georgia and Ukraine. Russia was willing to be accommodating toward the revolutionaries because their opponents, successive Presidents Askar Akayev and Kurmanbek Bakiyev, had been unable to maintain control over the situation and, more important, Moscow had accumulated a number of complaints with regard to each of them.

Akayev, for all his growing authoritarianism, seemed overly democratic, having allowed hundreds of NGOs with links to Europe and the United States to operate in the country. As former president of the Kyrgyzstan Academy of Sciences, Akayev had come from an academic background, and he differed in mindset from the other post-Soviet presidents of Central Asia. Bakiyev, who was toppled in 2010, had lost the trust of the Kremlin through his continual deceit, especially regarding the U.S. military base in Manas; he had promised Moscow he would close the base, but then broke his word. The Kremlin eventually dropped its support, coming to his aid only once, when it allowed the airplane carrying him into emigration in Belarus to transit Russian territory after a Kazakh airplane had first delivered him from Kyrgyzstan to Kazakhstan.

After the fall of Bakiyev's regime, the Kremlin spent some time sizing up future presidential hopefuls, although it was more concerned over the prospects that Kyrgyzstan might switch from a presidential system of government to a parliamentary system. Russia was used to working with authoritarian leaders in the region, and the switch to a parliamentary system could thus hold surprises for future relations. The Russian authorities figured that such attempts to transform the political system would put Kyrgyzstan at risk of yet more destabilization. President Medvedev described a parliamentary system as "not suitable for either

Kyrgyzstan or Russia," and said that attempts to introduce it could lead to "disastrous consequences."[52]

During the political upheavals that shook Kyrgyzstan throughout late 2011, many of its politicians repeatedly appealed to Moscow for support. They had their sights not on the president's post (which in the interim had been filled by Roza Otunbayeva, the revolutionary movement's leader), but on the now more influential post of prime minister. Moscow made no move to "sponsor" any particular candidate, however, and limited itself to promises. It is noteworthy that the Russian authorities coordinated their policy with that of Kazakhstan, where a final decision was also a long time in the making. It had appeared at one point as though Felix Kulov, Askar Akayev's interior minister and the man who had saved Kyrgyzstan from massacres during the Tulip Revolution (Kulov had been national security minister from 1987 to 1992 and prime minister from 2005 to 2007), would be the optimum candidate for both countries, but for a number of reasons, including his "political exhaustion," Kulov, for all his merits, was not the final choice. There were other hopefuls as well, but all of them to one degree or another needed the approval of both Moscow and Astana. In the end, it was Prime Minister Almazbek Atambayev who was elected president at the end of 2011 with 63.2 percent of the vote. His pro-Russian position played a substantial part in the victory. Indeed, in Bishkek and other towns in Kyrgyzstan throughout the 2000s, I heard all sorts of people say that the most popular politician in the country was Vladimir Putin.

In Kazakhstan, Uzbekistan, and Turkmenistan, however, no politician who runs into difficulties (or achieves success) would ever openly demonstrate a clear pro-Russian position. "Russia has lost its means of direct contact with future generations of administrators in the Central Asian countries and cannot hope that the elite there will have any real understanding of the situation in Russia."[53]

Another sign of Russia's nonintervention in the affairs of its neighbors is that it has had no dealings with the open or secret opposition groups and figures there. The view that "Russia has been positioned in particular to develop discreet contacts with different secular political groupings…" is debatable.[54] Of course, the Russian intelligence services do gather information on local political intrigues and pass it on to the leadership, but no practical action has followed. Again, the only exception is Kyrgyzstan, since it has become a routine occurrence there for the opposition to take power.

None of the above-mentioned opposition figures from Kazakhstan, Tajikistan, or Uzbekistan has received support from Moscow. The Kremlin has had contacts with critics of the different regimes, but only if they have not been involved in open and public uncompromising confrontation with the authorities and have not been demanding regime change. Akezhan Kazhegeldin, who was Kazakhstan's prime minister from 1994 to 1997 and had openly opposed Nazarbayev, did not receive Moscow's support, nor did Nazarbayev's son-in-law, Rakhat Aliyev, or Uzbek opposition politician Mohammed Salikh, who was a serious rival to Islam Karimov in the country's first presidential election, and they all emigrated to Europe. The Central Asian opposition could never count on Russia's help, although Kazhegeldin recalled in 1998 that when he had been in Moscow, he had met with "potential observers and allies" and with people who "were willing to support [me],"[55] although he mentioned no names.

None of the Central Asian opposition figures had been granted political asylum in Russia and so could not remain there without the risk of being handed over to the authorities in their own countries (the only exceptions were members of Turkmenistan's opposition). Former foreign minister Avdy Kuliyev (1990–1992), the family of former foreign minister Boris Shikhmuradov (until 2000), former deputy prime minister Nazar Suyunov (1991–1994), and a few others managed not only to settle in Moscow, but even to continue their struggle against the Ashgabat regime, albeit on a very limited scale. Kuliyev, for example, produced four issues of a small circulation magazine, *Erkin Turkmenistan*, and Suyunov headed the executive committee of the Russian Association for Ties with Compatriots, Rodina, but their activities in Russia had no impact of any kind on the situation in Turkmenistan. Turkmenistan opposition figures had contacts with Russian human rights activists, meeting especially frequently with journalist Vitaly Ponomaryov, who described in detail how he had tried to help Avdy Kuliyev return to Turkmenistan in 1995.[56] For his part,

Nurmukhammed Khanamov, Turkmenistan's former ambassador to the United States and now head of the Republican Party, chose emigration to Austria, where he continues his opposition activity. Khudayberdy Orazov, former deputy prime minister and now head of the Vatan Party, is also still active and currently lives in Sweden.

Askar Akayev, who emigrated to Moscow with his family, has left politics behind and returned to academic work. After becoming a senior researcher at Moscow State University, since 2009 he has also been coordinating the Russian Academy of Sciences' subprogram, Complex Systems Analysis and Mathematical Modeling of Global Dynamics.

RUSSIAN INERTIA

In refraining as it has from intervening in the domestic affairs of the Central Asian countries, Russia has been all the more distanced from any involvement in mending bilateral and multilateral relations among them. The inertia Russia has demonstrated in this regard can be explained by Moscow's initial conviction that the Central Asian countries would automatically stay within the Russian orbit; now it simply does not have either the strength or the resources to intervene in relations among the countries of the region. I would add to this the low level of professionalism among the personnel who work in the Russian embassies of the region, their ignorance of local languages and traditions, their perception of the Central Asian countries as being of only secondary priority for Russian diplomacy, and their belief that most problems can be settled at the economic level, which has also been part of the post-Soviet approach to the region.

Russia has lost its ability to be a mediator for intraregional relations, especially on unsettled border issues. This is one of the main issues for regional stability, and it concerns nearly all of the region's countries. Once the artificially set borders of the Soviet republics suddenly became international borders, old conflicts were rekindled from as far back as medieval times.

There is tension along the entirety of Uzbekistan's borders. In 2009, Uzbekistan erected seven-meter concrete pillars and dug trenches three meters deep along some stretches of the border with Kyrgyzstan. Earlier, it had mined parts of the borders with Kazakhstan, Tajikistan, and Turkmenistan and had sown antipersonnel land mines along the stretch with Kyrgyzstan's Batken. Uzbekistan (unofficially, of course) has territorial claims against Kazakhstan (Shymkent), Tajikistan (Khujand), and Turkmenistan (Tashauz and the surrounding area). These unsettled border disputes have been exacerbated by intraregional transborder migration driven by differences in living standards between the inhabitants of these countries. Moscow initially attempted to play the role of mediator in these border issues but without success, underscoring the fact that it now was dealing with not the former Soviet republics but independent countries having their own national interests and ambitions. It would be naïve to imagine that these countries would "seek to realize their territorial claims against each other via local armed conflicts, seeking support from Russian military formations acting under the auspices of KSOR," the Collective Security Treaty Organization's Collective Rapid Reaction Force.[57] In the view of the author of this comment, Ukrainian scholar Rustem Zhangozha, even a hypothetical interpretation could not include such a possibility for the foreseeable future.

The failures of Russian mediation attempts have been manifested in the water issue, which is crucial for the survival of all of the Central Asian countries and peoples, and which climate change (in particular the melting of the Pamir glaciers) threatens to make worse.

The region had had its share of conflicts over water and land during the Soviet period as well. In the 1980s, Tajiks and Kyrgyz clashed over the villages of Borukh-Tangi (1982) and Matcha-Aktakhyr (1988), with the tension growing even higher in 1989–1991.[58] The water issue became so serious that there was even talk of redistributing water resources in Central Asia's favor by reversing the flow of Siberia's Ob River to make its waters run south. This "project of the century" drew sharp criticism from scientists and part of the Russian intelligentsia. Back then, Soviet writer Sergei Zalygin had been one of the main opponents of the project, and biologist Nikolai Reimers said that the project "went counter to the scientific laws of world development," but it nonetheless was broadly supported across Central Asia. Reimers noted that Central Asia loses 49 cubic kilometers of water every year and said that an increase in water resources would only help to push the birthrate even higher and would prevent society from modernizing.[59]

Central Asian advocates of the project asserted that the "campaign against the reversal of the Siberian rivers is based on an invented demagogic platform that has nothing in common with science," and, pointing to the resolution by the Communist Party Central Committee and the government, noted the need for "further study of the environmental and economic aspects of redistributing the water resources." "We believe," they wrote, "that the Ob-Aral canal could become a miracle that people will create with their own hands."[60]

Kyrgyzstan and Tajikistan have been in a better position by virtue of their geographical location, inasmuch as the rivers of the region (the Amu Darya, Syr Darya, and Vakhsh) originate there. Uzbekistan, Turkmenistan, and Kazakhstan all suffer water shortages in summer. During Soviet times, floodgates would be closed over the winter months, and Kyrgyzstan and Tajikistan would receive their electric energy over feeder lines running from Kazakhstan and Uzbekistan.

It continues to be all but impossible to find a solution to this issue in a mutually acceptable way. According to many estimates, water demand in the region is predicted to grow by 40 percent over the next ten to fifteen years.[61] The amount of irrigated land has increased by 7 percent since the mid-1990s. Water resources are used very inefficiently: 40 percent of the water used for irrigation either evaporates or is lost to filtration. Per capita water consumption in Central Asia is ten to twenty times greater than in the developed countries: 1.5 cubic meters of water is used for each 100 kilograms of raw cotton in Israel, while the figure in Central Asia is six to ten cubic meters.[62] Resolution of the water shortage problem will demand better use of the water resources and an end to widespread resource-intensive practices. This is why the attempts to resolve the water issue have so far been unsuccessful.

The conflict between Tajikistan and Uzbekistan intensified after the construction of the Roghun Hydroelectric Power Station on the Vakhsh River. The Russian company RUSAL (with which the Tajik authorities had signed a contract in 2004) was named to carry out construction (preparations for which had begun back in 1976). Tajik authorities had insisted that the dam be built to a height of 335 meters, while RUSAL and the Uzbek authorities considered a height of 260 to 280 meters to be adequate. Uzbekistan had also wanted the dam to be built of concrete, while the Tajiks preferred to use rock. In reality, the issue boiled down to the fact that the Uzbek authorities believed (and not without reason) that such a high dam would give Tajikistan absolute control over the water flow and would make Uzbekistan completely dependent upon its neighbor for water resources. Characteristically, Russia did not attempt to act as mediator in this conflict and agreed with the Uzbek position from the very beginning. In the end, Dushanbe canceled the contract in 2007 and at the same time refused to sell RUSAL an aluminum plant in exchange for the Russian investment. Ignoring Uzbekistan's position, Tajikistan resumed construction of the dam.

Moscow has backed away from intervening in water resource disputes, assuming (and not without reason) that in any case it had no optimum solution to offer. It is telling that Russia had not taken part in an international seminar on water resource use in Bishkek in 1995 attended by representatives of Kazakhstan, Kyrgyzstan, Turkmenistan, and Uzbekistan, as well as experts from the United States.[63]

Although it is true that the participants in the August 2006 Eurasian Economic Community (EurAsEC) summit in Sochi had decided to draft a conceptual plan for the efficient use of water and energy resources (a special group had even been set up)[64] and that Russia had proposed a similar concept for water and energy resource utilization at the EurAsEC interstate council meeting in October 2007, the matter nevertheless went no further.

Meanwhile, help and mediation services began to be offered by the Americans and Europeans. The United States allocated $39 million for cross-border irrigation projects before 2008.[65] The European Union launched the European Water Initiative, currently coordinated by Italy and the European Commission. The EU should learn from the successes and failures of the previous irrigation projects by Mercy Corps and the Swiss Agency for Development and Cooperation (SDC) and the United Nations Development Program (UNDP).[66] EU support has given Tajikistan confidence in its standoff with Uzbekistan. In particular, Struan Stevenson, head of the European Parliament's environmental protection group, who visited Tajikistan in 2011, called the dam project safe and said it was vital for Tajikistan, which was "suffering from a permanent energy crisis." In June 2011, while visiting Europe, President Rahmon received an initial loan from the European Bank and a $21 million grant for developing the energy sector.[67]

Russia continues to "squeeze itself out" of involvement in what is one of the biggest issues in the Central Asian region. The grandest final chord in this story came at the sudden initiative of Yury Luzhkov, then mayor of Moscow, who was known for his foreign policy extravagance and in 2002 attempted to essentially revive the seemingly forgotten project to reverse the flow of the Siberian rivers, even writing a book on the subject, *Voda i mir* (Water and Peace).[68] Luzhkov's idea was supported by Nursultan Nazarbayev, who, speaking in Astana in 2006, called for the project's revival. In 2008, Uzbekistan submitted the design for a navigable canal linking the Ob River, the Syr Darya, the Amu Darya, and the Caspian Sea. However, the cost of implementing such projects has increased dramatically. Preliminary estimates put the cost of reversing the rivers at $40 billion, while the super canal was estimated to cost $100–150 billion.[69] The preliminary cost estimates for these grandiose projects make it highly unlikely that they could be implemented in the foreseeable future. Even if the money were to be found, reversing the rivers or building a trans-regional canal would make the countries in the region completely dependent upon Russia—something neither they nor outside actors would want to see happen. Thus, as in the past, such projects remain utopian dreams.

CONCLUSION

The influence of Russia on the Central Asian countries continues to decline. Moscow no longer has any real ability to push through the decisions it would prefer or to influence local political dealings. Now that they have shaken off their historical nostalgia and the burden of their Soviet past, Central Asian elites feel sufficiently independent to pursue their own interests without fearing that doing so might displease Moscow in the process.

Russia no longer has a *presence* in the region. Although it plays a specific part in Central Asian politics, it nonetheless is an outside actor. It does not choose the local regimes and is increasingly forced to adapt to them. Moscow does not play the vital role of mediator. Its role today is that of important ally and partner, the extent of its cooperation determined by each individual country's specific interests. Russia cannot even adequately protect the rights of the ethnic Russians in the region, showing just how limited its capabilities have become.

CHAPTER 2

REGIONAL INSTRUMENTS OF INFLUENCE

RUSSIA'S REGIONAL RELATIONSHIPS

For all the importance that Russia attaches to its bilateral relations with the Central Asian countries, it has nonetheless made concerted efforts to develop regional relations as well, by creating and using international organizations to bolster its own influence and authority in the region. Official Russian documents systematically refer to the importance of "making use of the potential" of the CIS, Collective Security Treaty Organization (CSTO), Eurasian Economic Community (EurAsEC), and Shanghai Cooperation Organization (SCO).[1] The SCO lies outside this paradigm in that the initiative to set it up came not from Russia, but from China, although its stated strategic goals are identical to those of the pro-Russian organizations.

The activity of these shaky and ineffective organizations has dwindled to a critical low in Moldova, the South Caucasus, and Ukraine. Belarus has long shaped its relations with Russia based on a special model that banks on the possibilities that the establishment of a Russian-Belarusian Union State could offer. For this reason, the existence and activity of the CIS, the CSTO, and EurAsEC have come to depend above all on getting the Central Asian countries involved, and it is in this direction that Moscow has concentrated its efforts to pursue post-Soviet integration under the aegis of Russia. To use these institutions for the purpose of reinforcing Russian-Ukrainian or Russian-Azerbaijani relations had appeared to be a dubious, perhaps even impossible prospect.

Central Asian expert Roy Allison has written that Russia is pursuing a policy of "protective integration" by proposing an integration model with guaranteed benefits and patronage, but only as long as Moscow remains the nucleus of such integration.[2]

This model appears perfectly natural from Moscow's perspective, if only because no organization could be viable as an effectively functioning body in the post-Soviet space without Russian participation. The only attempt to build an influential international organization without Russia's involvement had been GUAM (Georgia, Ukraine, Azerbaijan, and Moldova, which later became GUUAM after Uzbekistan joined), but the endeavor proved to be a failure.

Russia's dominance or attempts to dominate one organization or the other is no guarantee in itself that disagreements would not arise among the various participants. Russia continually finds itself in a position of having to try to maintain consensus among members of the organizations, and it has not always been successful. At the same time, at least under the current authorities, it still gives its support to the existing organizations and attempts to establish new ones.

ATTEMPTS AT A CUSTOMS UNION

One example of this kind of hoped-for new organization is the Eurasian Union. The idea for this had been initiated by Russia in 2011, and the first efforts in this direction began with EurAsEC, which gave rise to the idea of the union. In 2007, Russia decided to establish the Customs Union with Belarus and Kazakhstan, which then created the first supranational body of the post-Soviet space, the Customs Union Commission. The benefits and drawbacks of the Customs Union have been assessed in various ways. Umirzak Shukeyev, deputy prime minister of Kazakhstan, said that reciprocal trade between Customs Union members had increased by 57 percent in his country alone.[3] At the same time, some critics have said that Russia is losing up to $1 billion a year through the Customs Union. In addition, Russia's share of all of the customs duties levied within the Customs Union is 87.97 percent.[4] Many of the decisions concerning the Customs Union's operation were made during what Shukeyev called "off-the-record discussions."[5] Independent outside observers have given conflicting assessments of the Customs Union and its work, with some seeing it as a step toward integration and others as "a kind of fence that we have erected around the three countries' economies."[6]

Beginning in January 2010, the Customs Union introduced a common customs tariff, and as of July 1, 2011, it dispensed with customs formalities along the borders shared by the three member countries.[7] The Customs Union began working at full capacity in January 2012, but it will still be quite some time before the full extent of its potential benefits becomes clear. Some thorny issues, such as migration, have yet to be resolved. The free movement of labor policy was introduced in 2012. This has resulted in little visible change for Russia and Kazakhstan, but the number of labor migrants to Belarus has grown noticeably. If Kyrgyzstan or Tajikistan were to join the Customs Union, the free movement of labor would have an impact on the stream of migrants coming from these countries.

THE COMMON ECONOMIC AREA

The Customs Union had not yet begun operation when the presidents of Russia, Kazakhstan, and Belarus met in Almaty in late 2009 and approved a plan to set up the Common Economic Area (CEA). Over the course of the following year the legal foundations for the CEA were drafted, and seventeen basic agreements were signed. It was said at the time that the participants would need an additional four years to get the CEA working. Over that time, to get the planned organization up and running, they would need to sign more than 50 agreements and implement more than 70 different measures, including optimizing and coordinating the economies of the participating countries, establishing a common financial market to carry out a coherent currency policy, creating common energy and labor markets, harmonizing national legislation, and much more. The participating countries would open their national markets to each other on a reciprocal basis and sign an agreement on mutual recognition of licenses. Finally, the CEA's effectiveness would depend directly on whether the participants would agree to a common trade policy with respect to third countries.

Further steps to develop the CEA have included common public procurement rules, nondiscriminatory rules of access for member countries to each other's banking and insurance markets, and equal conditions for investment activity. There have also been plans to introduce common market (or, put another way, equally profitable) prices for gas beginning in 2015. This would be a particularly complex undertaking, inasmuch as energy prices have been one of the most important and sensitive issues in relations between Russia and its partners.

There has been talk in Kyrgyzstan about possibly joining the CEA. Tajikistan has hinted that it might be willing to join just the Customs Union. However, Armenia or Abkhazia could beat these countries to it. Giving membership to Abkhazia, which has not been recognized as a sovereign state by the international community, would inevitably create problems, given that all of the countries in the post-Soviet space remain firmly committed to the principle of territorial integrity.

The whole idea of establishing the CEA has always hinged upon securing the involvement of Ukraine. Without Ukraine, the project would be of lesser benefit and would appear less attractive in the eyes of real or potential participants. Furthermore, securing Ukraine's involvement would be evidence of the Kremlin's ability to influence the second most important post-Soviet country. So far, however, for a number of reasons (including differences in the energy sector), Moscow's attempts to lure Ukraine into joining the CEA and the Customs Union have not achieved the results it had sought, and this looks unlikely to change anytime soon. Although Ukraine has on numerous occasions hinted that it could possibly participate and has spoken of the importance of integration, when push comes to shove such words have always turned out to be nothing more than diplomatic niceties. "Ukraine's participation would give the CEA far greater weight and strength, and the emergence of a strong economic space of this kind would make our countries more competitive on global markets," said Yermukhamet Yertysbayev, adviser to the president of Kazakhstan. Otherwise, "we demand of Russia that the entire border [with third countries] be tightly closed as far as customs checkpoints go, so as to ensure that the economic union can function effectively."[8]

Ukraine has behaved in a somewhat similar manner to Uzbekistan, which has reiterated its desire for integration without ever actually definitively committing itself. This implies that if Tashkent ends up deciding not to join the Eurasian Union, its borders with Kazakhstan would be closed "in terms of customs checkpoints."

Overall, the development of the Common Economic Area has proceeded in such a way as to doom it to be nothing more than a mere idea or even a mythical concept, a sophisticated hint of integration under way. The CEA, if it does indeed take shape, would not begin to fully function until after 2016, and its future membership remains unclear.

One small step on the road to the Eurasian Union's creation was taken at the CIS summit in October 2011, when the leaders of Armenia, Belarus, Kazakhstan, Kyrgyzstan, Moldova, Russia, Tajikistan, and Ukraine signed an agreement to establish a free-trade zone (Azerbaijan, Turkmenistan, and Uzbekistan decided to postpone a final decision on whether to sign the agreement). The free-trade zone is to be less significant than the Customs Union. According to Yevgeny Vinokurov, director of the Eurasian Development Bank's Center for Integration Studies, the establishment of a free-trade zone will not bring any changes to Russia's trade relations with its neighbors; the flow of trade with Kyrgyzstan, for example, has so far remained unchanged.[9] Still, it is a step forward in the pursuit of integration.

Prior to 2011, integration mechanisms had in practice been mostly formal and produced little result. EurAsEC, the Customs Union, and other bodies had been hampered in their work by the various difficulties in bilateral relations between Russia and its partners, in particular in the energy sector and other areas; the integration efforts themselves were generally only "noncompulsory" half measures. Although numerous documents have been signed and approved, the process of actually structuring a durable integration chain of authority has been left for the indefinite future. At times, it appears as though Russia has concluded that turning ineffective old organizations into something of real quality is becoming an impossible dream, and that it is prepared to accept the situation as it is. One loss or tactical mistake that Moscow may be said to have made was the Kremlin's unflagging hope of attracting the greatest possible number of countries into the integration process. However, the trend in relations between Russia and its neighbors during the 2000s has been more in the direction of greater distance from Russia than closeness, as reflected in Moscow's cooling relations with Tajikistan, Turkmenistan, and Uzbekistan.

SPEEDING UP INTEGRATION

It gradually dawned on the policymakers in Moscow that integration should focus more on speed than on the number of participants, since to proceed at too slow a pace would inevitably weaken Russia's position. The Kremlin decided it was time to take decisive action.

It has been suggested that the burst of Russian activity in the post-Soviet space had more to do with the election season in Russia itself, in that the ruling elite was hoping that a show of effort in this direction would win votes for United Russia in the 2011 parliamentary election and for Vladimir Putin in the 2012 presidential campaign.

This view is debatable, however, because the outcome of the elections had been determined by purely domestic factors. Indeed, the idea of close cooperation with the Central Asian countries would hardly be likely to attract much support among the Russian public, with its increasingly nationalist leanings, anti-migrant stance, and fondness for such slogans as "Russia for Russians."

In 2005, for example, only 12 percent of the populace in Russia favored an alliance with Kazakhstan (versus 25 percent in Belarus),[10] while support for allying with the other Central Asian countries is probably even lower. Such negative views are also a reaction to the large scale of migration from these countries. The perception of Central Asia today among the Russian public is reminiscent of the situation in the early 1990s, when people had seized upon the idea that Russia would stand to benefit if it freed itself of its Muslim-populated outlands.

The Eurasian Integration Project proposed by Vladimir Putin in 2011 marked the first significant direct step toward the creation of the

Eurasian Union. The project's goal was to achieve maximum rapprochement between the former Soviet republics most ready for it, under the aegis of Russia. Presidents Alexander Lukashenko, Dmitry Medvedev, and Nursultan Nazarbayev signed the Declaration on Eurasian Economic Integration in November 2011, which is to culminate in the establishment of the Eurasian Union in 2015. They also signed the Agreement on the Eurasian Economic Commission, and on January 1, 2012, this commission became the common and permanent supranational body for managing relations within the Customs Union and the Common Economic Area. On that same day, twelve agreements on the CEA and a number of other regulatory documents also came into force. Supranational organizations will also regulate the common market. Putin, still prime minister at the time, said that this was the "most direct path to creating the Eurasian Economic Area" and that "removing trade barriers would create a continental market worth trillions of dollars, from which not only Russian business but also European business would profit." When exactly all of this would happen is difficult for the experts to predict at present.[11]

In Putin's words, the goal was to "turn integration into a stable and long-term project that is comprehensible and attractive for the business community and the public and does not depend on the various ups and downs of circumstance," adding, "we are not talking about reviving the USSR in any shape or form."[12]

According to analyst Sergei Shiptenko, "the Eurasian Union does not cancel out the previous stages of post-Soviet Eurasian integration."[13] It is interesting that Shiptenko equates post-Soviet integration with Eurasian integration, although a difference between the definitions might have been expected, given that Eurasia is not identical to the Soviet Union as geopolitical concepts.

As the project exists today, the Eurasian Union is essentially a union between Russia and Kazakhstan with weak and economically helpless Belarus tacked on because its government hopes to use it as a means for building more advantageous relations with Russia. "Alexander Lukashenko is attempting by all means possible to bargain the best possible conditions for his country's membership in economic groups, using political bargaining as a way of offsetting resource shortages and a lack of liberalism in the economy."[14]

It has been suggested by some figures in the Russian government that the future Eurasian Union could be expanded by taking in countries from outside the region (Mongolia, for example, or even Cuba or Vietnam).[15] This would be highly unlikely and even a somewhat comical prospect. Although Putin and his colleagues have proclaimed the Eurasian Union's openness, it is unlikely to attract other countries and will remain limited in scale.

I am talking here not about the post-Soviet space in general, but specifically about Central Asia. The Eurasian Union will not have much of an impact at the regional level. Its creation will have no effect on Turkmenistan or Uzbekistan and will probably not affect the situation in Tajikistan either.

The general plan proposed by Moscow is straightforward: to proceed from the Customs Union (Belarus, Kazakhstan, and Russia) to the Common Economic Area and from there to the Eurasian Union. Although this may appear convincing enough from the outside, "the logic and principles ... of the integration project are set out in rather superficial fashion."[16] First, only the bodies organized within the Customs Union and CEA frameworks have any real substance, and second, it is not at all clear what conditions would have to be met for other countries to join the Customs Union (it is still too early to speak of them joining the CEA). Third, the benefits that individual countries could expect from joining are also far from entirely clear.

There is no doubt that all of the countries are interested in expanding their markets, yet even with the agreements on the CEA's creation only recently signed, politicians and economists in Kazakhstan and Russia were already raising many questions about the wisdom of the project in the first place. Misulzhan Namazaliyev, director of the Central Asian Free Market Institute, for example, has stated that the Customs Union works to the interest of Russia. "Small countries such as Kyrgyzstan, Tajikistan and even Ukraine have no need to join this kind of union. Even Kazakhstan loses out by joining the Customs Union."[17] Andrei Chebotarev, director of the Almaty-based Alternativa Center for Topical Studies, said that "the Eurasian Union benefits Russia most of all" because it "enables Russia to regain its influence in the Central Asian region," seeing as "the CIS has long since lost its integration potential."[18]

Rafik Saifulin, former adviser to the president of Uzbekistan, said that Uzbekistan has a choice in the current situation: develop its multi-vectoral foreign policy, which could gain benefits for Uzbekistan in the form of U.S. investments but be complicated by actions taken by Russia, or focus on maintaining close strategic relations with Moscow. According to Saifulin, these Russian "actions" could involve the use of the same means of influence that Russia has already applied in other post-Soviet countries that have flaunted Russian national interests, suggesting that Russia could even stop transit shipments of supplies via Uzbekistan to Afghanistan.

In December 2011, Islam Karimov basically rejected the idea of Uzbekistan's joining the CEA and openly voiced suspicion that the Kremlin had been pursuing creation of the CEA primarily for political aims. Speaking in Karshi, he said, "Unfortunately, there are some forces in the former Soviet space that still cherish plans to revive the empire we knew as the USSR in a new form."[19] This was clearly a reference to Putin, who had called the Soviet Union's collapse "the biggest geo-political disaster of the century."[20]

At best, the CEA will bring together four countries, two of which (Belarus and, in the future, Kyrgyzstan) will play a supporting role. It will therefore be primarily a continuation of the bilateral relations between Russia and Kazakhstan, even as Kazakhstan's economy increasingly shifts toward China, which is its main trading partner and accounts for 20 percent of its exports and almost 30 percent of imports.[21] The most important foreign investor in Kazakhstan is the United States, with U.S. companies accounting for up to 30 percent of foreign direct investment.

The highly asymmetrical nature of the CEA makes it very difficult for its members to maintain parity. The GDP of Russia is eleven times that of Kazakhstan. This inherent inequality was in evidence when the parties were setting up the Eurasian Economic Commission, where Russia was given 57 percent of the votes under the so-called balanced voting system in spite of the opposition of the other members.[22] There is nothing unusual about a system of this kind—well-known practical examples abound. But the asymmetry of the CEA only reinforces the understandable apprehension Moscow's partners feel for Russian "political hegemony," which was already present in the consciousness of the Central Asian elites and was further exacerbated by Putin's comment that integration should go ahead based "on values, *politics* [italics added], and economics."[23]

Talk of the economic significance of the CEA cannot camouflage the political subtext that Moscow would prefer to pass over in silence. Economic cooperation is not possible without political cooperation, which, with an economically dominant Russia, would raise the question of Russian political hegemony. Uzbekistan's view of this prospect was noted above, but it is clear that Kazakhstan does not want to return to being under Moscow's wing (nor do any of the other countries, for that matter). In April 2012, in an interview with TV channel Vesti-24, Nazarbayev stressed that the intention had been to create an *economic* union by 2015.[24] Alexei Vlasov, director of the Center for the Study of Socio-Political Processes in the Post-Soviet Space, expressed the cautious and ambiguous view that "the post-Soviet space should concentrate on economic integration and leave political consolidation to develop as it can."[25]

The United States and the West in general have not taken a clear position on the CEA. The reaction to the new project has been very calm, since Russia does not in any case have the clout to create an international organization that would be capable of altering the situation in Central Asia or radically strengthening its own position. What's more, Russia's economic potential is not so great as to make it the only realistic partner for Kazakhstan or for other potential CEA members. At the same time, the CEA is perceived as being another attempt by Russia (perhaps its last) to create an organization that would be under its control, to raise its geopolitical standing, and to try again to give tangible form to its yearnings for the past. Zbigniew Brzezinski was withering in his comments on this point, calling the concept of a Eurasian Russia and a Eurasian Union "absurd" and saying that it "definitely makes one wonder about just how realistic Putin's views are."[26]

Although the CEA assumes that the current authoritarian regimes in the region, including Russia, will be in place forever, the behavior of the

Central Asian regimes indicates that they are less interested in cooperating with Moscow than in systematically looking for other, more advantageous partners. If the continuing slide in relations between Russia and Tajikistan, Turkmenistan, and Uzbekistan is any indication, interest in the CEA will continue to fade, especially since the participants themselves admit that it will take time to test and prove the effectiveness of the project. Nazarbayev, for example, has decisively rejected the idea of making the ruble the common CEA currency even in the distant future, saying that there is "no need to hurry with this matter" and calling the idea of a common currency "a question for the future."[27] He particularly emphasized that "we first need to prove that the economic space we establish is advantageous and equal in nature."[28]

It also cannot be completely ruled out that political change could occur in the region. How the new leaders who will ultimately take power in Kazakhstan and Uzbekistan would treat the Russian project cannot be predicted.

Russia, which has faced change since the end of 2011, must also answer questions. The events of 2011–2012 (the parliamentary and presidential elections and the mass public protests they set off) raise the question of Russia's political future; in particular, how likely it is that its political elite will remain committed to the Eurasian and post-Soviet policy dimensions and whether there will be change in Russia's foreign policy priorities (such as its willingness to continue supporting Alexander Lukashenko). The question is one of Russia's willingness in general to continue paying for its political influence in Central Asia, no matter what regime is in power.

THE DEMISE OF EURASEC

The newly launched integration project will likely be unable to reverse the economic situation and will clearly have no impact on the political situation in the region. For all of Russia's activeness, this "new integration project for Eurasia" has every chance of ending up every bit as much a phantom as its previous incarnation, EurAsEC. The Eurasian Union could become the swan song not only for the Putin regime's integration strategy, but also for Russian policy in general in the southern regions of the post-Soviet space.

The battles that have been fought in establishing the Eurasian Union could completely devalue the remaining pro-Russian organizations in Central Asia, above all EurAsEC. As Olzhas Khudaybergenov, director of the Kazakhstan-based Center for Macroeconomic Research, said, "As the EurAsEC countries are gradually drawn into the Eurasian Union, EurAsEC will cease to exist."[29]

In any case, EurAsEC's activity has always been limited and its future prospects unclear. The organization was formed in 2000 by Belarus, Kazakhstan, Kyrgyzstan, Russia, and Tajikistan. From the beginning, Russia had been given a 40 percent voting share in the EurAsEC decisionmaking process, while Belarus, Kazakhstan, and Uzbekistan each were given 15 percent and Kyrgyzstan 7.5 percent, which gave the "Central Asian leaders some political benefits of 'protective integration.'"[30] Armenia, Moldova, and Ukraine cooperated with the group as observer countries. Uzbekistan, with its typical inconsistency, first joined the organization, then left it. At first glance, the organization would appear to be impressive: it covers 15 percent of the world's inhabited landmass, and in 2010 it accounted for 4.4 percent of world GDP, 25 percent of the world's natural gas reserves, 8.5 percent of the oil reserves, and also more than 20 percent of the world's freshwater reserves and forested areas.[31] The EurAsEC market represents about 181 million consumers.

EurAsEC has faced numerous tasks, from "developing common financial and energy markets" and "coordinating the principles for successful introduction of a common currency" to "rapprochement and harmonization of national legislation." The organization's practical activities have been limited, often amounting to little more than Russia helping other members. In 2011, when the Belarusian economy was in paralysis, Moscow transferred $3 billion to Minsk via EurAsEC, formally presenting the deal as cooperation within the organization's framework. In 2011, also via EurAsEC, Moscow promised a $106 million loan to Kyrgyzstan, which faced severe economic difficulties.[32]

EurAsEC's main mission (as stated in 2000 when the organization was set up) was to "take decisive steps towards mutual cooperation in the aim of developing real integration."[33] The organization set about establishing a common customs union and putting the CEA in place. Thus, EurAsEC has served as a kind of "cocoon" for subsequent integration projects. Its effectiveness rests on the results of those subsequent projects, or rather, of the main project: creating the Eurasian Union. Unlike the unwieldy CIS, which is centered on the past, EurAsEC, for all its shortcomings, is a much more forward-looking organization.

THE COLLECTIVE SECURITY TREATY ORGANIZATION

In setting up EurAsEC, Russia pursued primarily economic aims. Another of its projects, the Collective Security Treaty Organization, focused on political and military cooperation and was designed to compensate for Russia's declining economic and financial influence. On May 15, 1992, Armenia, Kazakhstan, Kyrgyzstan, Tajikistan, and Uzbekistan signed the Collective Security treaty. They were joined in 1993 by Azerbaijan, Belarus, and Georgia. The treaty looked like a pale imitation of the Warsaw Pact, which had kept its signatories reliably under the thumb of the Soviet Union. Psychologically, the new treaty reflected Moscow's hopes of yet being able to restore the Soviet Union. Perhaps this had been true initially. It is quite probable that in the early 1990s, the political elites in the post-Soviet countries still had the sense that participation in this pro-Russian bloc would help them to maintain their domestic and external security and stability. Compared to the amorphous CIS, the treaty appeared more solid and specific, and created the illusion that Moscow was ready to guarantee the former Soviet republics security in return for their loyalty.

It is true that there were also some doubts about such regional security guarantees. The conflict continued unsettled in Nagorno-Karabakh, separatist movements emerged in Abkhazia, South Ossetia, and Transnistria (which Russia not only did not attempt to prevent, but even encouraged), and tensions continued to rise in Tajikistan.

Skepticism over the treaty's effectiveness gradually grew, and the CSTO itself began to look more like an overtly political instrument in Russia's hands. As a result, when the members extended their membership in the organization in 1999 for the next five-year period, Azerbaijan, Georgia, and Uzbekistan decided to drop out and did not sign the agreement. Azerbaijan left over the unresolved Nagorno-Karabakh conflict, Georgia in protest over Russian support for the Abkhazian and South Ossetian separatist movements. Uzbekistan, which had claimed the role of regional leader in Central Asia for itself, feared that the treaty would make it dependent upon Russia and at the same time limit its possibilities for building relations with the United States and China. For its part, Beijing took a wisely indifferent attitude toward the treaty, realizing that it posed no threat to Chinese influence, while the United States viewed it as an obstacle to its own efforts to enter the region.

In 2002, in a bid to give the alliance more substance and put it on a par with influential international organizations, Russia proposed transforming the treaty into the Collective Security Treaty Organization. The establishment of the CSTO solidified Russia's special status in the post-Soviet space, especially in Central Asia. For the countries of the region, CSTO membership could be a kind of bargaining chip in dealings with outside actors, above all the United States. When Uzbekistan's President Islam Karimov came under fire for his suppression of the unrest in Andijan in 2005, for example, "offended" by Washington, he reduced the level of relations with the United States and demonstratively joined the CSTO.

According to its charter, the CSTO is to work to "strengthen peace and regional security, and defend on a collective basis the member countries' independence and territorial integrity." The organization's main areas of activity include "fighting international terrorism and extremism, illegal trafficking in drugs and psychotropic substances, organized trans-border crime, illegal migration and other threats."[34] It is difficult to judge exactly by what measure the CSTO would be up to such tasks, given that it has never taken part in any military conflict, drug trafficking is on the increase, and illegal migration is also becoming a more serious problem. In any event, the main responsibility for preventing drug trafficking and illegal migration belongs to other, more specialized organizations.

The military cooperation component relies on a CSTO military contingent that has been specially set up, the continued presence of Russian military bases in the member countries, joint military exercises, and supplies of Russian arms.

In 2001, an agreement was signed to set up a collective force, which initially consisted of four battalions, one each from Kazakhstan, Kyrgyzstan, Russia, and Tajikistan. By 2008, this force had been expanded to ten battalions: five from Russia, two each from Kazakhstan and Tajikistan, and one from Kyrgyzstan. It has 300 tanks and armored personnel carriers and operates out of the Russian Air Force base at Kant in Kyrgyzstan.

In 2009, the CSTO members decided to establish the Collective Rapid Reaction Force (CRRF) to pursue essentially the same mission as the CSTO itself (namely, to counter outside aggression, fight terrorism, extremism, and drug trafficking, and perform disaster relief work). The CRRF has a total of about 4,000 people and includes highly mobile military units armed with heavy armaments and air cover provided by ten airplanes and fourteen helicopters based at Kant.

At that time there had been some friction in relations with Belarus, and Moscow initially demurred at signing the agreements on the CRRF, doing so only later. Since Uzbekistan's relations with the West had begun to improve by then, it decided not to sign at all. Tashkent, which also opposed Kazakhstan's proposal that the emergency response ministries and interior and intelligence services of the member countries be engaged in the CRRF, declared that Uzbek military personnel would be delegated to the CRRF only for conducting individual operations.

The CRRF's creation turned the CSTO into an organizationally fully fledged military and political alliance. Over the years since it was established, the CSTO has carried out eight joint comprehensive military exercises, including Cooperation 2010, BORDER, and Cobalt 2010. In 2009, CRRF forces participated in the Alliance 2009 Kazakhstan military exercises for the first time.

From Moscow's point of view, one of the attractions of the CSTO is that its members purchase their arms and military equipment from Russia at domestic Russian prices. For the Central Asian countries, the possibility of buying arms at a discount is also very attractive.

Furthermore, the Russian weapons are simple to use and do not require that the troops be retrained, since the Central Asian officers are already very familiar with them from the Soviet period. The problem here is that these arms are becoming obsolete. Colonel Anatoly Tsyganok, director of the Military Forecasting Center and lecturer at Moscow State University, in his very interesting book, *Russia in the South Caucasus* (about the Russo-Georgian war of 2008), gave a critical assessment of the quality of the Russian weapons: "God forbid that we ever have to go into battle with what we possess at the moment."[35] In fact, in recent years Russia has begun having problems selling its obsolescent weaponry. It is being replaced by higher quality foreign-made arms, and even Russia itself has increasingly been buying weapons from manufacturers abroad.

If we assume that the Central Asian countries equip their armed forces for the eventuality of large-scale military action, it follows that they will ultimately buy the most effective weapons they can find. The possibility of armed conflict breaking out among countries of the CIS cannot be entirely ruled out. Armenia and Azerbaijan, still locked in confrontation over Nagorno-Karabakh, are mostly armed with Russian-made weapons, although Baku has already begun to diversify and modernize its arms. Georgia is equipping its armed forces with new weapons, and Uzbekistan is unlikely to make do with Russian guns and tanks forever. Russia could eventually lose its monopoly on military technical assistance, which will do nothing to enhance the CSTO's attractiveness. Also contributing to the declining interest in Russian arms is the talk that the United States is prepared to hand over a certain amount of its used military equipment in the region to the Central Asian countries after it withdraws its troops from Afghanistan.

The CSTO can be seen as the means for guaranteeing the continued presence of Russian military installations in the post-Soviet space. Russia uses the base in Gyumri in Armenia, where it deploys S-300 air defense systems and MiG-29 fighter planes. It has the Baikonur space launch center in Kazakhstan, as well as a test range for anti-missile systems in Sary-Shagan. In Kyrgyzstan, it has the air force base at Kant and the torpedo test base at Karakol on Lake Issyk-Kul. In Tajikistan, it has the 4th Military Base and the *Okno* fiber-optic system, and in Belarus, it has a radar station. Naturally, some Russian military bases remain outside the CSTO: Russia uses the Daryal radar station in Gabala in Azerbaijan, and its Black Sea Fleet is based in Sevastopol, Ukraine.

What foreign threats does the CSTO face? In 2006, Nikolai Bordyuzha, CSTO secretary general, said that at any moment it could end up facing the Taliban alone.[36] At the CSTO summit in February 2009 in Moscow, it was decided that the CRRF would respond to external threats, such as those from Afghanistan and Pakistan. Although such a scenario cannot be entirely ruled out, it is nonetheless not very likely. Of the CSTO members, only Tajikistan shares a border with Afghanistan. Consequently, in the event of a hypothetical invasion of Uzbekistan or (even less likely) Turkmenistan, those countries would have to fight back with their own means and forces.

Furthermore, the "rise in international terrorist activity at the start of the 2000s showed how poorly prepared the CSTO members had been for taking effective collective measures to ensure regional security."[37] Independent experts have expressed the view that the organization's bodies and committees are no more than "empty shells waiting to be filled with substance."[38] Although this assertion would not be easy to entirely prove or disprove, the question of just how effectively the CSTO would be able to perform its stated mission remains unclear.

The CSTO charter did not anticipate intervening in the domestic affairs of the member countries in the event of serious crises. The massacres in southern Kyrgyzstan in 2010 underscored the CSTO's institutional weakness and showed that it had no actual ability to prevent or resolve such conflicts.

This prompted Moscow to propose expanding the CSTO's functions to include supporting stability in the member countries. By the end of 2010, a new "crisis response strategy" had been devised that envisaged collective action to "protect the security, stability and territorial integrity of the member states, and also joint action to counter collective security threats and challenges and carry out disaster relief."[39] Obviously, the main point here was to organize emergency relief actions that might be required following domestic turmoil.

At a meeting with Belarusian President Alexander Lukashenko in 2011, CSTO Secretary General Nikolai Bordyuzha spoke of "improving the legal foundations" and the "possibility of making decisions and using the CRRF's potential to protect the constitutional regime in the member countries." Lukashenko noted that "we are talking not just about using the CRRF in the event of outside intervention, but also in the event of intervention in a country's internal affairs by other CSTO members, because ... there are many whose hands are itching to carry out a constitutional coup."[40]

Russia's desire to use the CSTO as a means for bolstering the regimes of the member countries is understandable. Despite the disagreements that may occasionally arise between these regimes and the Russian leadership, in principle Moscow is satisfied with them. They in turn anticipate that Moscow, frightened by the "color" revolutions of the 2000s and later the Arab Spring, would support them in their critical hour. In December 2011, at a meeting of the CSTO Collective Security Council, the member countries approved the "Regulation on response procedures for CSTO member states to emergency situations," which, in particular, authorizes using the CRRF if a situation arises that a member country cannot deal with and control through its own means and strength.[41] Thus, Russia now has an instrument for *legitimately* intervening in the affairs of its CSTO partners.

It is somewhat symbolic that the heads of EurAsEC and the CSTO formerly served in the Russian intelligence services. Grigory Rapota, secretary general of EurAsEC from 2001 to 2007, had formerly headed the Russian Foreign Intelligence Service, and Nikolai Bordyuzha, who has led the CSTO since 2003, had been in charge of the KGB personnel department between 1989 and 1991 and later became head of the Russian Federal Border Guard Service. Indeed, at one point or another, nearly all of the key political figures in the current Russian system, including the current president, have worked in the KGB.

As for the foreign policies of the CSTO countries, under the CSTO charter, the "member countries agree and coordinate their foreign policy positions in international and regional security issues."[42] This provision does not make the foreign policies of the CSTO countries uniform or totally dependent upon Moscow. In 2008, for example, CSTO members refused to recognize the independence of South Ossetia and Abkhazia (which had broken from Georgia), and Moscow, though offended, nevertheless understood. Sometimes, however, Russia does manage to push through the CSTO the decisions that it sees as important. In January 2012, for example, the CSTO countries signed an agreement stipulating that "outside countries may station military bases on the territory of CSTO member states only with the agreement of all member states." The degree to which the possibility of an American military presence in the region irritates Moscow is no secret, as it would diminish Russia's contribution in maintaining security and could also lead some Central Asian countries to question the very need for the CSTO. Getting this decision approved was, therefore, a significant victory for Moscow.

The CSTO has, meanwhile, repeatedly stated its willingness to work together with the North Atlantic Treaty Organization (NATO). In 2003, the CSTO made attempts to establish cooperation with NATO in fighting drug trafficking, terrorism, and extremism,[43] but NATO responded cautiously, and no actual cooperation was ever discussed. Still, some individual CSTO members have developed stable and regular contacts with NATO member countries (in particular, the United States).

It should be noted that the number of countries participating in pro-Russian organizations has steadily been declining: twelve countries were in the CIS, nine in the CSTO, five (eight together with observers) in EurAsEC, and only three in the Customs Union. These low numbers reflect disappointment in cooperation with Russia under the framework of the organizations it has set up, as well as in cooperation among the former Soviet republics in general. Interest in such cooperation could hypothetically be rekindled if local business communities were to genuinely begin to believe that there are real advantages to be gained by participating in such projects. That could help to form something of a united Eurasian business elite in the post-Soviet space that would act as the driving force for cooperation. However, cooperation has so far been limited to the state level and depends entirely on the positions of the politicians in power.

THE SHANGHAI COOPERATION ORGANIZATION

Compared to the murky prospects of the organizations working in Central Asia under the Russian umbrella, the Shanghai Cooperation

Organization appears to be a more reliable, promising, and attractive body for the countries of the region. For as long as it has been in existence, not a single member of the SCO has ever questioned its participation in the organization.

The SCO was formed on the basis of the "Shanghai Five" (China, Kazakhstan, Kyrgyzstan, Russia, and Tajikistan), which had been founded in 1996 at Beijing's initiative. This group was set up to settle border issues, with its members selected under the principle, "only China and the countries with which it shares a border." The border issues were successfully resolved, and after Uzbekistan joined in 2001, the "Shanghai Five" changed its name to the SCO. Today, India, Iran, Mongolia, and Pakistan have observer status in the organization, while Belarus and Sri Lanka are "dialogue partners." The SCO was established in part as a reaction to Chinese and Russian apprehension about the U.S. presence in Central Asia. Such apprehension appeared especially serious to Russia, whose own position in the region has weakened.

Once the border issues had been settled, the SCO declared new official goals. But no tangible results of its activities have yet been seen, notwithstanding all of the optimistic proclamations made by leaders of the member countries. Typical in this respect was the statement by Chinese leader Hu Jintao, in which he listed the SCO's priorities as "the need to maintain good-neighborliness and friendship and build a harmonious region."[44] The results of the economic and political sides of SCO activity support the view of those who say that "the SCO's 'economic basket' is one of the emptiest around,"[45] and that most of the projects proposed at this stage exist only on paper. However, the SCO's "basket" is slowly beginning to be filled with substance. The organization is primarily an instrument for China to extend its economic influence, and Beijing has skillfully combined cooperation within the framework of the SCO and bilateral relations. "More economic ties within the SCO are based on the principle of bilateral relations between China and other members and not on the principle of multilateralism."[46]

One accomplishment by the SCO has been the Development Fund, established at China's initiative, which has already made small grants and loans to Kyrgyzstan, Tajikistan, and Uzbekistan. Over recent years, China has handed out $12 billion in preferential loans to the Central

Asian countries.[47] China's financial influence has been on the rise since
the global crisis of 2008. In 2011, the SCO (with ample support from
China) set about to establish the United Development Bank. Uzbekistan
was quick to express support for this project, although other countries in
the region have been more restrained in their response.

China prefers to characterize the promotion of its own interests
in cautious and diplomatic terms. Reporting on the results of economic cooperation between China and Central Asia, for example,
Xinhua News Agency said in June 2011 that "... a balance has been
reached between supply and demand within the SCO. China can offer
large financial reserves and advanced technology, while Kazakhstan,
Kyrgyzstan and other countries have abundant natural resources. The
results achieved from our many years of cooperation highlight the
benefits we can all gain from pooling our resources in this way."[48] It is
noteworthy that this report from China's official news agency does not
even mention Russia, an omission that can be taken as indicating that
China uses the SCO nearly exclusively to pursue its own interests.

At the 2009 SCO summit in Yekaterinburg, China supported the
Russian idea of rejecting the U.S. dollar as an international currency
and returning to the use of national currencies for paying debts. Beijing
then immediately opened a $10 billion credit line for SCO members. At
the same time, Hu Jintao signed a strategic partnership declaration with
Kazakhstan's Nursultan Nazarbayev, and the leaders agreed to increase
the size of the bilateral trade between the two countries to $40 billion by
2015. They also signed an agreement to carry out a $1 billion yuan-tenge
currency swap, and Li Ruogu, chairman and president of the Chinese
Export-Import Bank, announced Beijing's willingness to advance credit
to Kazakhstan's economy in yuan.[49]

Russia has no choice but to go along with this policy of preferential
yuan-denominated loans, giving tacit agreement to China's financial
expansion. Presidential aide Sergei Prikhodko denied seeing this as a
threat, and said, "if our Chinese partners show greater flexibility in the
SCO region and propose their own instruments, this is something we
can understand and support."[50]

One important point should be noted: unlike Russia, China steers
clear of the corruption practices common in business dealings in Central

Asia and monitors the use of the money it hands out. In this respect it has an advantage over Russia, whose businesses are forced to play along with the region's corruption.

Moscow has also been lobbying for large regional projects in which it could play a major part. Speaking at the SCO summit in Astana in June 2011, then president Medvedev said that a "road map" should be drafted and approved by the end of the year for multilateral cooperation to carry out important regional projects, which he listed as including the formation of a venture fund, creation of a unified business cooperation center, and establishment of a special SCO account for developing projects of this kind.[51]

At the same time, it remains unclear what benefits Russia could expect from participating in such projects. Their scale and the costs involved (a large portion of which would be borne by China) could devalue Russian efforts in similar projects that it hopes to pursue through the Eurasian Union. The Central Asian countries would be faced with the dilemma of deciding whether the SCO or the Eurasian Union would offer them the greater benefits, in essence having to tacitly choose between China and Russia.

Kazakhstan supports the proposed large projects, hoping to gain maximum benefit from them through its position as a transit country and to preserve an optimal balance in relations between Russia and China. Addressing the same SCO 2011 summit, Nursultan Nazarbayev proposed the idea of a transnational Eurasian energy space with a unified system of pipelines, high-voltage electricity transmission lines, and a trans-Eurasian transport route linking western China and Western Europe. Interestingly, China would already be prepared for such a route: construction of the Beijing-Urumqi high-speed rail line in Xinjiang is proceeding at a rapid pace. Nazarbayev also proposed drafting SCO project forecasts for the periods up to 2030 and 2050.[52] This was not an empty appeal, inasmuch as the drafting of such predictions would not only outline possible paths for the SCO's development, but would also clarify the way its member countries see the future of the organization and the kind of dividends each country hopes to gain from its participation in the group. Kazakhstan has great hopes for this project. Although the proposal has not yet been approved, it will be sooner or later, since in addition to Kazakhstan, China is interested in carrying out this work.

The SCO's economic component is intertwined with the political component, although by no means do the two necessarily coincide. China does not regard the SCO as a political instrument, while Russia has been keen from the start to bolster the political component of the organization to turn it into a group able to engage in dialogue with Western countries and international organizations (particularly NATO), or even be their opponent. The SCO's purpose, as Russia sees it, "is to contest and exclude the United States as much as it is to order the relations of all relevant powers."[53] Russia's National Security Strategy to the year 2020 lists as a priority objective strengthening the SCO's political potential. China, however, does not seek to turn the SCO into a rival to NATO; it has no need for such a thing. As Moscow itself has pointed out, "the SCO, unlike NATO or the Collective Security Treaty Organization, lacks the identity of a military bloc."[54]

The SCO is not about to start intervening in its members' internal affairs, and it is unlikely to be able to prevent any hypothetical "color revolutions" that Moscow so greatly fears (but to which Beijing has taken a rather calm, even indifferent, attitude). Summing up the SCO's position during the conflict in Kyrgyzstan at the organization's summit, Nursultan Nazarbayev frankly admitted that "we observed the situation but could not do anything."[55] The SCO's only visible contribution to stabilizing the situation in Kyrgyzstan had been the project to build a new residential development in the Osh Region's Kara-Suu district under the aegis of the SCO.

It is hard to predict how the SCO would react should Islamist forces use the instability in some countries to attempt to seize power. Most likely, this would be considered an internal affair of the country concerned. The SCO cannot be drawn into a conflict between one of its members and a third party. After its brief war against Georgia in 2008, Russia made an attempt (doomed to fail from the start) to draw the SCO into its confrontation with the West in the South Caucasus. At the SCO summit in Dushanbe, Dmitry Medvedev presented a draft document condemning Tbilisi's actions and referring to the "genocide of the Ossetian people." The Chinese delegation flatly rejected the wording of the document, in keeping with China's position of diplomatic but strict nonintervention in the Russian-Georgian conflict. As a result of the Taiwan issue, the Chinese had acquired a totally negative attitude toward separatism in general. Moreover, many in China remember that in the 1960s, when the breach in Sino-Soviet relations was at its peak, Moscow had tried to play the separatism card in Xinjiang. In April 1962, influenced by Soviet propaganda, more than 60,000 people left Xinjiang and crossed into the Soviet Union.[56]

However, it would be wrong to abstract the SCO into having no political dimension at all.

> The SCO has repeatedly denied that it aspires to become a military alliance or a "NATO of the East." Nevertheless, over the past decade, contacts between its member states related to matters of security have grown noticeably. Since 2003, the SCO has held a series of joint military exercises, dominated by Chinese and Russian forces. The military chiefs of the SCO members met in Shanghai in April 2011 for what is planned to be a regular forum to boost defense and security cooperation.[57]

The core security issue is Afghanistan, which sends ripples of tension out in all directions, including Central Asia. Muratbek Imanaliyev, secretary general of the SCO in 2009–2010, said that "there is a clear awareness that Afghanistan is still one of the sources of threats to our security."[58] Medvedev said that one of the SCO's key tasks is to "put in place an effective system for reacting to threats to our region's security and stability."[59]

However, awareness of the threats has not given rise to genuine cooperation between the SCO member countries, which, aside from some general declarations on stability, security, and preventing terrorism, have little to show in the way of genuinely feasible joint projects. For example, Kyrgyzstan's then president, Roza Otunbayeva, noted in 2011 that the SCO "has great untapped potential for preventing conflict" and proposed establishing a "security belt" along Kyrgyzstan's border with

Afghanistan.[60] This remained just an idea, however, and did not lead to any concrete action. A statement made by Leonid Moiseyev, Russia's presidential envoy to the SCO, was very telling: "The SCO member states all take the principled position that, while they are ready to work on Afghanistan along the perimeter of its borders, including through implementation of the potential that observer countries present, they would be prepared to work within Afghanistan itself only individually and predominantly on economic issues."[61] Although on the one hand this approach may appear justified, on the other hand the decision not to cooperate within Afghanistan is evidence of the limited capabilities of the SCO. It would not be possible to establish a security system around Afghanistan while completely disregarding its internal affairs. The fact that China had begun to establish its own economic ties with Afghanistan long ago is significant: since 2002, it has allocated $2.5 billion in aid to the country and in 2007 won the tender to mine copper in the Aynak district, a project in which it has invested $3.5 billion.[62] Tajikistan is also organizing its own cooperation with Afghanistan in the electrical power industry. Russia, for its part, has continued to exhibit relatively little direct interest in Afghanistan.

The situation in Afghanistan is particularly intriguing in light of the upcoming withdrawal of NATO troops in 2014. The common view in the Russian media and among some Russian analysts is that Russia, China, and even India will subsequently set about to resolve the conflict, but there is no evidence to support this. Beijing has repeatedly stated that political activity in Afghanistan would be possible only within the framework of the United Nations. "Going beyond the conventional strategy of engaging Afghanistan bilaterally, Beijing is considering an alternative SCO-based approach that could ease regional concerns while still serving Chinese interests."[63]

At the same time, Beijing hopes that SCO participation in stabilizing the situation in Afghanistan could facilitate solutions to its own internal problems in the Xinjiang Uighur autonomous district, where separatists are continuing to operate under slogans of Islam and to maintain contacts with Islamic radicals in Central and South Asia. Thus, the view that the "security policy profile of the SCO is in flux" can be supported.[64]

One way that has been suggested to help stabilize the situation in Afghanistan is admitting it into the SCO as an observer country. None of the SCO members opposes this idea, and Kazakhstan, Russia, and Tajikistan particularly support it. The questions are, however, what specifically the SCO would gain from the presence of Afghanistan among its members, and whether Afghanistan is ready to join the organization. The SCO's 2011 summit ended with no decision made on Afghanistan's entry into the organization as observer.

It is true that direct engagement of Afghanistan in the SCO's work would not be likely to have any fundamental impact on the level of involvement by SCO member states, including Russia and China, in the country's internal affairs and would also have little impact on the situation in Afghanistan. After years of civil war and as the world's main drug supplier, the country cannot become a full-fledged member in any organization until it has eased its domestic tension. It is noteworthy that the 2011 SCO summit in Astana, which debated the entry of new members, adopted a decision to approve a standard memorandum on the obligations of states applying to join the SCO. Afghanistan is unlikely to want to commit itself to many of these obligations. Talks were held with Afghan President Hamid Karzai in the 2000s on the country's possible entry into the SCO, but few doubt that once the coalition troops withdraw, the resulting government in Kabul will include members of the Taliban movement, and cooperation with the Taliban is not on the SCO's agenda for now.

Finally, there is another aspect to the invitation for Afghanistan to join the SCO that relates to the question of the U.S. presence there. As has been reported, the Americans plan to leave a few military installations in place after the troop withdrawal, including the modernized air base at Bagram. Russia has reacted negatively to this idea, Beijing has been restrained in its response, and Central Asia ambiguous, with Kyrgyzstan and Uzbekistan, for example, agreeing in principle to the presence of U.S. military installations on their own soil. Under such circumstances, "Afghanistan's inclusion on the list of prospective observers in the SCO ... could be evidence of attempts to raise the level of understanding on the Afghanistan issue between the United States and NATO on the one hand and Russia on the other,"[65] in a sort of U.S.

appeal to Russia to agree to the presence of U.S. and NATO bases in Afghanistan on a long-term basis. Thus, Moscow's willingness to see Afghanistan in the SCO could be taken as indirect agreement to the emergence of a whole network of American military bases in direct proximity to Central Asia's borders. Moscow has an interest in the American presence, which acts as a restraining force on local Islamic radicals.

Along with Afghanistan, candidates for SCO membership include India, Mongolia, Pakistan, Turkmenistan, and even Iran. Pakistan had applied to join in 2006, Iran in 2007 and 2008, and India in 2010. The SCO's enlargement and the inclusion of such giants as India and Pakistan would transform the organization's nature completely. The SCO would not have a single clear leader or be dominated by the China-Russia tandem in this situation. Its priorities would become much broader, and it would theoretically transform into one of the most influential global political actors with far greater potential than that of the Russian-established CIS or the CSTO.

It is true that for now, due to their territorial disputes, the entry of India and Pakistan into the SCO is far from certain;[66] chances are also slim for Iran, locked as it is in constant confrontation with Europe and the United States, and with the Central Asian countries preferring to distance themselves, put off by Iran's Islamic revolutionary ideology.

Moscow, for its part, has supported SCO enlargement in the apparent hope that a reformatted SCO, in which Russia would be one of the leaders, would give a significant boost to Russia's geopolitical standing as the SCO becomes comparable to NATO and the European Union in terms of political clout.

China strongly supports allowing Mongolia and Turkmenistan to enter the SCO; the inclusion of these countries would give Beijing new opportunities for developing its economic ties with them. The SCO could therefore eventually become a huge but nonfunctioning organization with a built-in and consolidated "parallel mini-SCO" in the form of China, Mongolia, and the Central Asian countries. This mini-SCO would address specific and practical tasks, while the "big SCO" would become a political tribune for discussing utopian ideas and projects. In this sense it would be not unlike the BRICS group, which Moscow is also trying to present as an alternative to Western alliances. Leonid

Ivashov, president of the Academy of Geopolitical Problems, expressed the exotic view that "the SCO could become the organization to consolidate the civilizations of the East."[67] A continually expanding SCO would not so much consolidate Eastern countries as it would create differences among them, which could lead to breakdowns in the organization itself and ultimately its collapse.

CHINA'S UTILIZATION OF THE SCO

It might seem somewhat out of place to analyze the SCO in a chapter studying pro-Russian regional (and international in the broader context) organizations active in Central Asia (the SCO is not in the same league as EurAsEC, the CSTO, or the Eurasian Union), but to view the SCO as "the Chinese master key to Central Asia" or the means for Beijing to establish its "dominion" would be overly simplistic.[68] Strategically, China needs the SCO, not only to promote its economic interests in the region, but also to affirm its influence across the broader span of Central and South Asia. Beijing, with its characteristic patience and outward modesty, follows a cautious policy line, taking pains to stress its policy of nonintervention in the internal affairs of its neighbors. I have heard Chinese colleagues speak on numerous occasions of the deep-seated historical and cultural differences between China and Central Asia that will prevent China from meddling in its neighbors' affairs (in private conversation, Chinese politicians and experts love to mention that they have more than enough problems of their own to tackle).

The dynamic of China's utilization of the SCO has been straightforward and consistent: at the first stage was the "Shanghai Five" to settle border disputes; the second stage was its transformation into the SCO to provide a basis for economic cooperation; and the third stage has been to gradually acquire a political dimension. China's role has grown at each stage, as evidenced by the way that the emerging outline of the SCO's cooperation with the United States has begun to appear closer to a kind of U.S.-Chinese cooperation. In the view of Chinese analyst Pan Guang, director and professor at the Center for International Studies in Shanghai and the Institute of European and Asia Studies at the Shanghai Academy of Social Sciences, mechanisms are emerging that "could reduce the possibility of the conflicts between China and the United States in Central Asia, while bringing into full play the potential cooperation between the United States and the SCO."[69] His words contained nothing unexpected other than the fact that Russia was not mentioned in any context. Guang, who is also director of the SCO Studies Center in Shanghai, sees the SCO as being no more than an instrument for China to pursue its own aims—in this case, to reach an understanding with the United States.

Moscow realizes that the SCO is an instrument of Chinese policy. Russia is losing ground to China, beginning to play "second fiddle" at the SCO and having secondary importance as a partner to the Central Asian countries. Russia is incapable of operating as an equal with China within the SCO, although neither Beijing nor Moscow will admit as much anytime soon. Central Asian politicians also remain silent about this new pecking order, although all of them (including, of particular importance, Kazakhstan's leader, Nursultan Nazarbayev) take it to be a given. Where China is dynamic, Russia appears to be taking a more passive, and to a certain extent even defensive, approach.

Still, Russia has a tremendously significant card to play, which although it might not have direct relevance to cooperating under the SCO, nevertheless enables Russia to position itself as China's equal, or even its superior. That card, of course, is the Russian nuclear arsenal, which remains a symbol of the country's power. Russia imparts a kind of virtual "security umbrella" to the SCO (especially if it should expand in the future), enhancing the organization's international prestige. This is convenient for Beijing as well, which finds having an ally of this kind to be to its advantage. The SCO could theoretically become a unique organization having four nuclear powers as members: Russia, China, India, and Pakistan. Only Russia's nuclear capability has a real geopolitical dimension, however, although Russia's nuclear arsenal is steadily losing value (as are nuclear weapons in general), inasmuch as they are not required for regional conflicts and it would be difficult to imagine a situation in the world today when one side or the other would be so bold as to use them.

It would probably be of some interest to note the comments expressed on the SCO by young scholars from the member states at a roundtable discussion organized by Moscow State University and the Peoples' Friendship University of Russia in 2011 during the presentation of a new youth structure known as the Inter-University SCO Model. Rinat Zinganshin of the Institute of Oriental Studies of the Russian Academy of Sciences said that "the SCO could become the means through which the former Soviet republics could establish a union state," while Alexei Karpenko, another Russian participant, said that "China and Russia are more adversaries than allies within the SCO, as they battle for influence in Central Asia." A participant from Uzbekistan, meanwhile, observed that "Russia joined the SCO so as to stop China from increasing its influence in the region."[70] The roundtable took place as part of the work of the SCO University, set up as pilot project in 2010 with more than 59 Russian universities taking part.

CONCLUSION

The SCO is an alternative to Russian regional projects that are appearing increasingly less cogent as Chinese influence continues to grow. Pro-Russian organizations, including the CSTO, to which Moscow has tied its military-political ambitions, are losing ground to the "Chinese project": "The Shanghai Cooperation Organization moved into its second decade with an ambitious agenda."[71] The pro-Russian organizations could end up in a situation in which, although they would remain on the Eurasian political map and function under Russian auspices, they would play a supporting role, helping to increase Chinese influence. The prospects for cooperation between the SCO and EurAsEC, and with the Eurasian Union and the CSTO, seem unclear, if only because these very same Central Asian countries belong to these organizations as well. Vladimir Vinokurov, director of the Center for Military-Diplomatic Analysis and Assessments, said that a gradual merging of the CSTO and the SCO would be to Russia's advantage.[72] This is not entirely true, since in such a merger the CSTO would simply disappear, taking on the appearance of a subdivision of the SCO, thereby in fact coming under

Chinese control. To assume that under the framework of the SCO, the CSTO would remain an independent organization completely subordinate to Russia would be mistaken. Beijing simply would not allow it (although the CSTO and the SCO did put forward an initiative to work together to establish anti-drug, anti-terrorist, and financial security "belts" along the borders of Afghanistan, as noted above, no practical steps have as yet been taken).

The international organizations that Russia has established have been rather ineffective in producing results and are largely symbolic in nature. They have had little impact on the internal situation in the Central Asian countries. These organizations, above all the CSTO, have had slightly more influence on foreign policy, but even then the results have been far from those desired. Furthermore, as Russian analyst Andrei Grozin has rightly noted, "the Central Asian republics themselves have no concrete, thought-out strategy, not only with regard to the SCO, but also to the other regional military-political projects."[73] The countries of the region often see these blocs as "protection just in case," not even so much against the threat of foreign attack as in fighting their adversaries on the domestic front, above all the Islamist opposition.

The multinational Russian policy instruments face a varied future: EurAsEC will disappear; the CSTO will remain capable of conducting military exercises and being on guard against the external threat (from the Taliban), but will continue to lack the ability to intervene in internal conflicts in member states; interest in the CSTO will gradually wane.

The organizations that Russia has endeavored to establish in Central Asia are incapable of reversing the main trend toward a declining Russian influence in the region. The economic dependence of Central Asia upon Russia is weakening, and Moscow is now pinning its greatest hopes on the Eurasian Union that it is in the process of creating.

CHAPTER 3

RUSSIA AND ISLAM IN CENTRAL ASIA: PROBLEMS OF MIGRATION

THE IMPACT OF ISLAM

Russia's relations with the Central Asian countries are defined by several factors: political, economic, cultural, and others. Each of these is highly important, and it would be difficult to establish any kind of hierarchy among them. This chapter will focus on the Islamic factor. Although it might not seem obvious, Islam is becoming increasingly important in relations between Russia and Central Asia.

The potential impact of Islam on this relationship can be seen in three aspects: the re-Islamization of society, the conformance with Islamic norms, and the spread of Islam into Russia.

The Re-Islamization of Society

Central Asian countries (as well as Russian republics in the North Caucasus) are undergoing a process of re-Islamization. This process is most pronounced in Tajikistan and Uzbekistan, where Islam has become not only an important factor of socialization, but also an instrument of state policy. Politicians in Kyrgyzstan are also increasingly appealing to

Islam. This behavior was particularly obvious during and after the second Kyrgyz revolution in 2010. Former Kyrgyz prime minister Omurbek Babanov said that "the true values of Islam will serve to strengthen the society and contribute to the preservation of peace and harmony in the country."[1] President Almazbek Atambayev, when he was prime minister, spoke about "formation of the correct interpretation of the canons of Islam."[2] Many members of the Jogorku Kengesh (Parliament) began to pray in the Parliament building, hoping that simple Muslims would notice this gesture. Several Kyrgyz politicians began to express their wish for the Hizb ut-Tahrir al-Islami Party (Islamic Party of Liberation, or IPL) to be legalized. The possibility of establishing an Islamic autonomy in the South is also being seriously discussed.[3]

Since the first years of Uzbekistan's independence, the appeal of Islam there has been popular and understandable.[4] While building a strictly secular state, the Uzbek ruling elite defined Islam as a historical and cultural heritage and the moral and spiritual basis of the country's culture. At the same time, the authorities feared that Islam would become a weapon of political struggle. As Islam Karimov stated in the mid-1990s, "we will never allow religious slogans to become the banner of the struggle for power, intervention into politics, economics, and law. We see this as a serious threat to our country's security and stability."[5] Leaders of all of the other Central Asian countries have made similar statements; for example, in 2004 the president of Turkmenistan said, "We will not use religion for political purposes and will never let anyone use it for the sake of personal ambitions."[6]

However, by the late 1990s, secular leaders were forced to rethink the role of Islam and begin *the struggle for Islam*, which required them to formulate approaches to religion for use in political and ideological confrontation with their opponents. If the struggle for Islam had been characterized by the presence of a protesting Islamic opposition in the 1990s, by the 2000s it had become one of the results of the re-traditionalization of society. This general process of re-traditionalization, symbolized by the change in the standing of women,[7] was combined with the declining education level and external influences to force the government to "intercept" religion and use it as an instrument of its own policies. The ruling elite began to form a circle of loyal clergy around it and turned mosques into its own political strongholds. "President Karimov has been actively promoting religion and religious activities through the construction of mosques, support of the *hajj* to Mecca … and the granting of considerable financial and political clout to the official Islamic clergy, who in turn remain under tight control."[8] While Uzbekistan did not renounce the principle of secularism, it reacted to the Islamization of society by essentially merging Islam with politics.

The secularity of the Tajik government has always been relative. The civil war and the subsequent peace agreement with the United Tajik Opposition, which was dominated by Islamists, legalized the role of Islam in Tajik political life. As in neighboring Uzbekistan, the Tajik regime, especially President Emomali Rahmon, began to advocate Islamization (although formally supporting secularism). Rahmon supports the establishment of a system of religious education, attempts to install control over mosques, and requires loyal clerics to interpret his political course. In 2009 Rahmon organized a symposium on "The Legacy of Abu Hanifa and His Importance in the Dialogue Between Civilizations," where he made a quasi-theological speech underscoring the commitment of Tajik society and its government to the ideas of Hanafism, a "bridge across different cultures and the basis for the dialogue of civilizations for the benefit of all mankind."[9] About the same time, rumors circulated in Tajikistan that Rahmon intended to assume the title of imam, which would simultaneously make him both secular ruler and spiritual leader of the country; however, those rumors were never confirmed. In 2010, Rahmon realized that he was losing control over the Islamization process and that parallel Islamic structures were operating independently from him in the country. In response, he launched a campaign to limit the influence of religion, although this proved to be very difficult to achieve. The increasing activity of the Islamic Renaissance Party (IRP) of Tajikistan made it clear that the Islamization of Tajik society had already become an irreversible process. Although the IRP had been marginalized in the 2000s, it was recently given a second chance and is now increasingly active.

"The divide between the new Islamic organization and movement and the old, 'secular' power structure inherited from the Soviet era certainly represents a challenge to the new states, in the sense that any such polarization of society presents a challenge,"[10] John Schoeberlein wrote ten years ago. "In societies that have no tradition of political parties Islam manifests itself on an official government level and within the secular opposition."[11] It is revealing that "those clerics whose views are shaped by the main body of Hanafi legal interpretation tend to be most accommodating toward the regime, but even Hanafi clerics ... seek ways to reinterpret the dominant Hanafi literature ... so that it increases their ability to engage in independent political action. Thus, their attitude toward the relationship of the state to religion is often much closer to Salafi thinkers...."[12]

The increased political role of Sufi orders, primarily such as Naqshabandiya and Yasaviya, which consist of thousands of *murids*, serves as yet more evidence of the re-Islamization of Central Asia. Naqshabandiya alone has about 30,000 followers, which, again, is strikingly similar to what has been taking place in the North Caucasus, where the orders of Naqshbandiya, Qadiriya, and Shadhiliya exert an even greater influence on public attitudes and even the behavior of politicians than in Central Asia.

WITH LEADERSHIP CHANGES COMES AN INCREASED ROLE FOR ISLAM

At least two Central Asian states, Uzbekistan and Tajikistan, have become Muslim, completely abandoning the Soviet legacy. Once the inevitable leadership change occurs in Uzbekistan, the role of Islam in the political life of the country will grow. The strict control that Islam Karimov established over Islam is likely to weaken with his departure, which will increase the influence of the religious opposition. I have had the opportunity to speak with Russians of various social groups (officials, drivers, teachers, and others) living in Tashkent, nearly all of whom were confident that the process of Islamization of society will only intensify with time. Russians, alien to the "Islamic society, united by historical ties, culture and traditions,"[13] fear re-Islamization in Kyrgyzstan, and now in Kazakhstan as well.

In the 1990s (and among some experts in the 2000s) there was a widespread belief that with respect to the degree of influence on the state by Islam, "Central Asia stands out mainly because of its Soviet past."[14] This assertion, however, did not stand the test of time. Central Asia went as could have been anticipated: once the totalitarian regime that had hung on by force disappeared, traditional norms of socialization began to recover and be legalized, while Islam and nationalism filled the ideological vacuum.

One of the more typical features of Islamic tradition has returned to Central Asia: the merging of religious and secular (primarily political) interests. "The familiar Western distinction between religious and political attitudes and activities … becomes irrelevant and unreal. Political dissatisfaction—itself perhaps socially determined—finds religious expression.…"[15] This feature distinguishes Islam from other monotheistic religions, in particular from Christianity (although the Russian Orthodox Church also addresses social and political issues, albeit in a less obvious form). Secularity in the European Christian world has always differed from that of the Muslim world, where the concept of "Islamic secularity" encapsulates the possibility or even the necessity for secular and religious law to coexist so that government positions can be approved by religious figures. Such principles have been restored in nearly all of the post-Soviet Muslim states, along with widespread shariaization and actual (informal) abandonment of secular principles in the structure of government.

The distinctions between the countries of the region are underscored by the differing degrees of influence of Islam in society and extent to which the ruling elites appeal to it, which makes the concept of "Central Asia" even more dubious. The ruling elites of Kazakhstan, Kyrgyzstan, and Turkmenistan have not allowed Islam to influence their domestic policies and do not call the secular nature of the state into question. However, even in Kazakhstan, the role of religion as a source of ethnic identity has been growing. In November 2011, after visiting the opening of the Karaganda Cathedral Mosque (which can accommodate 4,000 people), Nursultan Nazarbayev declared that he considers himself a Muslim.[16] The surge of radical Islam in 2010–2011 may turn out to have been a turning point for Kazakhstan. People attending events in Kazakhstan during 2011, no matter what the purpose, were placing the problems of Islam at the center of attention. In previous years, that would have been unimaginable.

The Kazakh elite never completely abandoned its religious identity, which not only does not conflict with a commitment to Eurasianism, but even reaffirms it. Kazakhstan has continued to develop relations with Muslim countries, although not very energetically. At the 7th World Islamic Economic Forum held in Astana in 2011, Nazarbayev proposed creating a platform for dialogue among ten leading economies of the *umma*, an Islamic international innovation center, a special fund to support small and medium enterprises under the Islamic Development Bank, and a regional fund and food pool headquartered in Kazakhstan.[17] In 2011, the Organization of Islamic Cooperation (formerly the Organization of the Islamic Conference) held its meeting of foreign ministers in Astana.

Apart from their religious identity, the elites of Central Asia (excluding Tajikistan) emphasize the Turkish heritage of their people. "The Turkish chessboard is only one of several that political grandmaster Nursultan Nazarbayev is playing on simultaneously."[18] In an address to the people of Kazakhstan delivered in early 2012, Nazarbayev emphasized in particular that "Astana is the capital of the CIS and of the Turkish world."[19]

THE RISE, AND FALL, OF THE IDEA OF PAN-TURKISM

Following the collapse of the Soviet Union, the Turks of Central Asia immediately turned to Turkey, hoping that their cultural and linguistic affinity would ensure economic, financial, and other assistance from Ankara. By the late 1990s, the idea of pan-Turkism faded (due to disappointment in Turkey, which treated the Central Asian Turks as its younger brothers, reminding the latter of Soviet times) and was replaced by nationalist sentiments. However, the idea of the unity of all Turkish peoples did not disappear; new life was breathed into it at the end of the first decade of the twenty-first century. On the one hand, this was evidently a consequence of the multivectoral foreign policy of the Central Asian states, under which the option of Turkey was only one among many others: Russian, Chinese, American, Islamic, and European. On the other hand, Turkey and its partners had already gotten accustomed to each other and had recognized common interests and opportunities. Finally, Turkey acquired new strategic momentum by attempting to become a regional power (which in this case should be defined broadly): Turkey has been active in the Caucasus, and in 2010–2011 it increased its influence in the Middle East. In the early 2000s, the Turks began to strive for expanded relations with the Central Asian countries. Although these states have greeted Turkish ambitions with caution, on the whole they have been positive. This is especially true of Kazakhstan, which hosted a large-scale Turkish summit in Almaty in October 2011.

The effect of overlapping Muslim and Turkish cultural influences has been cumulative. The Hanafi Madhab school of Sunni Islam is dominant in both Turkey and Central Asia. According to theologians, this should bring Turkic peoples even closer to each other. The Hanafi school is considered to be the most tolerant and "liberal" version of the Islamic theology and *fiqh* (jurisprudence). Hanafi *ulamas* claim, and politicians have followed their lead, that the Hanafi school is a barrier to radical Islamic ideas and the Salafi movement.

The situation in Tajikistan is unique. The cultural and linguistic identity of the majority of its population is the same (or nearly the same) as in Iran. At the same time, there are religious differences: in contrast to Shia Iranians, the majority of Tajiks practice Hanafi Sunni Islam. Only 12 percent of Tajiks are followers of Shia Islam (in the form of Ismailism).

ALIENATION FROM RUSSIA

In recovering and adapting old identities or building new ones, the Central Asian societies and states have increasingly become alienated from their former colonizer, Russia. *Homo sovieticus* is becoming a thing of the past and is being replaced by *homo islamicus*. The concept of "homo islamicus" does not completely capture the essence of the new "Central Asian man." The young people there, who base their judgments on the technological wonders that fall into their hands (iPhones, computers, cars, and so on) have an almost pious interest in the West. Meanwhile, members of the older generation, especially those who live in cities, have not forgotten their Soviet youth and believe that life was safer and quieter in the Soviet Union. Therefore, *homo islamicus* has acquired a number of identities, which are nevertheless still dominated by the component of traditional Islam.

Homo islamicus must not be confused with *homo post-sovieticus*. A new, "non-Soviet" society is forming that already sees the Soviet past as being archaic. Schools have long been using maps without a Soviet Union. In a relatively short period of time, Russia will face elites of a qualitatively new sort that have emerged from a transformed Muslim, and at the same time more technocratic, society. Their closeness to Russia will not be as "intimate" as among the current Russian-speaking and Soviet-educated presidents and prime ministers. The Russian impact on the policies of Central Asia will diminish even more.

Conformance With Islamic Norms

Russia's relations with the countries in the region have been affected by the presence and increasing influence of Islamists. This concept of Islamism is rooted in a religious and political opposition that agitates for society and the state to be transformed to conform to Islamic norms. Islamism in Central Asia has largely been reactionary, in that it presents a response to social and economic problems, the lack of reform, widespread corruption, and dictatorial government that suppresses political protest. "Elementary norms of the rule of law have ceased to be implemented in most of the Muslim countries of Central Asia. Lawlessness has often become the norm and attribute of public relations. In response to this complete lawlessness the Muslim population ... was forced to appeal to the rules of Islam."[20] Local Muslims and their activities were actively encouraged by international radical Islamic organizations based abroad.

Dozens of Islamic organizations have been active in the region. The largest is Hizb ut-Tahrir al-Islami (HTI), although such organizations as Akramiya, Adolat Uushmasi, Islam Lashkari, Nur, Tovba, Izun Sokol,

Ma'rifatchitlar, Takfirshirlar (Uzbekistan), the East Turkestan Islamic Movement, United National Revolutionary Front of East Turkestan, Jundullah (Kazakhstan), and Bay'at (Tajikistan) should also be mentioned. In Tajikistan, the Islamic Renaissance Party operates legitimately. However, the majority of Islamic organizations in Central Asia are, in fact, small-scale groups, or even cells. The Islamic Movement of Uzbekistan (IMU), also known as the Islamic Movement of Turkestan, which had been very active, was recently crushed by Uzbek security services, prompting most of its members to move to Afghanistan. It is yet to be seen whether this movement will be able to regain its strength.

HTI's cells exist in nearly all Central Asian states but are mostly concentrated in the Ferghana Valley: in Namangan, Ferghana, and Andijan provinces of Uzbekistan; in Osh, Jalalabad, and Batken provinces of Kyrgyzstan, and in Sughd Province of Tajikistan. Before 2011, the Islamists had been marginally active in Kazakhstan, operating only in its southern and southeastern regions. However, the situation has been changing. In the spring of 2011, there were two explosions in Aktobe, Kazakhstan, that, according to security authorities, had been organized by Islamists or with their participation.[21] Another explosion occurred in Atyrau in October 2011. The Jundullah (Allah's warriors) organization claimed responsibility for that one, stating that the act had been in response to the law on religion adopted in Kazakhstan in 2011. There were threats of more terrorist attacks unless a provision of the law that prohibited performing the five daily prayers in government institutions was overturned. A few days later, another act of terrorism took place, this time in the southern part of the republic, in Taraz, resulting in several deaths. Certainly, although the HTI has not put down deep roots in Kazakhstan, some cells have nevertheless been formed there already, with both Uzbek and Kazakh members. It is interesting to note that the extremists print their leaflets in Russian, anticipating an "international audience."

A number of Kazakh experts have come to believe that one reason for the sudden activity by Islamic extremists has been the influence and infiltration into Kazakhstan of Islamists from Russia. Kazakhstan has become "a potential starting point for public preaching."[22] Although this is something of an exaggeration, it nevertheless has to be recognized that certain ties exist between the Russian and Kazakh Islamic radicals, which could have an impact on both Kazakhstan and on the regions of Russia that border it.

ISLAMISM'S ROLE WILL BE MORE ACTIVE

Since no radical socioeconomic or political changes are to be expected in Central Asia for the foreseeable future, Islamism will remain on the stage in the region and, depending on the situation, will most likely become more active and will remain a force for all of the local regimes and their foreign partners to reckon with.

Experience has demonstrated that Islamism will be impossible to suppress by force alone, while any liberalization would open the way for the Islamists to make use of democratic institutions, especially elections, where they would be able to achieve significant success. Finally, they could easily take part in government coalitions in some of the Central Asian countries, given a particular balance of power. Islamism in Central Asia is thus a potentially political and de facto legitimate force that must be reckoned with, especially in light of the Islamist successes during the 2011 Arab Spring revolutions, their subsequent political achievements, and their rise to power in a number of countries.

Moscow would obviously be prepared to pursue relations with any regime, even an Islamist one (or one in coalition with Islamists). The possibility that such regimes could appear in Central Asia should not be underestimated, especially in light of the fact that "Islamism can formulate a long-term foreign policy that is different from ideological slogans,"[23] while its followers, especially moderate ones, appear ready to accept compromises.

The emergence of Islamists in the power structures will not be something extraordinary for Russia. Moscow has experience in dealing with Palestinian Hamas, Lebanese Hezbollah, and Egyptian Muslim Brotherhood. In addition, moderate Islamists are in power in Turkey, with which Russia has established a very cordial relationship. Thus Islamism cannot be regarded as an obstacle in developing relations between Russia and the Central Asian countries. In the same vein, the

United States and several European countries are in a dialogue with Islamists, including the Taliban, in the Middle East and South Asia. "Moscow is also suspected of having maintained a clandestine intelligence relationship with the IMU."[24] This statement is difficult to prove, but it is also not possible to refute such information.

A THREAT TO RUSSIA'S ALLIES

Not being a threat to Russia itself, the Islamists pose a threat to Russia's allies in the region. Although not consolidated, an active extremist force has been formed in Central Asia. In its struggle it is willing to resort to terrorism and is, to a limited extent, capable of engaging in military action. In 1999, extremists committed acts of terrorism in Tashkent against President Karimov. In 1999 and 2000, extremist groups consisting of 200–300 militants broke into the territory of Kyrgyzstan. In 2004, suicide bombers detonated explosives in Tashkent and Bukhara. The Jamaat al-Jihad group took responsibility for this act. In 2005, the Akramiya group organized an uprising in Andijan that lasted for days. In 2006, the IMU's militants attacked border posts in the Batken Province of Kyrgyzstan.

Central Asian authoritarian rulers declared the Afghan Taliban as the main source of the Islamist threat. They believe that local opposition would not last a single day without the Taliban's help. These rulers refuse to admit that the main reason for the rise of Islamist radicalism is their own failures in domestic policy. The Central Asian governments cultivate the sense of fear of radical Islamism and portray themselves as the only force capable of withstanding destabilization.

However, Islamism appeared and became popular in the region even before the Taliban came to power in 1996. Neither the civil war in Tajikistan, nor the 1991 events in Uzbek Namangan, when supporters of the Adolat movement rallied for the declaration of Islam as the state religion, was connected with the Taliban. Already at that time, the Adolat movement and its activities "had become uncontrollable."[25]

Undoubtedly, the Islamic opposition does cooperate with the Taliban. Members of the HTI and IMU are trained in camps in Afghanistan.

Several Taliban emissaries operate in Tajikistan, Uzbekistan, and Kyrgyzstan. Although financial support is also provided, its role is not significant. The Taliban and the Central Asian Islamists have a common goal: the establishment of an Islamic state.

At the same time, specific goals are more divergent. Some activists concentrate on the establishment of a national Islamic state in Uzbekistan and Tajikistan. Others are more inclined toward the Islamic caliphate with its core in the Ferghana Valley. Both stand in favor of sharia law. The Afghan opposition is not completely united either. The Pashtuns aim to create an Islamic state in Afghanistan; the Pakistani- and Arab-connected groups call for the formation of a cross-border Islamic state. The "Islamic internationalists" constitute a minority among the Taliban members, but they form its most irreconcilable wing and are the main opponents of the coalition between NATO and the government of Hamid Karzai.

AFGHANISTAN'S IMPACT ON THE REGION

Inevitable and also unpredictable changes in Afghanistan will have both a direct and indirect impact on the situation in the region and consequently Russia's standing there. Russian analyst Dina Malysheva suggests two outcomes of how the ongoing transformation in Afghanistan will affect Central Asia: one is pessimistic (Taliban-2), and the other optimistic (Peaceful Afghanistan). The first scenario predicts that Afghanistan will "get immersed in internal civil strife," which will lead to the "proliferation of the civil war ... to the territory ... of [the] Central Asian states." The second one is more congruent with the interests of the Central Asian states: "the implementation of a program of reconciliation and national reintegration ... with the result that local authorities will be capable of maintaining stability independently."[26]

It seems that the consistent implementation of both scenarios is not possible in the coming decade. The internal conflict in Afghanistan began with the overthrow of King Mohammed Zahir Shah in 1973 and has lasted for more than forty years already. It is not possible to say what its final outcome will be. French expert Gilles Dorronsoro, optimistic about the conflict's prospects, notes that "a combination of two critical problems threaten to undermine the mission of the U.S.-led coalition in Afghanistan: the failure of the counterinsurgency and the disconnect between political objectives and military operations."[27] This situation cannot be resolved in the medium term. Therefore, the withdrawal of coalition forces (mostly American, as most allies have already begun to withdraw) is being carried out in parallel with the search for a way the United States can preserve its presence in Afghanistan. In 2011, a joint U.S.-Afghan agreement was adopted providing for the establishment of four additional U.S. military bases on a long-term basis. Thus, a third intermediate scenario seems to be more likely: that the role of the Taliban will increase to the point that it can participate in the ruling coalition. In its recommendations, the Regional Network of Strategic Studies Centers Working Group on Reintegration, Reconstruction, and Reconciliation in Afghanistan, which operated until 2012, repeatedly pointed to the need "to move from currently fragmented contacts and patchy discussions to more formalized dialogue with the Taliban."[28] The Taliban in Afghanistan will continue to be a long-term factor. Therefore, it will exert a sustained impact on the situation in Central Asia. Apart from that, no matter how the conflict ends, the Taliban will proclaim itself the winner on the grounds that it was able to counter the most powerful state in the world.

All scenarios, including the intermediate one, provide for a continuing U.S./NATO presence in Central Asia under the umbrella of the military operation in Afghanistan. This will make Russia face "a risk of losing its strategic advantage and pushing Central Asia ... away from Russia's sphere of influence."[29]

How can Russia use Afghanistan to preserve its influence in the region? It is clear that Moscow's best option is for Afghanistan to remain unstable. Russia was not threatened by the Afghan "Islamic threat" during the Soviet intervention (1979–1989) or later, after the Taliban came to power. The story about the Taliban's "Northern Campaign" to Kazan, as well as pictures of Afghans in turbans and with Kalashnikovs posing in front of Lenin's Mausoleum on Red Square are nothing but journalistic banter. Nevertheless, the Southern threat remains a comfortable and significant justification for the Central Asian regimes to cooperate with Russia in the name of self-preservation. International terrorist movements, including al-Qaeda, operate in Afghanistan. In the absence of these movements, the political unions, in which Russia claims to be the leader, would lose their value.

The Central Asian regimes are well aware of this when, recognizing the Islamist threat coming from Afghanistan, they sometimes admit that it is somewhat exaggerated. While scaring themselves and the society with the Taliban, Central Asian leaders do not see in it a pretext for strengthening Russia's political and military presence. For example, in the mid-1990s Uzbekistan believed that Moscow was deliberately exaggerating the Taliban threat in order to reduce the flow of foreign investment into Central Asia.[30] Relations between Turkmenistan and the Taliban remain friendly. Turkmenistan's former president, Saparmurat Niyazov, was in constant contact with Taliban representatives. Until the September 11, 2001, attacks, whole eulogies to the Taliban were published in Central Asian newspapers. "Armed clashes, looting and robbery…have all ceased to occur on the territory controlled by the Taliban. They seek to establish order, peace, and harmony in their country."[31] (In private conversations, people in Central Asia told me that the Taliban are honest people who do not take bribes. They are sincere believers. When I asked them why the production of heroin has increased so much during their reign, the response was: "After all, everyone wants to eat.")

Russia's attitude toward the internal situation in Afghanistan remains unclear. On the one hand, Russia continues to express its support of the U.S.-led coalition; on the other, it avoids real participation in the process of resolving the Afghan crisis. Perhaps the only concrete step Russia has taken was its 2009 decision to allow transit of military-technical cargo through its territory. In 2011, Afghanistan received 30 percent of all military and civilian goods through the Northern Distribution Network. It is probable that, irrespective of whether the coalition withdraws its troops, this route will still be heavily used.

Russia has not yet determined the degree of its participation in Afghan affairs. Clearly, its policy will continue to focus on partnerships in combating drug trafficking, reconstructing Soviet-era enterprises, and supplying military-technical equipment connected with the repair of Soviet-era weapons. The statements by the Russian-controlled CSTO and CIS regarding the organizations' concern about the situation in Afghanistan are nothing but blatant propaganda. In addition, NATO does not seek to cooperate with these organizations. This is confirmed by Article 4 of the Lisbon Summit Declaration, adopted on December 5, 2010, which implies that NATO does not count on help from the CSTO or the SCO. This excludes these organizations from the process of conflict resolution in Afghanistan.

Russia's chances to participate in future large-scale energy projects that may significantly contribute to the modernization of Afghanistan are low. This includes its participation in the trans-Afghan gas pipeline, which will connect four states: Turkmenistan (gas exporter), Afghanistan, Pakistan, and India. Russia continues to hope that Gazprom will participate in its construction. However, the Turkmen Foreign Ministry clearly expressed its skepticism after Dmitry Medvedev visited Ashgabat in 2010 (Turkmenistan relies on other, non-Russian sources of financing). Moreover, the United States and the European Union are also reluctant to accept Russia's participation. They support diversification of energy routes.

Thus, Russia's role in the Afghanistan-Central Asia-China-United States-Europe-Muslim world group is unclear. It is unlikely that this situation will change in the coming years.

LITTLE FALLOUT IN CENTRAL ASIA FROM THE ARAB SPRING

What was the impact of the Arab Spring on the region? What is its impact on the countries where the same political "patriarchs" are still in power, as in Egypt, Libya, Syria, Tunisia, and Yemen? The events that have transformed the Arab world did not make any significant impact on Central Asia, Azerbaijan, or Russia's North Caucasus. The revolutions in Kyrgyzstan (in 2005 and 2010) occurred before the Arab uprisings. The violent and bloody Kyrgyz uprisings gave the leaders of Kazakhstan, Tajikistan, and Uzbekistan an additional excuse to show their subjects the advantages of stability, which they identify with their own rule. In this context, the Arab Spring was used to scare the population, as was justifiably the case with the civil war in Tajikistan.

However, in the second half of 2011, the situation in the Middle East and North Africa began to change. The "Arab Spring" was replaced by the "Islamic Summer." The Islamists were the ones who benefited from the revolutions. They managed to secure remarkable political victories: in the parliamentary elections in Tunisia in October 2011, Ennahda got 40 percent of the vote; radical Islamists connected with al-Qaeda control half of Yemen; the National Transitional Council that came to power in Libya proclaimed the formation of an Islamic state; and finally, in Egypt the Muslim Brotherhood and the more radical al-Nour Party achieved victory in the parliamentary elections. Mohamed Morsi, who came from the Muslim Brotherhood, became the president of Egypt. Islam has won and completely legitimized its right to participate in the political process.

In this context, the triumph of the 1978–1979 Islamic Revolution in Iran; the victory of the Palestinian Hamas movement in the 2005 elections; Turkey's moderate Islamist Justice and Development Party, which has been in power there since 2003; and Islamists' participation in the parliaments of most Muslim states can all be remembered. Against this background, the secular regimes in Central Asia look paradoxically like an exception to the "Muslim rule."

The success of religious parties in a key Muslim region makes an inevitable impact on Central Asia. There, local Islamists gained additional momentum to continue their struggle for the Islamization of state and society. Russia, where some Muslims see in the Arab Spring confirmation of the feasibility of the Muslim model of development, can face a similar problem.

The Spread of Islamism Into Russia

Since the mid-2000s, Islamists from Central Asia began to penetrate into Russia. The significance of this process should not be exaggerated, but it would also be shortsighted to ignore it. How does it manifest itself? The fact is that the Russian regions that border Central Asia—such as Astrakhan, Kurgan, Omsk, Orenburg, Tomsk, Tyumen, and several other oblasts, as well as Bashkiria—and also have a significant Muslim minority cannot be religiously and ideologically isolated from their southern neighbors. There is a narrow (18 km) isthmus in the Orenburg Oblast, which borders Kazakhstan. This isthmus separates the "Muslim Republic" of Bashkiria from Central Asia and, therefore, from the rest of the Muslim world. In the *Atlas of the World's Religions*, Bashkiria, Tatarstan (adjacent to it), and the Central Asian states are all painted in the green "Islamic" color.

Russia's southern border became permeable to religious radicalism. On the one hand, the penetration of radicals from Central Asia is limited and cannot make a decisive impact on the mood among Russia's Muslims. It is also clear that in contrast to the movements in the North Caucasus, the Central Asian Islamists cannot destabilize the political situation in Russia. On the other hand, this penetration is growing steadily, in particular due to the instability in the North Caucasus and the growing interest among young Russian Muslims in Salafi Islam.

The North Caucasus remains the main source of Islamic radicalism in Russia. However, similar sentiments are also widespread in Tatarstan (in Naberezhnye Chelny, Almetyevsk, Nizhnekamsk, Kukmor); Bashkiria (in Agidel, Baimak, Oktyabrsky, Sibay, Ufa); in the Volga region (in the Nizhny Novgorod, Samara, Saratov, Ulyanovsk oblasts); in Mordovia; and also in Russia's southern regions, which are geographically close to the Muslim Caucasus. Small groups of five to ten radicals consist of Russian citizens: Tatars, Bashkirs, and people from the North Caucasus (that is, internal migrants).

MIGRATION'S ROLE IN SPREADING EXTREMISM

The flow of immigrants from Central Asia contributes to the spread of radicalism. The number of radicals among these immigrants is increasing. In the 2000s, because of migration, the ethnic composition of Islamists in Russia has become more international. This became typical for the southern Urals and southern Siberia, in particular for the Chelyabinsk, Kurgan, Orenburg, Penza, Perm, and Tyumen oblasts and also for the Far East.

Migration is one of the factors that has a significant impact on relations between Russia and Central Asia. There are no precise data on how many migrants enter Russia from Central Asia, as most of them come illegally. Various sources place the number of migrants from Kyrgyzstan at between 400,000 and 1 million (500,000 according to the Kyrgyz Ministry of Internal Affairs), and from Uzbekistan between 600,000–700,000 and 1–2 million.[32] According to Bakhodir Matlubov, minister of internal affairs of Uzbekistan, 220,000 Uzbek migrants worked in Russia in 2007.[33] The number of incoming Tajik workers is unknown. In November 2011, *Novaya Gazeta* gave three estimates at once: 1 million, 1.5 million, and 2 million people.[34]

Migration from Central Asia is a consequence of local crises, unemployment, and the lack of land and water. The dynamics of the populations in Russia and in the countries where most of the migrants to Russia originate are noteworthy. In 2010, the population of Russia was 141.9 million, while the populations in the three Central Asian countries where most of the migrants originate (Kyrgyzstan, Tajikistan, and Uzbekistan) collectively totaled 41 million; by 2025 the populations are projected to be 140.8 million in Russia and 51 million in the three Central Asian countries; and by 2050, 126.7 million in Russia and 62 million in the three Central Asian countries.[35]

Migration binds Kyrgyzstan, Tajikistan, and Uzbekistan to their former imperial center. Up to 33 percent of the working population of Uzbekistan travels to other countries (predominantly Russia) to work, and the money these workers send back amounts to between 15 and 59 percent of the country's GDP.[36] According to statistics from the Central Bank of Russia, Tajik migrant workers sent remittances of $2.2 billion to Tajikistan in 2010, with the GDP of the country at $5.6 billion.[37] In 2011 Tajik migrants sent $2.96 billion home, which is $444 million more than in the record-breaking year of 2008, accounting for 45.5 percent of the country's GDP.[38]

Closer Ties vs. Mutual Irritation

The impact of migration on the relations between Russia and its southern neighbors has been contradictory. While migration has helped reinforce ties between the Russian and Central Asian societies, at the same time it has contributed to feelings of mutual irritation and rejection. The attitude toward migrants in Russian society is generally negative, which helps foster the rise in nationalist sentiments. If Russian irritation had previously been directed mostly against people from the Caucasus, it now has come to apply to Central Asians as well. Dozens of nationalistic organizations operating in Russia demand that the migrants be expelled from the country. Migrants have regularly been homicide victims, usually in an exceptionally cruel manner. In late 2008, for example, a small far-right group killed a native of Central Asia, cut off his head, and threw it into the regional administrative council building, promising to do the same with the officials unless they suppressed migration.[39] According to Rashid Nurgaliyev, former Russian minister of the interior, 7,500 extremist websites are operating in the country and spreading xenophobia. Based on the data of the well-respected Levada Center, the share of Russians advocating the idea of "Russia for Russians" was 13 percent in 1994, 33 percent in 1998, 55 percent in 2002, and since then has never dropped below 50 percent.[40]

In July 2010, Vladimir Zhirinovsky, head of the Liberal Democratic Party, proposed a ban on labor migration from countries where population growth is not limited by the government (a direct reference to Central Asia). During the December 2011 parliamentary elections, the party's main slogan was "We support the Russians!"

The Russian government has been inconsistent in its policy toward migration, as it well understands that in light of the current demographic situation, the country cannot get by without a constant influx of laborers; 10–12 percent of Russian GDP is produced by migrants.[41] The federal and local authorities are faced with two problems: the legalization of migrants and their adaptation to Russian culture.

Government's Policy Questioned

The Russian Orthodox Church has become concerned about the problem of Muslim migration. Vsevolod Chaplin, the chairman of the Synodal Department for the Cooperation of Church and Society of the Moscow Patriarchate, noted that the government's migrant integration policy has not been sufficiently effective.

Although 2 million migrants come to Russia every year, only 300,000 formalize their status; 12–15 million foreigners are in the country, but only one in ten is employed legally.[42] In 2007, the Federal Migration Service conducted a special campaign to legalize migrants who had entered Russia before January 15, 2007 (this applied only to citizens of the CIS who work in occupations that experience labor shortages). Over six weeks, 200,000 workers were legalized, while the number of "official" migrants from Uzbekistan alone amounted to 344,600 (compared with 111,000 in 2006).[43] Obviously, the legalization mechanism for migrants has not been adequately worked out.

Russian migration agencies regularly conduct operations simultaneously in many regions of Russia under the code name "illegal migrant," during which hundreds of Tajiks and Uzbeks are detained and expelled. Such operations were carried out in 2011 in Gorno-Altaysk and in Sverdlovsk Oblast. In Moscow in 2011, authorities began to eradicate the illegal migrant "towns" that were populated mostly by Tajiks. These "towns" are actually settlements whose inhabitants usually live in abandoned buildings and huts, and negotiate with the local authorities for electricity, running water, and communications. There is usually an informal local administration and healthcare system in such settlements as well. Several of these settlements were destroyed by the police, but, as the leaders of these communities have assured journalists, they expect to find another similar place to live. It can be said that the efforts by Russian authorities to counter illegal migration have been mostly palliative measures, and the overall situation continues to deteriorate.

The Value (or Not) of Learning Russian

The second policy line, as noted above, is the adaptation of migrants. Nearly everything boils down to discussions on the need for migrants to learn to speak Russian. The language issue is especially relevant to the migrants from Central Asia. Many Tajiks and Uzbeks, especially young ones, have a poor command of Russian and few of them can write in Russian. Based on data from the Center for Migration Studies, only 50 percent of the migrants are able to complete official forms in Russian, while a third of them speak no Russian at all.[44] As Konstantin Romodanovsky, director of Russia's Federal Migration Service, stated, "A command of the Russian language would establish the conditions for a secure and comfortable life. If a Central Asian does not know a word of Russian, how would he understand the command, 'Stop, or I'll shoot!'?"[45]

Under the law that came into effect on December 1, 2012, it is compulsory for labor migrants to have a test certificate confirming their knowledge of Russian. In 2010, more than 3,500 foreigners acquired the state certificate after taking a Russian language test. At the time, 1,247,000 foreigners were working in Russia.[46]

However, the difficulty is in the fact that, first of all, where the migrants from Central Asia would be able to learn Russian is not clear (this is not an issue for people from Belarus, Moldova, or Ukraine, where nearly everyone speaks Russian), and second, whether the migrants themselves would be interested in learning Russian. They usually do not exhibit much desire to learn the language. They come to Russia to work, not to spend their time studying. A few dozen words is perfectly adequate for them to perform simple labor. In addition, there are also always middle-aged and older workers (masters) among them who speak decent Russian and can serve as interpreters in case of difficulties. The people who have the ambition to remain in Russia permanently and subsequently acquire Russian citizenship usually already speak Russian and have a profession. They can establish their own businesses and send their children to regular schools. The language issue thus does not appear to be of great importance. Migrants will learn Russian only to the extent that they need to.

Teaching Russian to incoming migrants has scarcely gone beyond the stage of wishful thinking: neither schools nor teachers have been provided. The Federation of Independent Trade Unions has proposed that two centers be established for migrants in places of greatest concentration, but so far this idea is unrealized. In Tajikistan itself, there have been discussions about possibly beginning to offer such courses, but there, too, the idea has not been pursued.

Migrants usually arrive from Central Asia in groups and move into tight accommodations. A group leader who usually lives in Russia permanently (some acquire Russian citizenship), is in charge. The community leader establishes contacts with employers, communicates with local authorities (including the police), takes responsibility for all of the members of the group, and also frequently serves as imam. Recently, members of Hizb ut-Tahrir have been identified among these imams, although its members can also be found among average migrants. Russian Muslims have also been drawn into HTI cells. The opposite has also taken place, when Muslim migrant workers join radical groups that have already been formed by local "true believers" (Tatars or Caucasians). For example, in Tyumen Oblast, an HTI cell was discovered cooperating with Al-Ihsan, a local Muslim youth organi-zation.[47] Russian law enforcement agencies have obtained information that HTI cells are active in the Volga and Central federal districts, as well as in Siberia. As early as 2004, Rashid Nurgaliyev admitted that the HTI "has sprouted across Russia."[48] In April 2008, Nikolai Patrushev, director of the Federal Security Service (FSB), remarked that the HTI and IMU have shifted their activities to the Ural region.[49] These groups are not structured, and the activities of their members are limited. In the Ural, Volga, and western Siberia regions, they read and (as best they can) distribute HTI's *Al-Wa'y* review, as well as leaflets in Russian explaining the party's position. One of these leaflets was called "The Chechen Republic: How It Revived Islam in People's Souls." The FSB detained members of HTI cells in Tyumen in 2004, in Bashkiria in 2005, and in Krasnoyarsk in 2005. According to the local Ministry of the Interior, members of the HTI committed six crimes in Tatarstan in 2011. Tatarstan's minister of internal affairs, Asgat Safarov, believes that the rise in religious extremism has been directly connected to the growth of Muslim migration. In his opinion, "it is necessary to tighten control over the migration of people from the Caucasian republics and Central Asia, and with the cooperation of the migration and local authorities make a thorough check of all newcomers—where they came from and what religion they profess."[50]

In a number of Russian regions, propagandists from Central Asia have tried to use local mosques and madrasas to pursue their goals, usually choosing those that are well known for their radical orientation, such as the White (Gilan) mosque in Astrakhan Oblast; the historic mosque in Samara Oblast; the Rahman and al-Bukhari mosques in the Ural Federal District; the mosque at the Imam Fahretdinov Institute in Almetyevsk (Bashkiria); and the Nizhnekamsk mosque in Tatarstan. Natives of Central Asia have been seen around the mosque and madrasa in Buguruslan, near the border between Kazakhstan and Orenburg Oblast. According to information from law enforcement agencies, six militants who had been involved in terrorist attacks in Moscow (the 2002 Moscow Dubrovka theater siege and the 2004 Beslan school hostage crisis) were trained at this madrasa.[51] In October 2011, a group of four to six terrorists entered Chelyabinsk Oblast from Kazakhstan to carry out acts of terrorism in Ozersk, Snezhinsk, and Trekhgorny, where some of Russia's nuclear facilities are located. They were intercepted by the Russian Federal Security Service.

In 2011, according to Damir Mukhetdinov, deputy chairman of the Muslim Religious Directorate for European Regions, 7–8 percent of the posts of *imam-hatibs* in Russia were held by migrants from Tajikistan who had been naturalized in Russia.[52] This simultaneously testifies to their authority among the Russian Muslims and raises suspicions within the government agencies that scrutinize Islam.

Training With Extremists in the North Caucasus

Specific mention should be made of the Central Asian Muslims who have been establishing ties with radicals in the North Caucasus. Over the past decade, while these ties are not very extensive, they have become relatively regular. Hundreds of Chechens, Dagestanis, and Uzbeks have undergone combat training in camps run by the Afghan Taliban.[53] There, hatred for Russia (sometimes quite justified) has also been cultivated, along with religious education and training. Tajiks and Uzbeks have seen action with extremist groups in Chechnya and Dagestan, although in very small numbers. Those who had acquired some experience in real fighting in Afghanistan or at home acted as instructors for the others.

`At the same time, militants from Central Asia have been arriving in the North Caucasus at their own initiative; no structural cooperation has been observed between them and the local Islamists. The North Caucasian "Wahhabis" had no formal links to the HTI, and the appearance of HTI members in the region was noted only in the late 2000s. Nevertheless, in February 2011, two citizens of Kazakhstan were detained in Makhachkala, the capital of Dagestan, on charges of being involved in terrorist activities. "Mirror image" cases have also been reported, when Islamists from Russia have been found operating in Central Asia, in particular in Tajikistan. In 2009, 25 people (other sources suggest 40) escaped from the local prison; among the escapees were Caucasians who immediately joined the local militants fighting Rahmon's regime.

To combat the Islamic radicals, Russian and Central Asian intelligence services have established close cooperative ties. Once detained in Russia, members of the HTI, IMU, and other organizations are extradited to their countries of origin. Sometimes, however, members of the opposition have been handed over to Central Asian authorities under the pretext that they are extremists.

In the early 2010s, the "Islamization" of migrants began to affect the situation in the regions where their numbers are particularly high. Muslim migrant workers used to be indifferent to Islam: they would violate Islamic dietary laws, in particular with respect to alcohol; many did not practice the *salaf*, did not pray five (or even three) times a day, and did not fast during Ramadan. All of them, both young and older people, would explain their indifference by pointing to their living conditions, which gave them no opportunities to observe Islamic practices. Some of them were not even aware of the existence of mosques in Moscow.

However, the situation has gradually changed, and more migrants have begun to show their religiosity. This was primarily due to the creation of their own separate social environment having their own customs, mentality, and ideology (although, it is true, the opinion is widespread that Central Asian migrants are susceptible to both a stricter observance of Islam and alcoholism).[54] Migrants live in a culturally alien environment that treats them with increasing hostility. In the face of this hostility, migrants feel the need to join together to protect their interests. Under such circumstances, Islam becomes a consolidating factor. The new arrivals to Russia increasingly are young people who were born after the breakup of the Soviet Union, and for them, anything that relates to the old epoch is of no particular significance.

Influx of Muslims in Cities Creates Tension

The increasing number of people attending Russian mosques, especially in Moscow, reflects the fact that Islam is playing a greater role in the lives of migrants.[55] In 2010 and 2011, the number of Muslims who came to the Moscow mosque in celebration of *Eid al-Adha* (*Kurban-Bayram*) was 70,000 and 80,000, respectively, mostly people from Central Asia and the Caucasus. The thousands of Muslims created traffic jams and blocked access to apartment buildings; residents had to step over the heads of praying worshippers. In addition, people were annoyed (even disgusted) by the scenes of animal sacrifice, when goats were slaughtered right on the streets in front of passersby. The negative feeling is directed against the newcomers, rather than native Muslims, who have developed a form of behavior that does not make them stand out from other people. The Muslim migrants have also elicited irritation among their Tatar co-religionists.

Albir Krganov, the chief mufti of Moscow and the central region, admitted that Russian religious structures are unable to control "the Islamic training of migrants in prayer houses, markets, and apartments."[56] Ravil Gaynutdin, while noting that Russia should establish "centers of Muslim culture, combining the services of legal assistance to migrants, and teaching Russian language, customs, and traditions," proposed creating an advisory council of muftis of the CIS. Gaynutdin says that "Russia needs migrants because of the moral decay of the Russians."[57]

Because of the influx of migrants into the capital, the question of building new mosques (there are only five in Moscow) has been raised but remains unresolved, and increased tension will quite likely result from this problem in the future. The suggestion of establishing mosques for the "nationalities" (Avari, Azeri, Chechen, and others) has been made repeatedly, but so far Russia has only one Tajik mosque, which opened in Vladivostok in 2011.[58]

In autumn 2011, Muhiddin Kabiri, leader of the Islamic Renaissance Party of Tajikistan, made a visit to Russia (Moscow, Siberia, the Volga region, and the Far East). Before he departed, during the 9th Congress of the Party in September 2011, Kabiri had said that the party was "no longer confined to the Republic of Tajikistan, as it now appeals to Central Asian migrant workers in Russia."[59] In addition, Karomat Sharipov, head of the Tajik Labor Reserves public movement, stated that he would create the Muslim Party of Russia (there is no information, however, on whether he took any concrete steps in this direction).[60]

Muhiddin Kabiri spoke about "soft Islamization." The term itself would appear quite neutral, although it should be recalled that it had first been used by the Russian Islam scholar Ahmet Yarlikapov in the context of the situation in the North Caucasus.[61] In the long run, "soft Islamization" would lead to the archaizing of society, the incorporation of Islamic norms of behavior, and agitation to respect various religious rules and prohibitions.

Muslim migration has long since become a factor of domestic political life in Russian society, and it has been having an increasing impact on interdenominational religious relations. Muslim immigration to Russia is becoming strikingly similar to Muslim immigration to Europe, a topic for a future comparative study.

CONCLUSION

It is interesting that Russian politicians usually cite the figure of 20 million when talking about the number of Muslims in Russia, although the number of Muslims who are citizens of Russia is in fact slightly over 16 million. In other words, the number of Muslims in Russia is taken as a whole, without regard to which are "ours" and which are "newcomers." It would seem that the figure of 20 million is more accurate, as it provides a better understanding of the significance of the Islamic factor in the country.

The Russian establishment does not see Central Asia as a full-fledged segment of the Muslim world either politically or ideologically. They treat it primarily as former Soviet space, an attitude that brings significant negative side effects and ultimately leads nowhere. After more than two decades since the collapse of the Soviet Union, Moscow has built its policy upon two affiliations with the region: the old Soviet affiliation and the new Muslim one. It must be noted that Europe, the United States, and China have similar visions of Central Asia. On the one hand, it is seen as a Soviet relic, while on the other as an integral part of the Muslim world. The latter is especially pronounced when it comes to the presence of radical Islam there, which is regarded almost as the main feature of the region's civilizational identity.

Central Asia does not fit into the overall Russian strategy of dealing with the rest of the Muslim world as a global political actor (acknowledging the fact that the Muslim world is largely heterogeneous, one cannot ignore its role as a single actor). In a speech at Cairo University delivered on June 4, 2009, U.S. President Barack Obama spoke about the "tension between the United States and Muslims" and the "partnership between America and Islam."[62] The main thrust of Kremlin policy toward the Muslim world has been the desire to demonstrate Russia's "intermediary" position between it and the West, the attempt to play the role of a bridge, a kind of mediator. Russia's policy toward Iran is an example of this, and it was clearly demonstrated in 2012 in connection with the circumstances surrounding Libya and Syria. It is not the task of this book to judge to what extent this mediation effort was successful.

Islam as a factor in relations between Russia and the Central Asian states had long been considered only in the context of the general struggle against religious radicalism. Mutual understanding has been achieved in this direction. It can be said that the threat posed by radicalism led to rapprochement between Moscow and the Central Asian regimes.

There is a recurrent discussion about certain common (historical and quasi-Soviet) values and about Eurasianism, which includes an inter-religious Orthodox-Muslim dialogue. However, the Central Asian societies have been transformed over the past decade. They have become increasingly traditional, while their religious identity has strengthened. Islam has become an instrument for regulating relations within society, and local governments now use it as a tool in their domestic policies. All of these factors, as well as the strengthening of the "Islamic vector" in foreign policy, have made Central Asia increasingly distant from

Moscow. This process, most evident in Tajikistan and Uzbekistan, and to a lesser extent in the other countries, requires that the relations between Russia and Central Asia be reexamined.

CHAPTER 4

KAZAKHSTAN AND ITS NEIGHBORHOOD

Kazakhstan is the country with which Russia has developed the most stable and cordial relations since the breakup of the Soviet Union. The two countries' mutual interests have been based on the following factors: historical and geographical closeness; the relatively deep penetration of the Russian language and culture into Kazakh society; and mutual economic integration.

Located in the heart of Eurasia between Russia, China, and the Muslim world, Kazakhstan both differs from all of its neighbors and has features in common with them. Kazakhstan is obviously the only Eurasian state that is equally close to its neighbors and, at the same time, equidistant from them. Because of its sheer geographical size, natural resources, and human capital ("population quality"), Kazakhstan is a key country in the region and is the local center of gravity. Such factors are the source of Astana's broad ambitions, its claim to having one foot in Europe and the other in the Muslim world, and its desire to attain the status of something of a "global mini-power." As a consequence, Kazakhstan has been very protective of its sovereignty and has rejected any sort of patronage proffered by other states, which many of the outside players active in Central Asia did not immediately realize.

American experts from the Atlantic Council and the Central Asia-Caucasus Institute (CACI) proposed the "Central Eurasia" concept, under which the region is considered to consist of the three states of the

South Caucasus and the five Central Asian states. In such a context, researchers say that "Kazakhstan is arguably the most vulnerable of all eight countries to internal and external threats," with its vulnerabilities associated with "partition, invasion or collapse."[1] In our opinion, however, Kazakhstan is the *least* vulnerable state in the "Central Eurasian" region (itself a debatable concept), as has been proven throughout the history of its independent existence.

Kazakhstan's only external challenge, it might be said (assuming for a brief moment that the Kremlin would have ever taken the idea seriously), came more than twenty years ago from Russia, and even that was largely a product of the imagination of Alexander Solzhenitsyn. The dissident author proposed dismembering Kazakhstan and incorporating its Russian-dominated oblasts into Russia. However, Solzhenitsyn's proposal remained a product of political fiction and fantasy. Kazakhstan's neighbors (China and the Central Asian states) have never posed any real threat to its territorial integrity, inasmuch as all of them have an interest in Kazakhstan's remaining internally stable. As late as 2011, Kazakhstan had managed to escape social and religious turmoil, and avoid internal religious conflicts. There has been no civil war there (as there had been in Tajikistan), no attempted coup d'état as in Turkmenistan, and no Kyrgyz-type revolt or violent upheavals as those in Andijan and Osh. Finally, Kazakhstan has not experienced the destabilizing influence of a consolidated radical Islamist movement.

Kazakhstan appears to be the most prosperous state of Central Asia. Crossing the border into Kazakhstan from one of its southern neighbors, one is immediately struck by its comparative affluence. What is more, this appearance of success in Kazakhstan sometimes applies even in comparison with some neighboring oblasts of the Russian Federation (for example, Astrakhan Oblast).

Kazakhstan's success was first put to the test during the global economic crisis that swept Kazakhstan in 2008. Since the crisis had been brought about by factors that affected the entire world, Kazakhstan had by definition been unable to avoid it. Although it did suffer some losses, by managing to steer clear of disaster during the first stage of the crisis, Kazakhstan once again proved its viability. The second time it needed to prove its strength as a nation state was in connection with the outbreaks of social instability and the surge of religious extremism that arose in 2011.

PERIOD OF UPHEAVAL

Kazakhstan passed through a number of unprecedented upheavals in 2011, beginning with a strike in May in Zhanaozen, Mangystau Province (in the western part of the country), by oil-field workers demanding reinstatement of the 1,500 people whom the authorities had laid off, as well as better pay and improved working conditions.[2] The strike was declared open-ended, and some of the strikers announced a hunger strike and set up tents in the central square. When the government organized a rally of high school and local college students on December 16 (Kazakhstan Independence Day), they were met by workers shouting, "you celebrate, we grieve—go away!" Clashes ensued, which the police did not try to prevent. Then fighting spread, and the office of the local mine owner, the Uzen'munaigas Company, was set ablaze. In response, the police returned to the square and opened fire on the demonstrators. The gunfire continued until evening, when armored vehicles were sent into the town. According to official estimates, sixteen people were killed and more than 100 were wounded (data from opposition groups, in particular from the Socialist Movement Kazakhstan, list 73 killed and hundreds wounded).[3]

The crisis in Zhanaozen can be likened to the mass demonstrations of young Kazakhs in Almaty in 1986, which served as precursor to the transformation of Kazakh society and marked a turning point in the public's consciousness. The riots could also be equated with the 2005 demonstrations in Andijan, Uzbekistan, which though brutally suppressed, nevertheless had triggered widespread public dissatisfaction with the regime and had resulted in some loss of credibility by the government. In neither case had the authorities been prepared for such broad (though localized) protests, and even though they understood that in the end it would damage their popularity, the authorities still felt compelled to use extreme measures. Both Zhanaozen and Andijan forced the government to recognize not how strong, but how weak, they were. It should, however, be noted that long before the events in Zhanaozen transpired, certain Kazakhstan analysts had predicted that the political situation would destabilize.[4]

Without going into details, one important point must be made: the Zhanaozen crisis had no religious component. The protesters had not used Islamic slogans, and there was no credible information that they had been supported by Islamist groups.

Another trigger had been the activities of Islamist groups, which in 2011 carried out several deadly acts of terrorism. Their operations gained momentum, so to speak, in parallel with the labor strikes. In May 2011, a suicide bomber carried out an attack in Aktobe; on October 31, there were two blasts in Atyrau (one of which was set off by a suicide bomber). Investigators concluded that the explosions had been organized by the terrorist group Jund al-Khilafah. On November 12, 2011, a certain Maksat Kariev killed seven people, including two police officers, before firing a grenade launcher at the local National Security Committee branch building. Nurumakhan Isayev, deputy prosecutor general of Kazakhstan, announced that Kariev had been a "jihadist," adding that no direct link had been established between these attacks.[5] In the words of influential analyst Dosym Satpayev, the republic was beginning to turn into a "rear base" for the militants where they could go to "lick their wounds."[6] "Extremism has not been spreading across the country from any single center... acts of terrorism can happen in any city; there is no regional differentiation."[7]

In fact, compared with what has been happening with the rise of Islam across the rest of Central Asia and Russia, and especially in the North Caucasus, there is nothing noteworthy about the events in Kazakhstan, which only emphasizes the fact that Kazakhstan will not be able to avoid the activities of Islamic radicals operating in surrounding countries. Various sources have also indicated that Kazakh Islamists have established "working contacts" with Muslim Russian citizens who have planned and carried out acts of terrorism. Although it has become common to write about Central Asian radicals' influence on Russia, about Hizb ut-Tahrir and the Islamization of Muslim migration to Russia (see chapter 3, "Russia and Islam in Central Asia: Problems of Migration"), the opposite outcome, where Russian radicals are cooperating with Islamists within the borders of Kazakhstan, has also become more prevalent.

One particular but very important reason behind the acts of terrorism was the enactment of a restrictive new law, "Religious Activities and Religious Organizations," which prohibits religious activity outside officially designated areas, that is, closes down the "informal open houses of prayer," imposes stricter control over missionaries, and censors religious literature. Article 7, which prohibits prayer in public institutions, was a particular source of irritation for the radicals. This new law, initially proposed in 2008 as a replacement for a more lenient 1992 law, was mainly intended to prevent a rise in religious sentiment and to restrict the activities of Islamic opposition groups. Azamat Maytanov, press secretary for the State Agency for Religious Affairs, announced that "young people will learn about religion in official mosques rather than in obscure informal groups." "There are already plenty of mosques where prayers can be read. No one will complain about it."[8]

Mosque attendance in the country has increased. According to Radio Liberty, of the 30,000 people who attend mosque in Astana daily, 60–70 percent are civil servants. The number of women wearing the veil has grown significantly in cities across Kazakhstan, which provoked concern even from the Atyrau local university administration. Over the past two to three years, the Democratic Party Adilet has been markedly drifting toward the fold of Islamic movements. Just before the elections, Murat Telibekov, head of the Union of Muslims of Kazakhstan, joined Adilet; in November 2011 he declared, "People are beginning to realize that you can talk to the authorities only from a position of force."[9] I would also note such seemingly trivial details as the notice posted on the Almaty central mosque's website at the very end of 2011, pointing out that the New Year is not an Islamic holiday. Such a warning would have been unimaginable just a few years ago. Looking at this in the context of calls not to celebrate the New Year in Dagestan, the murder of a man dressed in a Santa costume in Dushanbe, and similar events, there is evidence of Islamic radicalization in the post-Soviet space (this trend can be generalized even beyond the post-Soviet space if the bombing of five churches in Nigeria just before Christmas is included), and also evidence that, despite the earlier view that Kazakhstan was "distanced" from the Islamic issue, it has now been drawn into the general Islamization trend. The HTI has been operating in Kazakhstan since 1998. As part of the *umma*, the Muslim states of the former Soviet Union are also affected by the trends within it, including the negative ones. The authorities in Kazakhstan, although perhaps with some delay, are beginning to wake up to this fact, which will have major implications for the country and society.

While the Russian language issue pales in comparison to the events in Zhanaozen or acts of terrorism, it is symptomatic of the situation in Kazakhstan as a whole. During the run-up to the extraordinary parliamentary elections in January 2012, several political parties had advocated programs and actions that smacked of nationalism. In September 2011, the so-called 138 Appeal had been signed by the Communist People's Party of Kazakhstan, the Ruhaniyat Party, the Azat Social-Democratic Party, and the Ak Zhol Democratic Party of Kazakhstan, calling for an end to the status of Russian as an official language under the current constitution (that is, its use in official documents on an equal basis with Kazakh).

These parties do not have much influence, and only one of them made it into Parliament (Ak Zhol, which is in the shadow of the ruling Nur Otan Party). In an effort to ease tensions surrounding the language issue, Nursultan Nazarbayev bluntly pointed out that "the constitution says that state authorities can officially use the Russian language alongside Kazakh. No one can violate these constitutional rules … the most precious things for us in the country are unity and harmony. Kazakh will gradually acquire its status as the state language. We have said that 95 percent of the population will speak the state language by 2020; there is no need to hurry."[10] Nazarbayev's irritation at the attacks on the Russian language is easy to understand, since the Russian-speaking population makes up 40 percent of the electorate and has traditionally supported the ruling party at the ballot box.[11]

However, it must be acknowledged that ethnic nationalist sentiments have continued to grow in the country. Ethnic nationalism and religion remain among the most important mobilization tools available for both the government and its opponents to use as needed. This situation is not unique to Kazakhstan. Indeed, ethno-nationalist sentiments are common throughout the post-Soviet region, including Central Asia, and if the domestic situation should deteriorate further, these sentiments will continue to spread and their slogans will become more polarized. This in turn would lead to increasing tension in Kazakhstan. As recent history has shown, whenever power is up for grabs, one or the other political force will almost inevitably appeal to ethnic nationalism or religion.

TRADITION AND SOCIETY'S PASSIVITY

In discussing ethics and religion, the role of tradition in the political life of Kazakhstan should be considered. Its importance should not be overestimated (in this respect, Kazakhstan differs strikingly from, for example, Uzbekistan); however, it also should not be completely dismissed. In any case, clan and kinship do play a role in appointments to high positions. Belonging to one of the *jüz* (three regional associations: the Great Ulu jüz—meaning "seven rivers"—in the southeast, in Zhetysu; the Middle Orta jüz in the central and eastern parts of the country; and the Junior Kişhi jüz in the west) plays a significant role as well. According to expert Konstantin Syroezhkin, "competition between the *jüz* at the elite level has played and continues to play an extremely important role in the life of Kazakh society."[12] It should be noted that the major energy reserves in Kazakhstan are located in land traditionally dominated by the Junior Kişhi jüz.

Neither the events in Zhanaozen nor the activities of the Islamist groups have garnered wide support among the public. This is not only because the authorities have managed to take preventive measures to stop the protests from spreading further, but also because the public in Kazakhstan was not prepared for them, absent the kind of social or religious solidarity or any broad-based civil or political opposition that would be capable of putting thousands of people into the streets, as happened in Russia. Evidence of the lack of any widespread societal appetite for protest may be seen in the results of the 2012 election (in which Nazarbayev's Nur Otan Party won a convincing and unsurprising victory) and also in the fact that the public never objected to violations committed during the process of preparing for and organizing the election. Joao Suares, the head of the Organization for Security and Co-operation in Europe (OSCE) Parliamentary Assembly observers' mission, said that "Despite the government's declarations that it wants to develop the democratic process in Kazakhstan and hold elections in accordance with OSCE obligations... the extraordinary parliamentary election does not measure up to the fundamental principles of democratic elections."[13] In Kazakhstan itself, this assessment had all the force of a voice crying in the wilderness.

The question of whether Nazarbayev's émigré political opponents had had any hand in the events of Zhanaozen or in religious extremist acts is still unanswered; nevertheless, the question of whether some of them may return to "big politics" remains open. If some of the politicians who have left the country (for example, former prime minister Akezhan Kazhegeldin) would not appear inclined to want to dive back into local political intrigue, the same cannot be said of others, such as Nazarbayev's son-in-law Rakhat Aliyev (who is married to his daughter Dariga and continues to monitor events in the Republic of Kazakhstan) or media oligarch Mukhtar Ablyazov.

Ablyazov, who fled Kazakhstan in 2009 amid accusations of money laundering and fraud, has retained some of his influence and has media resources at his disposal. At one point, Ablyazov cooperated with the government; then he became part of the opposition; and then he sought reconciliation with Nursultan Nazarbayev. In 2005, he financed the establishment of the People's Party Alga!, the successor to the Democratic Choice of Kazakhstan, which remains part of the non-systemic opposition and is not registered. He also funds the *Respublica* newspaper, which is critical of the government and is widely known outside Kazakhstan, having its editorial offices in Moscow. Ablyazov has been involved in some notorious scandals connected to financial fraud. Courts in Kazakhstan, Russia, and the UK have charged him with theft. Ablyazov's life story has been very similar in some respects to those of Russian oligarchs Boris Berezovsky and Mikhail Khodorkovsky. However, in contrast to Berezovsky, Ablyazov has never been a key member of the ruling establishment. And in the view of Central Asia expert Martha Brill Olcott, Ablyazov's influence is in no way comparable to Khodorkovsky's influence in Russia, for all of Ablyazov's pretensions of finding a similar role in his country. Also, he has never been able to pose a personal challenge to Nazarbayev.

A BLOW TO KAZAKH STABILITY

"The passivity of Kazakhstan's society," says scholar Nikolai Kuzmin, "cannot hide the fact that Kazakhstan has lost its stability since the events at Zhanaozen and that its instability is being felt in this country *more intensely than anywhere else* [italics mine]. . . . Last year, it became clear that from now on Kazakhstan will have to live in a world that has lost its familiar reassuring qualities of security, tolerance, and stability. Our society has had to face various forms of extremism, from acts of terrorism to public appeals that the use of the Russian language be banned."[14] At least psychologically, the citizens of Kazakhstan are not ready for this, and their reaction could be unpredictably sharp should such excesses be repeated. Martha Brill Olcott described the events in Zhanaozen as "a wake-up call for President Nazarbayev and the ruling elite of the need to make political change and strengthen political institutions so that the national leader can ensure a successful handover of power and guarantee himself a place in Kazakhstan's history."[15]

In evaluating the events in Zhanaozen, Karim Masimov (prime minister at the time) admitted, "This is the first time that a conflict of this level has broken out in Kazakhstan. There were many reasons for this conflict, some more evident, others deeper . . . the root causes of the situation reach deep." At the same time, he added, "Although in Zhanaozen there is social tension, throughout the country as a whole there is not."[16] For his part, Yermukhamet Yertysbayev, the adviser to the president of Kazakhstan, said that the authorities should respond to the events in Zhanaozen by "building a welfare state."[17]

Serious analysis of the events by leading political figures contrasted quite sharply with the numerous pronouncements in the official media to the effect that "the 2011 Mangystau crisis, which lasted for several years and has been greatly exacerbated over the past seven months, was the result of the hidden hand of the West at work."[18]

"Shock and awe has prevailed among the opposition" following the events in Zhanaozen. "The opposition acted too blatantly and carelessly, trying to escalate the situation and inflame hysteria and unrest." "They were allowed to run wild during the elections, but immediately after they ended and the new Parliament began to work, detentions, searches and interrogations followed."[19] In terms of the style and manner of presentation, these comments were strikingly similar to Putin's criticism of the Russian opposition. However, it should be noted that the media (which are associated with the Russian government) attempt to be more objective when characterizing the situation in Kazakhstan and do not blame local problems on any conspiracy of external forces.

The Zhanaozen crisis became emblematic of the overall social and economic deterioration and failures of the political system, in other words, of what has been called "authoritarian modernization." Inflation in Kazakhstan has been on the rise: in 2011, prices of all goods and services increased by 7.4 percent compared with the preceding year; food prices alone rose by 9.1 percent.[20] Corruption accounts for 25–30 percent of the country's GDP, and "is large enough to constitute a separate 'parallel economy.'"[21] As Alisher Sagadiev has written, "when average people experience a 'disruption' in income, they will not be as interested in the outcome of the *El Clásico* in soccer between Real and Barcelona as in which government financial faction will prevail in the next clan war." Masimov's wealth is valued at approximately $2 billion, and he owns a mansion in London that is worth $189 million. "Anything at all could set the unrest off."[22] If such statements might have sounded exaggerated before 2011, they are now backed by solid evidence.

ENERGY'S ABUNDANCE

All of the politicians in Kazakhstan recognize the need to implement changes. That's true even for those who find it psychologically difficult on a personal level to actually begin doing so, whether because they are satisfied with things as they are (those who are wealthy and happy) or because they have gotten too old (after long having lived blissfully in the instinctive hope that they would be able to avoid dealing with any "sharp corners"). Such sentiments were rooted in a number of factors: first of all, the availability of natural resources; second, the success achieved in reforms; and third, the tradition of social stability and the reliability of the political system.

According to data for 2011 from BP, Kazakhstan has reserves of 5.5 billion tons of oil and 3 million cubic meters of gas, which make it one of the top ten countries in the world (and second in the CIS) in the size of its hydrocarbon reserves. While Kazakhstan ranked 16 in the world in quantity of oil extracted in 2011, it plans to achieve a production of 130 million tons of oil (which would make it one of the top ten oil producers in the world) by 2020. Over the first eleven months of 2011, 65.4 million tons of oil were recovered, and 12.4 million tons of oil were refined, although the quality of the oil being delivered to the refineries has been declining due to its increasing weight and higher content of sulfur, which causes greater wear on equipment. Expansion of the Caspian Pipeline Consortium's pipeline has begun in Atyrau. When complete, it will stretch 1,510 kilometers from the Tengiz oil field to the Novorossiysk-2 Marine Terminal, and plans call for increasing the pipeline's throughput to 67 million tons of oil, of which 52.5 million tons will be from Kazakhstan. The Kazakhstan-China oil pipeline is to be expanded to 20 million tons, and a proposal has been made to build the Kazakh Caspian Transportation System (KCTS) pipeline from Kashagan through Baku-Ceyhan; that pipeline would initially have a throughput of 23 million tons, which potentially could be increased to 35–36 million tons.

Gas recovery over the first eleven months of 2011 totaled 36.1 billion cubic meters, of which 8.7 billion cubic meters were consumed and 7.9 billion cubic meters were exported. A total of 88.6 billion cubic meters of gas transit Kazakh territory: 56.8 billion cubic meters from Russia, 24.1 billion from Turkmenistan, and 7.7 billion from Uzbekistan. There are currently two pipelines to China, with a third under construction.[23]

Between January and October 2011, exports of fuel and energy products amounted to 78.2 percent of Kazakhstan's total exports, worth $58.1 billion,[24] which confirms the obvious conclusion that Kazakhstan's economy will continue to be based upon energy resources and will always be dependent upon hydrocarbon prices on the world market. On the one hand, this circumstance could condemn the country to a kind of "economic backwardness" and create the conditions for it to develop an inferiority complex. Astana is nervous about the fact that between 2000 and 2008, exports of oil and petroleum products increased from 53 percent of the total to nearly 70 percent, which is turning the country into a "natural resources appendage." On the other hand, however, both the availability of hydrocarbons and Kazakhstan's favorable geographic location could at least provide the long-term financial foundation needed for further development. "More transit pipelines will be needed in the future. ... Because of the economies of scale, road or rail transport of oil and gas is extremely expensive. This leaves pipelines as the only viable alternative for transporting significant values."[25] The question is whether the ruling class will be able to effectively capitalize on the country's geographical advantage. One way or another, the National Fund (which accumulates revenue earned from energy exports) now totals $70 billion, which the government has promised to spend on industry diversification and social programs.[26]

According to Daniil Kislov, head of the website Fergana.ru, "Kazakhstan's current ruling class has returned full circle to where it began: the authoritarian late-Soviet past that tolerated no competition," while Nazarbayev himself, "like many aging autocrats, lives on a completely different planet and follows a logic of his own."[27] Although there is a fair amount of truth in this judgment, there is also a share of exaggeration. Kazakhstan's ruling class is not monolithic, but contains competing groups. Nazarbayev himself, who can be credited with playing a part in building the new country of Kazakhstan (which had never previously existed as a state), is by no means completely isolated from the real situation in the country.

PLURALISM'S ORIGINS

The current situation can be understood only in the context of the history of independent Kazakhstan, where growing authoritarian tendencies over the past twenty years have not precluded the evolution of a certain political pluralism (as opposed to its neighbors Turkmenistan and Uzbekistan). This pluralism usually does not rise to the surface in political life, but in Kazakhstan it emerged in order to protect the interests of various economic groups and clans. Nazarbayev, though an authoritarian ruler, remained at the same time an intercessor between the various interest groups, which they generally found acceptable. Such a duality may perhaps be a characteristic of the regime in Kazakhstan, one that will remain even after an eventual transition of power.

In the opinion of Konstantin Syroezhkin, political "polycentricity has always been a feature of political life in Kazakhstan."[28] Nazarbayev has always had to deal with it, although he has repeatedly tried to overcome it. As he was consolidating his power, he took the decisive step of holding a referendum in 1995, which allowed him to extend his term as president until December 1, 2001. Under the new constitution adopted in 1995, the president's power was made independent and superior to the other branches of power, and authoritarianism took on its "classic form." Even in this context, however, latent polycentricity remained, and the separate groups continued to defend their interests under its framework.

In 2004 Nazarbayev, without going into detail, mentioned that 80 percent of GDP in Kazakhstan was controlled by "ten megaholdings," some of which are even "seeking power."[29] Obviously, this was an exaggeration, but it sounded a warning to those who had begun to take their own independence for granted. Although the idea of political modernization had been discussed in 2002–2006, it was soon concluded that such hopes had been misplaced. In the presidential election in December 2005, Nazarbayev got 91 percent of the vote.[30] This reinforced his decision in favor of personal power, while still retaining some vestiges of a managed democracy. The process of tightening the regime's control reached its climax in 2011. Kazakhstan's Majlis became a one-party parliament, with only one party, Nur Otan, able to participate in the parliamentary elections. Realizing that this could impede the transition of power and put him in an awkward position with respect to the West, Nazarbayev called early elections. Apart from Nur Otan (which got 83 seats), two other parties were elected to the Parliament: Ak Zhol with eight seats and the Communist People's Party of Kazakhstan with seven.

A partial return to the polycentric model had first become evident earlier, in 2008–2009, when several powerful groups began to
appear: "the Southerners," represented by Sarybai Kalmurzaev and
Umirzak Shukeyev; "the old guard," headed by Nurtai Abykayev; and
a third group consisting of representatives of the current government,
Karim Masimov, Timur Kulibayev, Grigori Marchenko, and Imangali
Tasmagambetov, who were in control of the national economy.[31] These
centers of power (as identified by Konstantin Syroezhkin) are to quite an
extent arbitrary. It would be more appropriate to discuss the influential
politicians who remain loyal to the president and certainly would have
rejected any implication that they belong to any such group. Moreover,
these groups (in particular the third one) can be further divided into
subgroups. In any case, in contrast to Uzbekistan, Turkmenistan, and
Tajikistan, there is a viable political process in Kazakhstan, represented
by outstanding figures, each of whom has his own supporters and political circles. Altogether, they constitute the political elite of Kazakhstan
that will make decisions on the economic and political development of
the country in the future.

Unlike Russia's ruling elite, Kazakhstan's ruling class has a better
understanding of the need for and inevitability of reforms, including in
politics, and does not suffer from a great, if complex, historic past (Soviet
or imperial); in fact, Kazakhstan has never even existed as a nation state.
Its ruling elite is not fixated on any sense of tradition, which it generally
views as a useful political instrument of convenience. It therefore hangs
its own survival and that of the country exclusively on the future and
modernization (which, in Kazakhstan, unlike in Russia, are more than
empty words).

Finally, Kazakhstan does not possess as vast a quantity of energy
resources as Russia, where the abundance of natural resources has fueled
political irresponsibility among the ruling class. To a certain extent,
Kazakhstan's approach more closely resembles that of the Persian Gulf
monarchies, which, having realized that their energy resources are finite
and cannot be the only foundation upon which to build prosperity,
are attempting to use "God's gift" of oil to develop their countries into
stable and modern states.

THE NEED FOR CHANGE

Kazakhstan's political and business elites have dispensed with their infantile self-assuredness of the 1990s and are preparing for the economic and political difficulties ahead. Prime Minister Karim Masimov (who following the extraordinary parliamentary elections in January 2012 retained his position, although many had expected him to lose) takes the view that "a second wave of the crisis will be inevitable and will come in 2012–2013." He is aware of the negative impact this could have and knows that Kazakhstan will require "macroeconomic stability" to overcome the consequences, with a "second priority of fighting unemployment."[32] Although Masimov's opponents have criticized him on many issues, he deserves some credit for having admitted that the country faces some difficult years, instead of sticking to a populist line. It is striking that when the prime minister made these points, per capita GDP was at $11,300 and unemployment was at only 5.3 percent—a level of development that would be an elusive dream for nearly any other CIS state.

The cautious, almost pessimistic, glimpse into the future by the Masimov, who stepped down as prime minister in September 2012 to become Nazarbayev's chief of staff, stands in contrast to that of the president, who expects the per capita GDP to grow to at least $15,000 by 2016, and the economy to grow at an annual rate of 7 percent, which would make Kazakhstan one of the higher-income countries.[33] Local economists and technocrats have preferred to remain silent on the chances that a 7 percent annual growth rate could be quickly achieved. But it is not easy to see how this could happen, given the inevitability of a crisis. However, according to official statistics, the GDP of Kazakhstan unexpectedly grew by 5 percent in 2012.[34]

In a wordy address to the people of Kazakhstan, President Nazarbayev spoke about the need to find an "optimal balance between economic progress and the provision of public goods," to "begin new large-scale projects in the sphere of re-division of our natural resources and infrastructure, which will manage this division," to achieve independence in electrical power generation ("the construction of the Balkhash thermal plant with a capacity of 1,320 MW, worth $2.3 billion"), to greatly increase the level of education and "social adaptation of young people," and other genuinely important problems.[35] The question remains how such grandiose plans could be implemented in the context of the looming crisis.

Kazakhstan's ruling class is aware of the need for change, and sooner or later changes will be made. They have a kind of handicap in the form of a priori support for Nazarbayev in Europe and the United States, countries that are willing to forgive Nazarbayev's regime much, seeing that, unlike its Central Asian neighbors, Kazakhstan is genuinely taking the path to reform. Nobody brings up "Kazakhgate"[36] or the 95.5 percent vote in the 2007 presidential election, which had no effect on Kazakhstan's heading the OSCE in 2010, the first Central Asian state to do so. The actions of authorities in Zhanaozen have not been compared to Tashkent's suppression of the demonstrations in Andijan in 2005, for which Uzbekistan was punished with criticism and sanctions.

In this respect, potential reformers have been given free rein, and they have support from outside. (That could be particularly important if during the introduction of reform the authorities are forced to take tough measures against those portions of the populace that are affected and whose living standards have declined for a time.) Reforms disrupt the accustomed stability. However, events in Zhanaozen have shown that the "hyperstability" in Kazakhstan tends to lead to stagnation and could threaten national security. As far-reaching reforms are implemented, the rivalry among the various economic, social, and political interests will intensify. The middle and lower levels in society will become more politically active, and there will be greater demand for a democratic and civilized system of government. If such a system does not emerge, the changes could bring about negative consequences, such as an explosion of social unrest that would be suppressed by dictatorial means. The ruling elite clearly would not be interested in seeing such an outcome.

The extent to which the elite will be prepared to risk reform will soon become evident. Although Kazakhstan will inevitably move in this direction, inertia and fear of political change will also have an effect, especially since economic reforms from the top down are not infrequently accompanied by attempts to preserve the customary distribution of power and the established balance of political forces.

THE SUCCESSION ISSUE

The expected change of government and the appearance of a new leader acquire fundamental importance in the context of proposed reforms. The question is, of course, when a successor to Nursultan Nazarbayev will be named and when that person will actually assume the president's chair. It is true that Yermukhamet Yertysbayev, speaking at the Royal Institute of International Affairs in London in January 2012 (on the eve of the elections), said that the incumbent president "has a mandate until December 2016 and has no plans to step down from office."[37] This can be taken both as an attempt to avoid giving a direct answer and as evidence that Nazarbayev has not yet made a final decision.

Different politicians have been mentioned at various times as potential successors to Nazarbayev. In 2009, it was Imangali Tasmagambetov, the *akim* (mayor) of Astana, and in 2010 it was Nurtai Abykayev, the chairman of the National Security Committee. Nazarbayev's daughter Dariga has also been on this list,[38] as have Karim Masimov and Jarmakhan Tuyakbay, who was chairman of the Majlis between 1999 and 2004 and subsequently joined the opposition. According to Yertysbayev, "Timur Kulibayev, the president's son-in-law, has the best chance to win the presidency in the future."[39]

The decision on a successor will evidently be made by consensus. Even if Nazarbayev appoints an "heir," he would do so only after taking the interests of the elite into account. So far, Nazarbayev has not clearly indicated whom he would entrust to be his successor. After the unexpected death of Saparmurat Niyazov in Turkmenistan, the ruling class there managed to agree on a future head of state within quite a short period of time. Even though there had been no fewer than two candidates for the position, the local politicians were nevertheless able to avoid a split by selecting Gurbanguly Berdimuhamedov president within a matter of days (if not hours).

This kind of quick decisionmaking will be more difficult to achieve in Kazakhstan (which despite the authoritarianism of its system remains "polycentric"), if for no other reason than that there are more politicians with ambitions among the elite than there are in Turkmenistan. The decision, however, will be agreed to consensually. Kazakhstan's next leader will not be a dark horse from the ranks of the minor politicians in the country, but someone whose name has long been familiar in both politics and society. It should be recognized that the new president will find it very difficult to gain credibility. First, he will be compared to the first president, who had managed to lay the foundations of a nation state, avoid conflicts as they formed, and build relations of trust and mutual respect with the country's neighbors. Second, he will bear primary responsibility for the upcoming reforms and for the way the country copes with crisis conditions.

Reforms in Kazakhstan will likely be accompanied by a partial influx of young blood into the elite, which could lead to friction between the generations in the ruling class, with impacts on both the domestic situation and the country's foreign policy. Positions of authority in the government will begin to be staffed by graduates of American and European universities who have experience working abroad and are fluent in English. These young civil servants will have had no Soviet past and most of their experience will have been in the post-Soviet environment.

As Martha Brill Olcott noted, "Although Kazakhstan could never have achieved the twin goals of the democratization and market reform in the space of a decade, it wasted the opportunity to make genuine strides in that direction."[40] Whether the "new start" will succeed will become evident over the next year or two. If reforms, including political reforms, are postponed (contrary to the assurances of the current president), development in Kazakhstan may come to a standstill, or could even be rolled back, leading to social and political instability.

RUSSIAN INTERESTS IN KAZAKHSTAN

The course that events take in Kazakhstan will be of particular interest to Russia. The mutual trust between Kazakhstan and Russia remains strong compared to the other countries in the region, despite their national "selfishness" in economic relations. These relations appear to have only gotten stronger since Vladimir Putin came to power in 1999, perhaps because Nursultan Nazarbayev had from the beginning been the only Central Asian leader to treat the new Russian president in a friendly manner and without prejudice, thus contributing to Putin's authority in the post-Soviet space. Moreover, Nazarbayev had accepted the appearance of the Putin-Medvedev tandem as a natural event in Russian political life and had treated each of them discreetly.

The strength of the relationship between Russia and Kazakhstan has also largely been a consequence of the two countries' similar economic and political systems, harkening back to their closeness throughout history. Eurasianism has turned out to be a convenient ideology for both.

However, if we assume that these systems will continue to evolve, then Kazakh-Russian relations will correspondingly evolve as well, although this will most likely become an issue for the very distant future.

Positive progress toward integration was made between 2011 and 2012. In November 2011, Presidents Alexander Lukashenko, Dmitry Medvedev, and Nursultan Nazarbayev signed the Declaration on Eurasian Economic Integration (which is to culminate in 2015 with the establishment of the Eurasian Union) and the Agreement on the Eurasian Economic Commission, which as of January 1, 2012, became the common standing supranational body to regulate relations within the Customs Union and the Common Economic Area. However, regional integration is based primarily on bilateral relations between Kazakhstan and Russia (Belarus may be considered to be associated with them), and the future of integration and the Eurasian Union will depend entirely on the way these bilateral relations develop.

From the outside, these relations appear to be in good shape. President Nazarbayev and his prime minister have on numerous occasions declared that integration must be pursued through the Common Economic Area and Eurasian Union. Commenting on the victory of the Nur Otan Party at the parliamentary elections, Leonid Slutsky, chairman of the State Duma committee for CIS affairs, said that it "reaffirms the course of general integration with Russia and construction of the Eurasian Union."[41] At the same time, however, some Kazakh politicians and experts have been more cautious in their attitudes about the Eurasian Union and the perceived unconditional benefits to be gained by the country from integration with Russia.

One of the more difficult issues to address on the path to integration is the question of a common currency. In Masimov's view, "This is not something that should be expected over the near term.... It is a problem to be addressed in the distant future."[42] In order to establish such a currency, tariffs will need to be unified for the natural monopolies, which will take at least three years.[43] Thus, Masimov has in essence admitted that the Eurasian Union would be able to begin full-fledged operations only after such a decision has been made. In November–December 2011, Nursultan Nazarbayev stated repeatedly that there should be no rush to establish a common currency and that there should be no illusion that it might be the Russian ruble.

Obviously, no matter who replaces Nazarbayev, Kazakhstan's stance on the Eurasian Union will remain pragmatic, even cautious, especially since it is possible that the organization would just be getting on its feet as the second wave of the crisis hits, when Russia (and Belarus) might be tempted to impose protectionist measures that could create insurmountable difficulties for the process of integration. In anticipation of such complications, the supranational Eurasian Commission has been created. Under the framework of the Eurasian Union, both Kazakhstan and Russia will be able to pursue their own national interests even though they may not coincide with the other's.

CONCLUSION

The future, especially the more distant future, is impossible to predict. For now, politicians and experts in Russia remain certain that the upsurge in public awareness and increased activity by opposition forces since the events in Zhanaozen will compel the Kazakh authorities, no matter who they are, to introduce changes into domestic policy (similar views have been voiced in Kazakhstan). These potential changes in domestic policy will have an impact on foreign policy. What new trends will this bring to Kazakh-Russian relations, especially in light of the influx of a new generation of politicians? To what extent will Russia have an interest in the reforms in Kazakhstan, and in the diversification and especially the modernization of the economy that will require

Kazakhstan to focus on developing relations with technologically advanced countries? Finally, what will happen if the restructuring of the economy causes the political system to be significantly transformed?

In addition, potential changes in Russia need to be considered. It could turn out that the Kazakh-Russian relations (which had formed under different political regimes) will develop (or "reload," to use the buzzword) within a transformed political environment and with different foreign policy priorities. At the same time, it is clear that Kazakhstan has sought and will continue to seek relations as an equal, and to pressure it would inevitably bring about the opposite effect.

Kazakhstan has the chance to begin positive changes; under certain conditions, though more transparently, Russia could also get such an opportunity. However, it will be very difficult to take advantage of this chance. Whether reforms can be carried out successfully will largely depend upon the extent to which Kazakhstan can retain and strengthen favorable relations with its northern neighbor.

CHAPTER 5

KYRGYZSTAN— THE EXCEPTION

Each Central Asian country is unique in its own way. For independent Kyrgyzstan, its uniqueness has been its recent political history. Kyrgyzstan has been an exception in the region for the past decade: the country's first president, Askar Akayev, was a scientist and intellectual, unlike his counterparts, who were all from the Soviet *nomenklatura*; and Kyrgyzstan has been socially active, drawn to political pluralism—and passed through two revolutions.

Kyrgyzstan's uniqueness does not stop there. It is the only Central Asian country to be made up of clearly distinct southern and northern portions. Relations between the two are complex and resemble somewhat the relations between Tripolitania and Cyrenaica in Libya. The stability and well-being of the country will depend upon the way these relations develop. Another feature of Kyrgyzstan is that its leaders rotate, a process that emerged as early as the Soviet era. Turdakun Usubaliyev, a northerner, was the first secretary of the Communist Party of the Kyrgyz Soviet Socialist Republic from 1961 to 1985. He was then replaced by a southerner, Absamat Masaliyev, who held the top post until 1990, when he was replaced by Askar Akayev, who became president (there had previously been no such position). After Akayev was ousted in 2005, Kurmanbek Bakiyev (another southerner) came to power; he was overthrown in 2010 during the second Kyrgyz revolution. Then followed Roza Otunbayeva, who was interim president until 2011, when she passed her duties on to newly elected President Almazbek Atambayev. Both Otunbayeva and Atambayev are northerners. The ethnic makeup of Kyrgyzstan's population is complex and changing rapidly. According to the 2009 census, of the total population of 5–5.5 million, Kyrgyz account for 71 percent (64 percent in 1991), Uzbeks for 14.3 percent (13.8 percent in 1991), and Russians for 7.8 percent (12.5 percent in 1991). The situation of the Dungan people remains unclear. Some experts believe that their number has equaled the number of Uzbeks. In the South, Uzbeks officially account for 27 percent of the population (the figure is even higher in reality) and Russians for only 5.7 percent.

A political pluralism uncharacteristic for the region, a complex ethnic mix, economic backwardness, and growing religious radicalism have combined to make Kyrgyzstan a potentially unstable place and among the region's more vulnerable countries.

ATTEMPTS AT DEMOCRACY

There is, however, a paradox. Although many analysts predicted that Kyrgyzstan's attempt to build a parliamentary system of government after toppling President Bakiyev in 2010 would bring about a collapse, this did not happen. The idea of parliamentary democracy in Kyrgyzstan drew skeptical (if not outright negative) reactions from the country's neighbors and in Moscow. President Dmitry Medvedev said quite clearly, "Our friends in Kyrgyzstan have chosen this road, but I say quite openly that for Russia, and I am afraid for Kyrgyzstan too, this would be a disaster."[1]

However, the elections that followed (first the parliamentary and then the presidential election in 2011) were largely successful and trouble-free. They resulted in a coalition made up of the Social Democratic Party of Kyrgyzstan (SPDK), the Ata-Meken Socialist Party, the Ar-Namys Party, and the Republic Party, with Social Democrat Almazbek Atambayev moving from the position of prime minister to assume the office of president. The SPDK appears to have some predominance among the ruling establishment: the president, Speaker of the Parliament (Zhogorku Kenesh) Asilbek Zheenbekov, and former member and current Prime Minister Omurbek Babanov are among its members. However, the first coalition did not hold for long, and in November 2012 a new coalition was created.

Of course, it would be a mistake to assert that these parties all measure up to classic standards as political parties. To a great extent, they are based upon groups having regional or even familial clan affiliation, and some of them can be characterized as being more "southern" or "northern" in disposition. Nevertheless, pluralism among clans in politics has continued to find expression in the modern institutions of parties and parliament. Some parties, such as the Social Democrats, have more or less clearly articulated programs, and all can lay claim to being parties of the country as a whole.

No matter what the opinion of the Kyrgyz elite today, it is undeniable that it is made up of a wealth of prominent personalities and that the country's political arena has not yet been worn down, as it has in most Central Asian countries. Such figures as Askar Akayev, Roza Otunbayeva, current president Almazbek Atambayev, former foreign minister and current Secretary General of the Shanghai Cooperation Organization Muratbek Imanaliyev, Ar-Namys Party Chairman Felix Kulov, and Adakhan Madumarov could be mentioned, and the list goes on. Although each of these people may be of varying caliber (at least in terms of morals), the political palette in Kyrgyzstan is impressionistically colorful and effective. There is no "boring" ruling class in Kyrgyzstan cemented together by common corporate interests.

The October 2010 parliamentary elections involved the participation of 39 political parties, with no single party gaining a full majority (Ata-Zhurt won 8.87 percent; the Social Democratic Party 8.04 percent; Ar-Namys 7.75 percent; Respublika 7.25 percent; and the Ata-Meken Socialist Party 5.6 percent). This was not the only clear demonstration that political pluralism exists in Kyrgyzstan; the 2011 presidential election was also competitive, with the SPDK candidate winning 63 percent of the vote while his two main rivals (the heads of the Ata-Zhurt and Butun Kyrgyzstan parties, Kamchybek Tashiyev and Adakhan Madumarov, won 14.5 percent and 14.9 percent of the vote, respectively.

The Ata-Zhurt Party is the successor to Bakiyev's Ak Zhol Party. Many people in Kyrgyzstan still believe that if Tashiyev and Madumarov had been able to agree, a second round would have been inevitable.

To his credit, Atambayev was "not only able to get the support of the North, but also win over votes from the South, especially among the Uzbek population."[2] The latter circumstance requires some explanation. On the one hand, the local Uzbeks have always voted for northerners; on the other hand, however, this has been a sign of their trust in the government, which has been attempting (although not always successfully) to curb interethnic tensions in the country.

On the eve of elections, local councils of the Ata-Zhurt and Butun Kyrgyzstan parties attempted to unite into a single opposition bloc, stating that their main goal was to "establish interethnic harmony and the unity of the Kyrgyz people."[3] At the same time, both parties, including their leaders, are "southerners." Although confrontation between the government (represented, as noted above, by northerners) and the opposition may turn more or less acute over time, it would appear that, after two revolutions and the ethnic clashes of 2010, in which massacres by Uzbeks and Kyrgyz in Osh and Jalalabad left 476 people dead and hundreds wounded,[4] neither of the two parties is willing to split the country apart. One reason for this is that a parliamentary system has emerged that will sooner or later balance out representation for North and South, thus reducing the significance of regional affiliation of future heads of state.

In analyzing the situation in Kyrgyzstan, there are two extremes that should be avoided: first, the factors of clanism and regionalism should not be seen as absolute; second, Kyrgyz democracy should not be viewed with euphoria. Although the system of checks and balances that is taking shape in the country is still very fragile, the very fact that it held up after the tragic events in Osh and Jalalabad in 2010 demonstrates its potential: it cannot be denied that for more than two years Kyrgyzstan has been living under a *nonauthoritarian* political regime.

It is also important to take a balanced look at the state of Kyrgyz society today. After two presidents, Akayev and Bakiyev, were toppled in turn, a joke began to make the rounds in Bishkek: "What is revolution? Revolution is Kyrgyzstan's national pastime." The joke has a grain of truth to it in that it reflects the impulsive outbursts of social and ethnic frenzy that are part of the Kyrgyz national character and in some cases spin out of control or even lead to cruelty. But it cannot be denied that the Kyrgyz, unlike some of their neighbors, have overcome their inertness and developed a sense of self-worth and awareness that the "little people" are not just the objects of political life, but its subjects as well.

This situation has forced the authorities to become more accountable to society, which follows their actions closely. At the same time, as a country in which people are living under constant stress, Kyrgyzstan is extremely difficult to govern.

ECONOMIC SITUATION

Meanwhile, the economic situation in Kyrgyzstan remains very difficult. With a per capita GDP of $2,162, Kyrgyzstan was fourteenth among the CIS countries in 2011, above only Tajikistan ($1,907) and below Uzbekistan ($2,959).[5]

The national debt of Kyrgyzstan totals about $3 billion.[6] By early 2010, foreign debt had reached $2.23 billion. Kyrgyzstan ended 2011 with a budget deficit of $400 million.[7] Between 60 and 70 percent of the total economy derives from the shadow economy.[8] Unemployment is officially put at 8.4 percent, but according to unofficial data may actually be as high as 20 percent.[9] According to UN data, about 1 million people in the country face year-round food shortages. In 2011, the UN World Food Program sent aid to the country totaling $17.5 million (of which Russia provided $2 million).[10]

Of the 193 countries listed in the human development index for 2011, Kyrgyzstan ranked 126 (Russia was 66, Tajikistan was 127, and Uzbekistan was 117).[11]

Corruption continues to be a problem in Kyrgyzstan. According to data from the prosecutor general, in 2010 Kyrgyzstan lost 24 billion soms (around $500 million) due to corruption.[12] Swedish researcher Johan Engvall, who has studied this issue, said that "corruption in Kyrgyzstan is inseparable from state institutions." In his view, the main problem for the energy supply sector (which is in critically poor

condition) is not the condition of the infrastructure itself but the theft
of energy through a variety of schemes. The traffic police in the country
operate as commercial businesses. "I have not seen any real changes in
the style and goals of the new leadership," Engvall noted.[13] It will take
time and effort at a variety of levels to reduce corruption, especially considering the fact that essentially any politician who has business interests
can turn out to be corrupt.

However, the economic collapse that many predicted has not happened. At his first news conference on December 29, 2011, President
Atambayev said that "GDP is growing, we have held inflation in check,
and the rumors of an imminent default proved unfounded."[14] Indeed,
Kyrgyzstan's GDP grew by 5.7 percent (after having posted a drop of
0.5 percent in 2010), with the growth occurring in nearly every economic sector,[15] inflation declined by about 4 percent, and the budget
deficit, which had reached $460 million in 2010, also decreased by
$60 million.

The president promised to reduce expenditures by the agencies
under his direct authority by several million dollars,[16] and the size of
the apparatus of government was reduced by 20 percent. In keeping
with an order by Prime Minister Babanov, the State Development Bank
of Kyrgyzstan was established in March 2012 to encourage development, rather than to accumulate money. This bank is to be 100 percent
state-owned, and the government sees as its main objective the creation
of a climate that would be favorable for investment and could attract
wealthy donors.

Steps have been taken to fight corruption. In December 2011,
Atambayev signed a decree establishing an anticorruption department
under the National Security Committee. The financial police, which
had been a major source of corruption, was disbanded. A center was
established for public procurement in an effort to significantly reduce
the so-called kickbacks that were consuming up to 30 percent of the
funds allocated for procurement. Taxes were increased by 20 percent on
traders working at Kara-Suu and Dordoy, the largest wholesale markets
in Central Asia; at the same time, the traders were relieved of the need
for frequent and systematic checks, which essentially amounted to
extortion. Law enforcement agencies were reformed, and the traffic

police, famous for its graft (as has been typical in the post-Soviet space), was disbanded.

Despite all these efforts, the key to rooting out corruption in the post-Soviet space has not yet been found. Kyrgyz politicians have decided to make use of Georgia's experience, as well as of all of the reform achievements of the government there; of the former Soviet republics, Georgia has shown perhaps the greatest determination so far to resolve the problem. Delegations of Kyrgyz officials have regularly visited Georgia in order to gain firsthand experience of its reforms.

The main ideologist for reform in Kyrgyzstan is former deputy prime minister Joomart Otorbayev, a technocrat and an intellectual who was minister for economic development, foreign trade, and investment under President Askar Akayev. He later worked at the World Bank, where he drafted proposals for reform in several postcommunist countries including Mongolia, where the reforms were successfully implemented.

The question is the extent to which the current improvement in the Kyrgyz economy will represent a steady trend, and this, in turn, will depend on the degree of political stability and, to a large extent, on the situation in the South of Kyrgyzstan.

POLITICAL, SOCIAL, AND ECONOMIC PROBLEMS

Kyrgyzstan's political, social, and economic problems are particularly serious in the context of the chronic ethnic and political crisis in the South. People still remember the bloody events of 1990 in Osh,[17] and the events of 2010 have now added new tragedy to their memories. Although social and economic problems and political provocation all played their part, the extreme cruelty of these events had its roots in interethnic hostility that has been especially persistent and difficult to overcome.

The investigation of the events in Osh and Jalalabad continues. While no one doubts the need for an investigation, at the same time the attempts to establish a "single true version of events," combined with the mutual accusations and continual incidents erupting during the court hearings, have only served to further fan the flames of hatred. In February 2012, Prosecutor General Aida Salyanova, speaking at a meeting of the Zhogorku Kenesh, said that after questioning 48 politicians, including President Atambayev and former president Otunbayeva, she had come to the conclusion that they had "not performed their duties adequately, although they themselves did not commit crimes."[18]

The authorities today remain hostage to the 2010 conflict, which will long continue to affect the situation in the country.

The government has drafted a Concept for Ethnic Harmony based on the principle of coexistence among the different ethnic groups. By the end of 2011, eleven new multistoried apartment buildings had been built to house people who had lost their homes in the 2010 violence. Although Atambayev has said that the Kyrgyz authorities "should build modern cities, not large Osh villages," the people have nevertheless been trying to get into these apartments following ethnic lines. Efforts have been made to cleanse the mass media (particularly the electronic media) of materials that could provoke interethnic strife. Four memorials have been built for the victims of the ethnic violence, including one bearing the name "A Mother's Tears."

However, interethnic clashes have not ceased. The country's Interior Ministry has listed 147 potential hotbeds of conflict, while the State Committee for National Security has named "only" 29 such trouble spots. In the view of Tatyana Vygovskaya, director of the public foundation Egalité, 350,000–370,000 people in the country (about 10 percent of the population) are involved in interethnic confrontation (under normal conditions, it would not amount to more than 2 percent of the population in any country).[19]

The 40 percent decline in business activity at the Kara-Suu market was a clear indication of tension in relations between the two largest ethnic groups in the region. Uzbek traders have been oppressed, even overtly extorted.[20] Member of parliament Azamat Aparbayev stated that "there is no friendship between the Kyrgyz and the Uzbeks." In the best traditions of "black humor," he suggested that a law be passed that would condemn people to death "for inciting ethnic hatred."[21]

Kyrgyz and Uzbeks are not the only ones to have been caught up in interethnic conflict. Although the greatest tension has naturally been between the two largest ethnic groups, Tajiks and people from the Caucasus living in the country have also been drawn in, as have

Russians (in December 2011 Russian and Kyrgyz youths clashed in Maevka village). The media noted an episode that took place in the Osh City Court, when relatives of the victims in the case verbally attacked defense lawyer Tatyana Tomina, shouting, "Send this Russian home (to her own country)!"[22]

Presidential candidate Nurlan Motuev invoked the events of 1916, when the Russian czar crushed a Kyrgyz rebellion, killing, by some estimates, more than half the population. Motuev demanded that Russia pay $100 billion in compensation to Kyrgyzstan to avenge the deaths. Speaking with regret, he added that "the Kyrgyz are not as devout Muslims as the Chechens, … who look death in the eyes as they fight Russia."[23]

Ethnic Russians have continued to leave Kyrgyzstan, not just for economic reasons, but also out of fear for the country's stability and the increase in ethnic nationalism. In the twenty years since Kyrgyzstan became independent, 485,000 people have departed for permanent residence in Russia.[24]

The use of the Russian language has been declining in Kyrgyzstan, even though its equal status with the Kyrgyz language has been enshrined in three articles of the country's constitution. Article 10, for example, states that "the Russian language is an official language alongside the Kyrgyz language in the Republic of Kyrgyzstan." However, in 2012 the Zhogorku Kenesh debated prohibiting the use of Russian in official documents. Russian had been on the decline not just in the South, but also in the northern regions of Naryn, Talas, and Issyk-Kul, where the language had once been as common as Kyrgyz.

When Irina Karamushkina, a member of parliament from the Social Democratic Party of Kyrgyzstan, visited the Batken region in the South of the country and met with students there, she discovered that "they understand Russian, but already cannot speak it."[25] Social Democratic Party member of parliament Ryskeldi Mombekov has publicly stated that he never uses Russian to respond to any Russian journalist. "People call me a nationalist, but during these moments I am happy and walk with my head held high…."[26]

Russians remain essentially unrepresented in government. Among the members of the cabinet seated in December 2011, there is not a single

Russian. President Atambayev admitted that he was sorry to see this happen.[27] His regrets are understandable, if only because the Russian-speaking voters of Bishkek had supported him during the presidential election. Curiously, however, no one in the government or the parliament appears to have noticed the absence of the Russians. This ethnocracy contradicts the authorities' stated policy of building a democratic system of government.

Ethnic nationalism has been one of the main factors potentially leading to destabilization, and the authorities are well aware of this fact. However, it is unlikely that the interethnic tension that has been holding the country back can be overcome over the next few years, while the ethnic card is there as a trump card in the hands of any ambitious politician, common opportunist, or even criminal.

ISLAM—ON THE PERIPHERY OF POLITICS

Since it never played the significant historical role in Kyrgyzstan that it had in both Tajikistan and Uzbekistan, Islam had been on the periphery of politics in the country throughout the 1990s, although it is now becoming an important force in Kyrgyz political life. Kyrgyzstan has been characterized by inherent syncretism and the predominance of nomadic cultural elements, with the South being the most Islamized area of the republic and the Uzbeks its most Islamic-centered people. According to Ormon Sharshenov, chairman of the State Agency for Religious Affairs (SARA), of all of the mosques in Kyrgyzstan, more than 70 percent are concentrated in the South.[28] The fact that the Kyrgyz and Uzbeks have differing levels of religious commitment has been one of the causes of friction between them. The Uzbeks consider the Kyrgyz to be "bad Muslims," while the Kyrgyz accuse the Uzbeks of being fanatics.

To a certain extent, the revival of Islam in Kyrgyzstan that began after the collapse of the Soviet Union did not appear to be as intense and politicized as it had been among its neighbors. However, cells of Hizb ut-Tahrir and the Islamic Movement of Uzbekistan had emerged as early as the 1990s, and missionaries from other countries began to infiltrate Kyrgyzstan. In 1999, a large group of IMU militants entered the Batken Oblast of Kyrgyzstan, where for several days they battled Kyrgyz Republic military units that were supported somewhat by air from Uzbekistan.[29] Although the militant force was partially destroyed and its remnants scattered, this incident did make it clear that Kyrgyzstan will not be able to avoid the process of Islamic radicalization. Radical Islam first began to spread among the Kyrgyz people in the early 2000s, especially among the young (more than half of the country's population is younger than seventeen). Law enforcement agencies have registered 1,438 adherents to extremist organizations (other data put the numbers much higher).[30] In addition, there have been fewer interethnic disputes between Uzbek and Kyrgyz Islamists, in part thanks to Islamic solidarity. Significantly, HTI members now include not only Uzbeks but also Kyrgyz, including those from the North (previously indifferent to Islam). As early as 2002, several members of Hizb ut-Tahrir were detained by authorities in the Jalalabad Oblast, carrying leaflets and weapons.[31] Between 2006 and 2008, the number of HTI members increased from five thousand to fifteen thousand,[32] and by 2012, to about twenty thousand, perhaps more.

The Islamic factor first became actively manifested during the first Kyrgyz revolution. The HTI tried to influence the 2005 parliamentary elections. The organization even negotiated with seven of the candidates, who pledged if elected to lobby for the passage of laws based upon Islamic values. Five of the seven HTI followers were elected to parliament.[33] Subsequently, during the 2010 crisis, the HTI offered to support Bakiyev's opponents. They turned down the offer.

Although the greater portion of Kyrgyz society remains unprepared to accept Islamic behavioral norms and prohibitions, Islamization continues to intensify. Discord between those who champion Islam and their opponents will contribute to the growing social and ethnic tension. Islam will be used by various forces as a political tool, leading to increased conflicts within the elite, the majority of which is firmly committed to the principles of secularism.

DEPENDENCE ON OUTSIDE PLAYERS

Like the other Central Asian countries, Kyrgyzstan pursues a multi-vectoral foreign policy. The question is, however, to what extent does the country risk becoming hostage to this very policy? In the near future, Kyrgyzstan is fated to become dependent on foreign actors and its neighbors, and neither the political elite nor society in general has any illusions about this predicament. The question is, what form will this dependence take, and to what extent will it impinge upon the country's sovereignty? Dependence on outside players is a sensitive issue for any government for obvious reasons. As Atambayev said, "It is in the interests of some to have us on our knees and begging for money.... We must be a sovereign country."[34]

Russia

Kyrgyzstan's strongest ties are with Russia, and none of the country's leaders disputes the need to maintain those ties. People in Bishkek have been heard to say that Vladimir Putin is more popular in Kyrgyzstan than he is in Russia itself. There is Russian participation in all of the major projects under way in Kyrgyzstan, including construction of the Kambaratin hydroelectric power station, which will be the largest in the country, and the Naryn hydropower cascade. Russia is Kyrgyzstan's chief source of imports (33.4 percent) and its third-largest export market (18.2 percent).[35] Russian direct investment in the Kyrgyz economy more than doubled in 2010, coming to $95.9 million,[36] and Russia provides Kyrgyzstan with direct financial and material assistance. In January 2012, for example, it delivered military equipment worth $16 million to Kyrgyzstan's border guards.[37]

Finally, various sources estimate the number of Kyrgyz citizens working in Russia as between 700,000 and 1 million (though the latter figure seems high), who send home $2 billion every year. If this figure is correct, then it exceeds the entire national budget, which is about $1.8 billion.

The genuine interest that the leaders in Kyrgyzstan have toward developing cooperation with Russia can be seen in Bishkek's willingness to join the Customs Union and its positive view of the common economic space and even the Eurasian Union being established by Russia and Kazakhstan (any benefits that will accrue to Kyrgyzstan from participating in these organizations have yet to be proven). Aside from purely pragmatic motivations for participating, the Kyrgyz political mentality is characterized by an emotional attitude about them. "Many of us had our fathers and grandfathers fight for the Soviet Union, and if only for the sake of their memory we need to create this common economic space," Atambayev said.[38] If this view is perhaps a bit reverential, it does appear completely sincere, although (in my opinion) it only further confirms the belief by the Kremlin in Kyrgyzstan's enduring dependence on Moscow.

At the same time, not every Kyrgyz politician considers the country's participation in Russian projects to be without alternative or inevitable. For example, the Ata-Meken Socialist Party, which is a part of the ruling coalition, is skeptical about joining the Customs Union because it would mean that, first of all, Kyrgyzstan would need to bring its tariffs in line with the rates of the World Trade Organization, and second, it would lead to a price hike, especially in food prices. Kyrgyzstan's entry into the Customs Union would probably be contingent upon meeting a number of conditions and exceptions to the rules. Finally, in Kyrgyzstan (as in Kazakhstan) not everyone fully understands how the process of integration is to develop from the Customs Union to the Common Economic Space and then to the Eurasian Union.

The fact that some senior Kremlin officials regard Kyrgyzstan as essentially belonging to the Russian Federation has already created problems for relations between the two countries. Although it is understandable that Bishkek would take offense at such a view, the expression of such offense sometimes sounds rather infantile. Atambayev elicited snickers in Moscow when he said, "I will not ask for a cent from Russia. In time, it will be we who help them."[39]

Kyrgyzstan is the only Central Asian state where Moscow retains influence over internal politics. There is scarcely anywhere else in the region where it would be possible for a politician seeking high government office to visit Moscow on a regular basis in order to garner the support of a senior Russian official, the prime minister, or the president. In the chaotic days following the first Kyrgyz revolution in 2005, and especially after the second revolution in 2010, many contenders for top jobs in Kyrgyzstan made the trip to the Russian capital. The Kremlin would make it clear through the media or other means whom it found more (or less) acceptable. Kyrgyz politicians have to create an image both at home and in Moscow. It is known, for example, that Omurbek Tekebayev, leader of Ata-Meken, as well as Roza Otunbayeva, for a time Kyrgyzstan's ambassador to Washington and London, had been considered to be pro-Western. Any "jealousy" felt by the Kremlin is understandable. It had become accustomed to Kyrgyzstan's unequivocal attachment to Russia, and it often views any real or perceived desires on the part of Kyrgyzstan to develop relations with any other country as "adulterous."

During the presidential election in 2011 there had been rumors that Moscow might support an individual candidate, specifically Marat Sultanov, whose promotion had been lobbied for by Alexei Kudrin, Russian finance minister at the time,[40] or Adakhan Madumarov, who had shifted to an unambiguously pro-Russian position on the eve of the election.

A curious episode occurred on the eve of the election, when the Central Electoral Commission of Kyrgyzstan announced that candidates for president would not be able to use photographs showing them in the company of politicians from other countries to campaign.[41] In essence, this requirement was imposed as a warning to the politicians who were drawn to posing with Putin or Medvedev.

Despite numerous requests from the Kyrgyz government, Russia did not provide it with any direct military aid during the Osh ethnic clashes of 2010; the CSTO and the SCO both also remained on the sidelines. Russia's refusal to directly intervene in the conflict on the side of the "revolutionary government" can be explained in a variety of ways. First of all, intervention would have been problematic in purely military terms. Success in such military operations needs to be achieved within a matter of hours, or at most days. Otherwise, the intervening side, that is, Russia, would inevitably be drawn into internal strife and become involved in the civil war. Second, it would appear to be inter-ference in the internal affairs of a foreign state, an impression that Russia was reluctant to make after the 2008 war with Georgia. Third, even if it could be imagined for a second that the CSTO would actually get involved in the conflict, the appearance of Kazakh and especially Tajik soldiers in Kyrgyzstan would complicate the situation even further. Another point is that at the time of the crisis, the CSTO had not yet adopted documents that would legally formalize its intervention into the internal affairs of one of its members. Fourth, Uzbekistan was categorical in opposing the idea of sending in foreign forces, considered the Osh crisis to be Kyrgyzstan's domestic affair, and was unwilling to allow foreign troops to be deployed near its borders. Fifth, Moscow was confident that the new government would be able to restore order, albeit perhaps at a high cost. It must be noted that neither Russia nor Uzbekistan had an interest in seeing Kyrgyzstan divided and involved in civil war, which could destabilize the entire Ferghana Valley.

There is, however, an alternate version of these events, where Russia and Uzbekistan on the contrary had an interest in aggravating the situation, even if Kyrgyzstan were to split. According to Osh Mayor Melis Myrzakmatov, set to arrive from Andijan on the night of June 12–13, 2010, were "20 aircraft with a detachment of select troops ... tasked with the elimination of municipal and regional leaders, local internal affairs departments, local communication centers, municipal infrastructure and military forces," when a telegram allegedly arrived from Moscow saying, "you must create the Osh republic."[42] According to Myrzakmatov, Kyrgyzstan was saved from being split solely through his efforts and those of his supporters, who managed to prevent the invasion at great cost. This interpretation of the events, although impressive, is actually far removed from reality.

However, it cannot be ignored that the Kyrgyz authorities continue to attribute the cause of the conflict in the South to the intrigues of certain "third forces." Almazbek Atambayev has said that Uzbek President Islam Karimov once told him in an informal setting that certain forces "want a war to begin between Kyrgyzstan and Uzbekistan." Atambayev promised "to find the people who started this."[43] What forces these might be is difficult to say: Islamists, drug dealers, whoever. Most likely, Atambayev was hinting at the activities of the deposed Bakiyev, who was strong in the South and whose relatives stubbornly resisted the authorities. It is known that Bakiyev's son Maxim, a businessman, who during his father's reign had exercised complete financial control in the country and caused great agitation within society, had spoken with Boris Berezovsky in London and that Berezovsky had supposedly been ready to provide support to the Bakiyev clan in its continuing resistance to the government in the South. Strictly speaking, however, the Bakiyev clan cannot be considered to be a third party or an "external factor." In what he told Atambayev, Karimov seemed to be referring to something more serious, specifically certain mysterious external "enemies" interested in destabilizing the situation in the immediate vicinity of Kyrgyzstan. He probably was not referring to the Taliban, because he surely would have named them.

Although Russia's reluctance to get involved in the 2010 crisis caused some disappointment both within the new government and in Kyrgyz society, it did not lead to mutual alienation between the two countries. However, Kyrgyz-Russian relations did experience something of a decline beginning at the turn of 2011–2012 due to a number of factors. First, the Kremlin stubbornly continued to cast doubt upon the correctness of Kyrgyzstan's chosen path in building a parliamentary republic; second, the trend toward a multivectoral foreign policy in Kyrgyzstan continued to strengthen; and third, a number of actions that the new president had taken were seen in Moscow as extravagant. For example, Atambayev had invited the president of Georgia, Mikhail Saakashvili, who is greatly disliked in Russia, to his inauguration; as revenge for the snub, Chief of the Presidential Administration Sergey Naryshkin did not attend (Russia was represented by a low-level official instead).

Experts have called Atambayev's working visit to Moscow in 2012 a failure, some even pronouncing it an "absolute disaster."[44] The planned agreement to cede 50 percent of the shares in the Dastan defense industry plant and testing facility in Issyk-Kul to Russia remained unsigned after Russian Finance Minister Anton Siluanov refused to accept them in exchange for writing off $190 million of Kyrgyzstan's debt; a loan of $106 million from Russia via the Eurasian Economic Community failed to be confirmed; the question of preferential prices for Russian fuels and lubricants was not clarified; and several hydroelectric power

station construction projects on the Naryn River have come to a standstill. Moreover, plans for future joint oil exploration efforts in Jalalabad
remain unclear, and talks over selling the Kyrgyzgaz company to
Gazprom continue to drag on.

These unresolved problems will most likely be cleared up eventually. In the meantime, relations between Kyrgyzstan and Russia remain
strong. As Grigorij Mikhajlov wrote, "Moscow does not want to deliberately worsen the situation in Kyrgyzstan, nor does it intend to pay for
the country's upkeep."[45] While it would be senseless for Moscow to lose a
stable ally, Bishkek would also gain nothing from quarreling with Russia.

In such a context, the fuss over Atambayev's words about the possibility of a withdrawal of the Russian Air Force from the base at Kant seems
unjustified. Atambayev had called for shuttering the base, saying that
Russia owed only "measly rent" for four years and even then had not
paid it. Atambayev's remarks could be seen as being more of a tactical
move designed to balance the promised closure of the American base in
Manas. Kyrgyz authorities have been so cautious in their statements on
Manas that it is impossible to know for sure whether they will extend
the agreement with the United States in 2014. "The country's previous
authorities already did enough to spoil Kyrgyzstan's image abroad with
the biased attitude they took toward their international obligations,"
Atambayev said. "In order to mend this image, we simply have to fulfill
the agreements already concluded.... Our position is that ... we will give
the Americans six months' advance notification on ending the agreement and its terms, and from 2014, the base will become a large international civil aviation hub" in which anyone could invest.[46]

The United States

Meanwhile, in January 2012 small demonstrations of fifteen to twenty
people were held in front of the U.S. embassy in Bishkek, demanding
that the United States withdraw from the base on the grounds that it
was having a negative impact on the environment from aircraft jettison-
ing their remaining fuel on approach to the base.

For Kyrgyzstan, the base at Manas (now renamed the Transit Center) remains a symbol of its multivectoral policy. Bishkek sees it not as an alternative to Russian influence, but as evidence of both the Russian and the American vectors in its foreign policy. Muratbek Imanaliyev has called the Transit Center the "cornerstone" of Kyrgyzstan's foreign policy.[47]

Washington has remained generally calm about the Manas problem. In the first place, Russia is not likely to insist that the Americans leave, since the base is there primarily to help maintain order in Afghanistan, which is something that Russia also wants. Second, Kyrgyzstan also wants the base to remain, since it has already earned $1.4 billion from it so far.[48] The three countries will ultimately work out some form of consensus on the issue, although each of the sides will first have to endure quite a few more mutual accusations.

It has been speculated that Moscow is apprehensive that Manas could potentially be used in a conflict between the United States and Iran. However, this would hardly be possible due to the lack of any corresponding agreement between Bishkek and Washington.

Beijing has also not objected to the Transit Center, since it also considers the base to be an instrument for combating the spread of radical Islam, and in any case does not believe it to be directed against China.

China

The third vector in Kyrgyzstan's foreign policy after Russia and the United States is China, which, like Russia, is becoming of crucial importance for Kyrgyzstan's foreign economic relations. According to research carried out by the Central Asian Free Market Institute, of the goods being sold at Kyrgyzstan's two largest wholesale markets, Kara-Suu (located in the South of the country) and Dordoy (in the North), 85 percent and 75 percent, respectively, come from China.[49] Since tens of thousands of people in small and medium businesses are trading with China, relations automatically acquire great political significance, because any disruption in relations would inevitably impact all of these people and provoke their dissatisfaction. This single circumstance is indicative of Beijing's latent *political* influence on the situation in Kyrgyzstan and simultaneously explains Bishkek's desire to maintain stable relations with China. In addition, Kyrgyzstan attaches great significance to the re-export of Chinese goods, from which it earns $14 billion a year.[50]

China does not compete with Russia in Kyrgyzstan, since each of them occupies its own economic niche. China has respected Russian interests in the country, and Russia in turn has accepted the increased numbers of Chinese goods on the local market as a normal development. In this respect, Kyrgyzstan differs little from dozens of other countries, including some in Central Asia, where shops are filled with Chinese consumer goods.

Beijing refrains from meddling in local political intrigues, but no politician in authority in Kyrgyzstan would dispute the need to develop relations with Kyrgyzstan's powerful neighbor to the East. Although there had been some grumbling in Bishkek in the late 1990s and the early 2000s about the Chinese pressuring the country, referring in particular to the treaties signed in 1996 and 1999 under which Kyrgyzstan ceded nearly 500 square kilometers of territory to China,[51] this is now all in the past.

Qatar and Turkey

Kyrgyzstan's multivectoral foreign policy has not been limited to building relations with Russia, China, and the United States. Bishkek has also sought to establish good relations with other countries. Contacts have been revived with Turkey and Qatar. This process can be seen as a step toward the formation of a "Muslim axis," which could yield great benefits for the country. In March 2012, Prime Minister Babanov visited Qatar and signed three economic agreements. The parties discussed the issues of Kyrgyz agricultural exports and Kyrgyz labor migration to Qatar,[52] as well as the potential for establishing a special $100 million development fund.

Bishkek has also been looking for ways to develop relations with Saudi Arabia, which has expressed willingness to consider importing agricultural products from Kyrgyzstan.

Kyrgyzstan and Turkey have declared that "a new historical stage of relations" was beginning between them. During President Atambayev's visit to Turkey in early 2012, a plan was signed for cooperation between the two countries through 2013, and measures were developed to ensure the free movement of people, capital, goods, and services. The emphasis in cooperation was to include developing air, rail, and road shipping, and increasing the trade turnover between the two countries from $300 million in 2011 to $1 billion. In addition, Turkey has agreed to take on the training of Kyrgyz students, soldiers, and even diplomats.[53]

Turkey's interest in Kyrgyzstan has been growing steadily. At one time, in fact, Ankara had even hoped that it could acquire shares in the Dastan plant in exchange for writing off the debt, but this predictably was poorly received in Russia.

However, Kyrgyzstan's economic relations with the Muslim world will be unlikely to pose any serious alternative to its relations with Russia for the foreseeable future, although they may become very significant for Kyrgyzstan. By developing its agricultural product export industry, the country would not only diversify its economy, but would also reinvigorate it, thus promoting modernization and job creation. The experience of Mongolia will evidently be used in this endeavor, where Joomart Otorbayev was directly involved in planning the reforms.

The expansion of economic cooperation with the Muslim world is hardly likely to contribute to any significant increase in its political influence on Kyrgyzstan. Such would not be possible, inasmuch as the current political elite remains faithful to the principle of maintaining a balance between external "vectors." Kyrgyzstan will probably be less affected than its neighbors by the Arab Spring or the revolutionary assumption of power by Islamists. The two revolutions that occurred in the country in the course of a decade have served as a kind of "vaccine" for Kyrgyzstan against the potential of any new destabilization: Kyrgyz society needed to catch its breath.

Thus, both the old and new partners of Kyrgyzstan will probably act in parallel and complement each other, and in any case, for Moscow to suggest that Kyrgyzstan cannot choose between Russia and any other country would be imprudent.

Tajikistan and Uzbekistan

Perhaps least encouraging are Kyrgyzstan's foreign relations with its neighbors in the region, especially Tajikistan and Uzbekistan, with which Kyrgyzstan maintains minimal economic and trade ties. As noted above in previous chapters, relations have been hampered by an unresolved water issue related to the energy sector. In December 2011, Uzbekistan curtailed the gas supply to Kyrgyzstan, leaving the southern districts of Bishkek without heat and the pressure in the pipes greatly reduced. Tashkent explained this by pointing out that the pipeline simultaneously serves two countries (Kyrgyzstan and Kazakhstan), and that makes it vulnerable to rolling blackouts (although there were none in 2011). In 2011, Uzbekistan raised the prices of its gas (100 million cubic meters) to $290 per 1,000 cubic meters.

Such problems as border issues, ethnic disputes, and regular political clashes have not contributed to the development of economic relations either. With this in mind, it would appear that the Central Asian aspect of Kyrgyzstan's foreign policy is the least secure, and it brings the country many difficulties in addition to the benefits.

To some extent, Kazakhstan has been an exception in this situation, as certain positive prospects have emerged in Bishkek's relations with Astana. Meetings between the two countries were held at the presidential and prime ministerial levels in 2011 and 2012. At one of the meetings, former Kazakh prime minister Karim Masimov noted that relations had developed with Kyrgyzstan dynamically, although the "unrealized potential is great."[54]

An agreement was signed in September 2011 for Kazakhstan to supply gas to northern Kyrgyzstan at a price of $224 per 1,000 cubic meters. Kazakhstan had previously intended to raise the price from $195 to $281. The total volume of gas to be supplied is 240 million cubic meters.

Omurbek Babanov's visit to Astana in early 2012 when he met with President Nazarbayev was felt by many to have precipitated a breakthrough in Kyrgyz-Kazakh relations. Arrangements were made for Kazakhstan to participate in the construction of the Kambaratin dam and hydroelectric power plant and the Almaty-Kemin power

transmission line. The sides agreed to extend the allowed period of stay
for Kyrgyz citizens in Kazakhstan to up to ninety days without the need
to register; to reopen the "Kichi-kapak" and "Karkir" border crossings;
and to develop closer cooperation in the agricultural sector (in particular in supplying Kyrgyz dairy products to Kazakhstan). Such personal,
"minor" issues as these have a great impact on the lives of ordinary citizens, as problems in relations among nations can be reflected as difficulties in their personal lives.

Another issue that was discussed was accelerating the establishment of a Kyrgyz-Kazakh investment fund with an initial capital
of $100 million.[55] Thus, Kyrgyzstan can be said to have normalized
relations with its northern neighbor, and judging by the optimism
of politicians in both countries and by the rapidity with which the
signed agreements are being implemented, relations between Astana
and Bishkek can be singled out as a separate vector for Kyrgyzstan's
foreign policy.

CONCLUSION

No matter how Kyrgyzstan's relations develop with outside players, the
country's future will ultimately depend upon the domestic political
situation. Its desire to build a regionally atypical parliamentary system
does not preclude authoritarian leanings or the psychologically understandable yearning for a "strong hand" and a charismatic leader, another
"father of the nation," who would be able to rally society and guide it in
a tolerant but firm manner through all of the difficulties to come (and
Kyrgyzstan does indeed have willing candidates for such a position).

Between 2010 and 2012, the Kyrgyz government succeeded in
improving the stability of the country and avoiding conflict between the
North and South. Naturally, overcoming regionalism will be extremely
difficult, especially in light of the fact that the South (where there are
still many Bakiyev supporters) has felt largely marginalized since the fall
of Bakiyev. Despite the fact that the closest and most influential relatives
of the former president, including his son Maxim, have left the country,
the Bakiyev clan remains an important political force. The Ata-Zhurt

Party has gained a number of seats in parliament and has turned into a real opposition party. It has a strong presence in the South and is generally considered to be "pro-Bakiyev." Maxim Bakiyev had been responsible for stirring up friction between the North and the South, and during the March 2012 elections to the local *keneshs* (councils), he had tried to exacerbate the situation in the South and to negotiate with Madumarov. As Omurbek Babanov, commenting on the situation in Osh, noted diplomatically, "People who will want to divide the country into North and South will surely appear in the course of the election campaign."[56]

Reflecting on the prospects for parliamentarianism in Kyrgyzstan, Johan Engvall stated, "The Kyrgyz are flexible and adaptive people, so they have a chance to preserve the parliamentary system."[57]

Nevertheless, for all its vulnerability, contradictions, and mistakes, Kyrgyzstan, like a fiercely determined icebreaker, continues to plow ahead in new directions, trying to cut a new channel through the ice of Central Asian authoritarianism.

CHAPTER 6

TAJIKISTAN: AUTHORITARIAN, FRAGILE, AND FACING DIFFICULT CHALLENGES

In terms of internal and external security, Tajikistan has had more problems than most of the other countries of Central Asia. It is the only country in the region to have experienced a protracted civil war (from 1992 to 1997), which, according to various estimates, caused the deaths of between 23,500 and 100,000 people[1] (perhaps more) and devastated the economy. One reason for the mutual brutality associated with this war was the existing friction based not only on political affiliation, but also on regional, clan-based, interpersonal, and Islamic religious confrontation between those seeking to build a secular state and those wishing to establish an Islamic one.

ETHNIC AND LINGUISTIC EXCEPTION

Tajikistan is an ethnic and linguistic exception in Central Asia. Unlike most of the region's indigenous population, which is of Turkic origin, the Tajiks belong to the Iranian group. Although they have many features in common with their neighbors, they nonetheless maintain an ethnic and cultural identity of their own. The Tajiks are a sedentary people, which differentiates them in tradition, mentality, and behavioral norms from their until recently nomadic neighbors. The Tajiks are more religious, hence the earlier and more intensive revival of Islam that began during the late Soviet period and subsequently became politicized. It was in Tajikistan that the first and only remaining legal religious party in the post-Soviet space was formed, the Islamic Renaissance Party of Tajikistan (IRPT).

Events in Afghanistan (where ethnic Tajiks make up 27–38 percent of the population) have a greater impact on Tajikistan than on any other Central Asian country. The 1,400-kilometer-long Tajik-Afghan border zone is one of the most volatile in the Central Asian region. More than any country, Tajikistan wants to see peace in Afghanistan. The conflict in Afghanistan resounds as a constant tragic echo across Tajikistan. It is a role reversal: Few now remember that in the mid-1990s, Afghan politicians had in turn been concerned about the civil war in Tajikistan. It was in Kabul in 1995 that the first real peace talks took place between the warring parties in Tajikistan's conflict, under an initiative organized by then Afghan president Burhanuddin Rabbani and Ahmad Shad Masoud, an outstanding Afghan of ethnic Tajik descent. Film director and public activist Davlat Khudonazarov, who took part in the talks, said that the choice of Kabul as venue for the talks was also fortunate in that "the very atmosphere of this city in ruins was a warning signal to the Tajiks to give up armed confrontation and seek peace."[2]

AFTERMATH OF THE CIVIL WAR

The civil war ended in compromise between the Popular Front and the United Tajik Opposition (UTO, at the core of which was the IRPT) when they signed the General Agreement on the Establishment of Peace and National Accord in 1997. The Popular Front, however, believed that the deal represented victory. President Emomali Rahmonov (who later "de-Russified" his last name by removing the "ov") set about building an authoritarian regime along the lines of others already established in Central Asia. Three circumstances made him confident of success:

first, after years of civil war, ordinary people were yearning above all
for security and stability, which the majority of the public felt a strong,
strict regime could provide; second, Russia (which had in fact supported
Rahmon both during his battle with the opposition and as mediator
at the peace talks) tacitly backed the idea of establishing an authoritarian regime (essentially a dictatorship) in Tajikistan; third, Rahmon,
like the other Central Asian presidents, had positioned himself as the
bulwark against Islamic extremism and the only person who could save
Tajikistan from going down the Taliban road (the Taliban came to
power in Afghanistan in 1996).

Rahmon has been head of state since 1992, when he became chairman of the republic's Supreme Soviet. In 1994, he was elected to a
five-year term as president and was reelected in 1999 and again in 2006
(to seven-year terms, after the constitution was amended accordingly
in 2003). In setting about to consolidate his regime, he first removed
his rivals from among the members of the former UTO, thus rejecting
national reconciliation, and then gradually removed from power those
even among his allies who appeared capable of potentially becoming
rivals. Among those forced out of politics were Abdumalik Abdullajanov
(prime minister in 1992–1993), Safarali Kenjayev (founder of the
Popular Front, killed in 1999), Yakub Salimov (former interior minister), and Abdujalil Samadov (prime minister in 1993–1994, who died in
Moscow in 2004), and others.

Rahmon relied on a carrot-and-stick approach. After 1997, many of
the prominent opposition figures, including local warlords, were given
large land holdings, business enterprises, and some control over local
markets in exchange for abandoning political activities. UTO head
Said Abdullo Nuri, who had moved into a fine villa in the center of
Dushanbe, took a passive position. The IRPT controlled two seats in the
Tajik parliament. Gradually, however, Rahmon began to take a tougher
approach in removing his real and potential rivals. Mirzo Zeyev, for
example, former head of the country's Ministry of Emergency Situations
and one of the most prominent figures in the UTO, died in 2009 under
mysterious circumstances.

Not only did Rahmon establish control over the political and public
sectors of the country, but he also sought to regulate the daily routines

of the Tajik people and to intrude into their personal lives, thus making his regime more of a totalitarian administration than one that is authoritarian. In 2007, the Republic of Tajikistan adopted an unprecedented law on "Streamlining Traditions, Celebrations, and Ceremonies," which set standards for their observance and established an entire department and permanent local commissions under the auspices of the Executive Office of the President to bring order to these traditions. The purpose of the law was explained as being "to protect the social interests of the people of Tajikistan, to decrease the level of poverty and prevent excessive expenses ...," which in itself appeared quite reasonable. However, the very tone of this law and the petty meticulousness of its provisions were absurd and even ridiculous. Article 8, for example, proclaimed that "birthdays can be celebrated voluntarily only in the family circle."[3]

Pressure on the media increased. As well-known opposition journalist Dodojon Atovulloyev put it, "Tajikistan had freedom of the press until Rahmon.... Under Rahmon Nabiyev [the previous president], each issue of our newspaper, *Charogi Ruz*, would elicit calls to our office from the head of the presidential administration ... and dozens of officials were fired. Ministers trembled when they got a visit from our paper's journalists. [President] Rahmon's arrival in power was the day that marked the death knell for our free press."[4] The Reporters Without Borders index of press freedom ranked Tajikistan 122 out of 179 countries for 2011–2012 (it had previously been ranked 115).

INTERNAL CHALLENGES

The ruling regime faces several internal challenges: a permanent economic crisis, regionalism, domestic political confrontation, and the presence of radical Islam. These dangers are all closely interwoven: to a great extent, political confrontation has been rooted in regional friction (in the Sughd, Garm, Kulyab, and Gorno-Badakhshan regions) and the radical Islam espoused by the opposition (based primarily in the Garm and Gorno-Badakhshan regions). There had even been some separatist feelings noted in the Gorno-Badakhshan Autonomous Region during the years of civil war, although the region's ethnic diversity would have made it unrealistic for such ideas to actually be carried out.

After a peaceful interlude that followed the civil war, the Islamists gradually began to resume their activities. Although Rahmon at first tried to pretend that the problem had been due to the action of only a few criminal groups, after 2007 he began sending troops into the Rasht Valley (where the Islamist opposition forces enjoy substantial support) under a variety of pretexts (in 2009, for example, troops were sent there ostensibly to destroy the poppy crop, although poppies had never been grown in the valley in the first place).[5] The situation intensified in 2010, when rebels began to emerge in other parts of the country under the leadership of intransigent warlords Abdullo Rakhimov and Alovuddin Davlatov, dubbed the "Tajik Taliban," who engaged army forces in armed clashes in which both sides suffered casualties (specifically about fifty troops killed and dozens captured by the rebels).

Abdullo Rakhimov (Sheikh Abdullo), one of the more prominent UTO figures, refused to sign the Peace and National Accord Agreement in 1997 and left for Afghanistan in 1999. He returned to Tajikistan in 2009 and has resumed his struggle against the current regime. Although there are about 300 armed rebels active in the country, under certain circumstances they could be joined by tens of thousands of the dissatisfied and could also receive support from abroad.

Increased Islamist activity has been noted in Isfara, located near Batken in Kyrgyzstan, where in 1999 clashes had occurred with the Islamic Movement of Uzbekistan, and where young suicide bombers continue to be recruited.[6] There have even been instances of female suicide bombers: a native of Isfara, Mukhtarsrakhon Miramonova, blew herself up with a grenade during a clash with the police in 2010. The imam of the local Khojien mosque has admitted that "acts of terrorism occur one after the other, with people blowing up buildings, themselves, and people in the vicinity."[7]

Relations between the Islamic opposition groups and the regime are influenced by the position of the IRPT, which since the death of Said Abdullo Nuri in 2006 has been headed by Muhiddin Kabiri, a reformist who can be seen as a pragmatic opposition figure willing to engage in dialogue with the authorities. It is interesting to note that one factor prompting such dialogue has been the increasing popularity of the unrecognized Hizb at-Tahrir Party and the Bayat organization, which operate independently from the IRPT and pursue the goal of establishing a caliphate in Central Asia. This contradicts the ideology of the IRPT, which seeks to build an Islamic Tajik state. Kabiri's influence among Muslims has increased in recent years. It is telling, too, that he has devoted much of his efforts to supporting Tajik migrants in Russia, even traveling to Russia to meet with them.

A struggle for control over Islam has begun in Tajikistan, with each side vying to be recognized as the one true guardian of Islamic tradition charged with speaking on its behalf, and able to use it as a political instrument. Rahmon has attempted to "monopolize" Islam and has worked to broaden its hold on society by setting up a system of state-controlled religious education, building a huge mosque in Dushanbe for 100,000 worshipers (some data say 150,000),[8] and personally promoting the Hanafi school of Islam over the other branches, above all Salafi Islam. He proclaimed 2009 the "year of the Great Imam"[9] (in this aspect, Rahmon can be likened to Chechen leader Ramzan Kadyrov, who, although also a secular politician, supports the total Islamization of Chechnya).

However, Rahmon's declared Islamization policy then began to spin out of his control. A private religious education system emerged that was not under the jurisdiction of the president, while the sermons read in the mosques were not always in line with Hanafi Islam or official ideology. Not all of the clergy has been loyal to the regime. Rahmon soon realized that his bid to take control over Islam had failed and that Islam's consequent increasing influence in society was beginning to represent a threat to the regime itself. As a result, he began to implement measures aimed at curtailing religion's political influence. In 2010, he began to close mosques where non-loyal clerics were preaching,[10] ordered the 1,400 students studying in Islamic institutions abroad (including 200 in Iran) to return home,[11] and prohibited the wearing of traditional Muslim clothing by women in public places, primarily in state institutions. This de-Islamization reached a peak in 2011 with the adoption of a law setting forth Parental Responsibility for the Education and Upbringing of Children, prohibiting those under the age of eighteen from attending mosques unless accompanied by older family members.[12] The law drew fierce criticism from the Muslim faithful and has been violated en masse.

INCREASING AUTHORITARIANISM

Having lost the battle for Islam, Rahmon continued to strengthen his authoritarian regime, trying to remove any real competition to himself. In the February 2010 parliamentary elections, 70.6 percent of the voters supported the presidential National Democratic Party, which won 52 of the 85 seats. The IRPT (which came in second with 8.2 percent of the vote) won two seats, as did the Communist Party, the Party of Economic Reform, and the Agrarian Party. Not without justification, the opposition accused the authorities of having falsified the election results, prompting Rakhmatullo Zoirov, leader of the Social Democratic Party (which did not make it into parliament) to speak of a "usurpation of power."[13] It must be noted that the IRPT actually did garner many more votes than was officially attributed to it; the party itself mentioned the figure of 40 percent of the vote.

Rahmon's desire for absolute rule has sometimes gone to absurd lengths. It is now customary in Tajikistan to address the president as *Chanobi oli*, an expression identical in meaning to "Your Majesty." The political system has taken a nepotistic turn typical of Central Asian regimes, with nearly every member of Rahmon's family (and he has nine children) getting a high official post.

The regime in Tajikistan is somewhat reminiscent of the toppled regime of Kurmanbek Bakiyev in Kyrgyzstan. The Tajikistan News website has featured very apt and even provocative comparisons between Tajikistan and Kyrgyzstan. As the author of one comment wrote, "The Kyrgyz agreed among themselves, got together, and within a day sent Bakiyev packing. Yes, people were injured, there were victims, but they achieved their goal, at least, and kicked him out!"[14]

"After going through a stabilization period, Tajikistan has once again returned to the crisis point it was at in the early 1990s, when open struggles between the central government and the regional elites spilled over into civil war,"[15] journalist and analyst Sanobar Shermatova wrote in 2010. In 2010–2011, Rahmon—prompted by his survival instinct, no doubt—apparently realized that it would be dangerous to tighten the screws any further, all the more so with the country in such a desperate economic situation (according to the National Bank of Tajikistan, per capita income was $879 in 2009 based on current exchange rates,[16] and 45 percent of the people of Tajikistan live below the poverty line).

RECESSION

The economic recession in Tajikistan, aside from being a consequence of the collapse of the Soviet Union in general, was caused by the civil war, a chronic shortage of land,[17] environmental issues, and mistakes made by the local leaders. Another cause could be said to be the fact that the Tajik government had been insufficiently critical of the International Monetary Fund (IMF) demand that property rights during privatization, including land rights, be transferable to individual ownership, a mandatory IMF condition for credit to be issued for the national economy. This led to the collapse of collective farms, as the small owners found themselves unable to cultivate the land they had inherited or to operate reasonably as farms. The agricultural sector itself consequently collapsed, affecting most of the population.

Since in terms of the size of its reserves of water Tajikistan is eighth in the world, one likely economic cornerstone for the economy remains its hydroelectric potential, estimated at 527 kilowatt-hours (of which only 5 percent is currently being utilized). A number of hydroelectric power plants are operating in Tajikistan: the Nurek, Baipazin, Sangtuda 1, Sangtuda 2, Kayrakkum, and several others of smaller capacity. The Nurek power plant remains the most powerful of these, having a rated capacity of 3,000 megawatts (first attained in 1979).

The main new power generation facility is the Roghun hydroelectric power plant (currently under construction), which has been a cause of major economic and political clashes. The plant is being built in a seismically dangerous zone of the Ilyaksk-Vakhsh fault. There are 62 *kishlaks* (rural settlements) located within the territory affected by the project. It is known that the local population is highly religious.

According to the initial design, the dam was to have been 355 meters (1,165 feet) in height, which would have made it the world's tallest. In 1993, the project was frozen due to a lack of financial resources. In 2004, the Russian company RUSAL became the main investor in the project, but in 2007 the agreement was canceled for financial, technical, and, apparently, political reasons. RUSAL experts suggested reducing the height of the dam to 285 meters and making it out of concrete rather than rock-fill. After rumors emerged of RUSAL's refusal to pay so-called kickbacks (that is, large bribes to local politicians and senior officials), Dushanbe announced that it had decided not to sell the aluminum plant to RUSAL in exchange for its investments. On top of everything else, politics began to play a part in the debate over the fate of the Roghun hydroelectric power plant when Russia sided with Uzbekistan, which has been against having the dam at all.

After losing funding for the Roghun project, Rahmon issued a "patriotic initiative" in 2010 appealing to the Tajik people to donate money for construction. These funds were to be used to rehabilitate the project, for which purpose the budget had already allocated 650 million somoni. However, the absence of a project front meant that this money went unspent and began to decline in value, while banks had no commercial reason to accept it.[18] Construction of the Roghun dam came to a standstill, and Rahmon has not been able to find any wealthy investors to complete it.

Without the Roghun dam, it would be difficult to imagine how yet another ambitious and political goal could be achieved: the sale of electric power southward, to Afghanistan and Pakistan (which has already stated its readiness to help complete the Roghun project). This concept to supply electric power in such a way was formulated under the framework of the U.S. Agency for International Development's 2004 Regional Energy Market Assistance Program (REMAP), which anticipated that Tajikistan and Kyrgyzstan would become the main suppliers of electric power for "greater" Central and South Asia, including Afghanistan and Pakistan. This project is targeted at restructuring the entire energy system, and if implemented may further weaken Russia's position in the region.

Since August 10, 2011, Tajikistan has been supplying electric power to Afghanistan over the Sangtuda-Puli Humri power line, although in negligible amounts and only during the summer period (in winter, Tajikistan itself suffers an electric power deficit). Tajik electricity, however, is cheap (3.5 cents per kilowatt, as opposed to 7.5 cents for Uzbekistan's electric power).

The Central Asia South Asia Electricity Transmission and Trade Project (CASA-1000) envisions the provision of electric power from Tajikistan and Uzbekistan southward. Russia is shrewdly supporting this project, and the Russian company Inter RAO is preparing to participate as well. Once built, plans call for the Roghun dam to generate 13.1 TWh of electric power annually, which would not only fully satisfy Tajikistan's needs, but also provide enough surplus electric power to export.

Until recently, the supply of electric power southward had been monopolized by Uzbekistan, which now, because of emerging competition, is prepared to even increase the supply of power to Pakistan and Afghanistan, probably at a slightly reduced price.[19] Clearly, with all of its disagreements with Tajikistan, Uzbekistan will sooner or later need to find a way to participate in multilateral projects.

Aside from the energy sector, which is undoubtedly a dominant component of the Tajik economy, prospects should be considered for development of the mining industry. Tajikistan has deposits of uranium ore that are suitable for the production of nuclear weapons and fuel for nuclear power plants. In addition, there are deposits of gold in the vicinity of Penjikent.

There was a slight improvement in the economy in 2011, when GDP growth increased from 6.7 to 7.4 percent.[20] Foreign exchange reserves grew by 20.8 percent, totaling $801.6 million.[21] Although the rate of inflation has slowed, this should be attributed not so much to the efforts of the government as to the global financial crisis, which has caused food prices to decline globally. Although according to official figures the average monthly salary in Tajikistan exceeded $100, the generally low standard of living among the majority of the population is not reflected by macroeconomic indicators or official figures on increased salaries.

In any event, in a hint of the regime's new willingness to liberalize somewhat, it began dismantling the personality cult that had built up around Rahmon. In March 2011, photos and posters of the president disappeared from the streets, and at about the same time a number of the rebels were granted amnesty. Rahmon signed an amnesty law in honor of the twentieth anniversary of Tajikistan's independence in August 2011 that became the greatest the country had yet seen, affecting 15,000 prisoners, of whom about 4,000 were released. Mahkmadsaid Ubaydulloyev, speaker of the upper house of parliament and mayor of Dushanbe, appealed for personal rights to be respected and the law to be observed. Rahmon proposed that Articles 135 and 136 (slander and defamation) be removed from the Criminal Code and included in the Civil Code instead, which could be seen as opening the way to greater freedom of the press. (On January 12, 2012, an attempt was made on the life of independent journalist and opposition figure Dodojon Atovulloyev, although identifying exactly who gave the order has remained impossible to determine.)

Finally, in response to rising food prices in February 2011, Rahmon ordered that the country's strategic reserves of buckwheat, rice, and flour be released onto the market. Still, such measures have appeared to be nothing other than palliative. Public discontent has continued to grow, and social tension still runs high. Atovulloyev believes that the only way to change the current regime would be to "organize our own Tajik 'Tahrir.'"[22]

However, organizing another "Midan Tahrir" (that is, to replicate the mass protests on Cairo's main square that toppled Egyptian President Hosni Mubarak's regime in the spring of 2011) would be difficult, if not impossible. Rahmon's regime does have its supporters, above all among the numerous bureaucrats, each of whom in turn is backed by his own clan. The president would be able to count on the support of his hometown, Kulyab. The status quo is also satisfactory for the local drug trafficking mafia, which has incorporated a sizable number of bureaucrats as well. Thus, even if the opposition does succeed in organizing mass protests, it would encounter serious resistance. The situation in this case would be more reminiscent of the confrontation just before the civil war began, when the Islamic-democratic opposition had gathered on Shakhidon, one of Dushanbe's two main squares, and the regime's supporters had gathered on the other main square, Ozodi. Rather than leading to a painless regime change, a new confrontation could usher in a new civil war.

However, even if Rahmon's opponents are successful, it is by no means clear who would take over: the IRPT, the regional elites (who have felt slighted by Rahmon and his team and are fed up with the Kulyab clan holding power), and the local drug mafias all have their eyes on power, which does nothing to bring down the level of internal instability. The influence of the IRPT grew considerably between 2010 and 2012. Moreover, support for it among the public now surpasses the 5–10 percent that analysts had estimated previously, apparently because of the victories in the Arab revolutions in the Middle East won by Islamists, whom the IRPT sees as its ideological allies. Should the authoritarian regime fall, the IRPT would be prepared to assume the responsibilities of governing. Its criticism of the regime intensified noticeably, and the organization became more uncompromising in 2011 to 2012.

INFLUENCE OF OUTSIDE ACTORS

To what extent is the situation in Tajikistan being influenced by outside players (China, Russia, the United States, and its immediate neighbors, primarily Uzbekistan)? Obviously, none of these countries would want to see the situation in Tajikistan escalate to any great degree, not to mention see the country collapse. In the first place, it would destabilize the entire Central Asian region; second, it could open the way for radical Islamists with ties to their fellows in Afghanistan to take the stage and turn the country into another base for international terrorism; and third, it would inevitably initiate a new flood of refugees in every direction, which could affect neighboring countries, including Russia.

Thus, no matter how foreign relations might develop between outside actors and the Dushanbe regime, there is no one who would be prepared to provide support to Rahmon's opponents. Beijing is quite happy with the idea advanced by certain experts that Tajikistan "is trying to win itself the status of a Chinese province,"[23] while Washington has been increasing financial aid to the Tajik government and has incorporated it into its security strategy for the region. Neither the United States nor China would have any interest in seeing a hypothetical "Tajik Spring."

Russia, of course, also wants to see nothing of the kind. It hopes to keep Tajikistan within its sphere of influence by taking part in large-scale projects there (in particular, energy projects) and by providing military aid. The foundation for military cooperation between Tajikistan and Russia was laid during the civil war, when Moscow agreed to bear half of the costs of defending the Tajik-Afghan border.[24] This mutually advantageous cooperation played an important part in helping Rahmon remain in power. Subsequently, Rahmon was able to count on the support, if tacitly, of the Russian 201st Division, which had remained in Tajikistan and became the core of the Russian military base established there in 2004.

Since Moscow has decided to reequip the base with upgraded arms and equipment, Russian military hardware worth an estimated $1 billion will be handed over to Tajikistan, including 160 tanks (T-62, T-72), 140 armored personnel carriers, 169 infantry fighting vehicles, an artillery repair and maintenance complex, a mobile *Igla* air defense system, 30 *Shilka* and *Osa* air defense systems, and four helicopters.[25] Although these weapons might be obsolescent, they nonetheless will be of great assistance to the regime in battling its opponents domestically and can serve to defend the borders, including as "a deterrent in Tajik-Uzbek relations."[26]

MIGRATION

Migration is the other significant link between Tajikistan and Russia. One in three Tajik families has at least one family member working abroad, the vast majority of them in Russia. According to data from the Tajikistan Migration Control Directorate, more than 1 million Tajiks were in Russia at the end of 2011 (see different migration figures in Chapter 3). Most of them work in the Perm Krai, Sverdlovsk, and Orenburg oblasts, and in Krasnodar Krai[27] (there is even a newspaper aimed at them, the *Mukhodzhir*, which began appearing in Dushanbe in the spring of 2012). Migrants have sent nearly $3 billion home, which amounts to 45.4 percent of Tajikistan's GDP.[28]

In 2011, a dispute erupted between Russia and Tajikistan when Russian pilot Vladimir Sadovnichy was detained and arrested (together with Estonian citizen Alexey Rudenko), accused of smuggling aviation-related spare parts, illegally crossing the border, and violating international transportation regulations. After the Russian pilot was sentenced to eight-and-one-half years in prison, harsh criticism was expressed by politicians in Russia (including President Dmitry Medvedev) and nationalist sentiments grew among the Russian public. As a means of punishing Tajikistan, some State Duma deputies demanded that Russia deport Tajik migrants and introduce visa requirements for citizens of Tajikistan. The Russian police conducted a series of raids in which only Tajiks were detained, not migrants from other republics, and several hundred of them were deported.

Tension abated after Rahmon decided to release Sadovnichy and let him return home. Still, the fact that Moscow had demonstrated its willingness to use migration as a means of pressuring Tajikistan will certainly have a negative impact on future relations between the two countries and force Dushanbe to put more emphasis on a multivectoral foreign policy and to find countries other than Russia with which to form partnerships.

It should be recalled that the number of Tajik migrants working in Russia had declined by 150,000 to 160,000 in 2009 and that their remittances had decreased by a third, amounting to $1.8 million; 20 percent of the workers did not send any money home at all, while 40 percent sent reduced amounts. However, "despite the apocalyptic predictions of experts based on the declining amounts of money sent home and the massive numbers of returning migrants, Tajikistan has for the time being succeeded in avoiding the worst case scenario: impoverishment of the population and increasing social tensions."[29]

The conflict over the arrest of the Russian pilot came at a bad time for Moscow, during the latter half of 2011, when the Kremlin had been actively promoting the Customs Union and Eurasian Union projects and was attempting to induce Tajikistan, among others, to join. Nevertheless, the question of joining these organizations has barely even been considered by the upper echelons in Dushanbe; so far there have been only hints that Tajikistan theoretically might join.

In discussing the question of whether Tajikistan should join the Customs Union, let alone the Eurasian Union, Tajik analysts have also noted the fact that Uzbekistan has been negatively inclined toward such projects and have concluded that it would not be particularly advantageous for Tajikistan to join if Uzbekistan is not also involved. Certainly, if Tajikistan should agree to participate, although migrant travel to Russia would be made unencumbered, and prices on energy imports, grain, and certain other goods would fall, the cheap products currently being imported from China, Iran, and Turkey would be affected and the businesspeople involved in trade with those countries would be subject to financial ruin. As Hamrokhon Zarifi, the foreign minister of Tajikistan, said, "If Tajikistan were to join the Customs Union now, the benefits would be negligible."[30] Nonetheless, Russia continues to wait in the hope that Tajikistan will make a positive decision to agree to new forms of cooperation by joining the Customs Union and Eurasian Union.

RELATIONS WITH CHINA

Tajikistan's relations with China continue to develop. In 2011, 1,100 square kilometers of territory was transferred from Tajikistan to China, which was 0.77 percent of the total land area (although the Chinese had requested 28,500 square kilometers, which would have been as much as 20 percent of the total). In January 2011, the Parliament of Tajikistan ratified the Complementary Agreement Between China and the Republic of Tajikistan on the China-Tajikistan Boundary, which put an end to this sensitive issue. The degree of the Chinese economic activity and the extent to which the government supports it is such that, according to Maxim Gusarov, "official Dushanbe wants the country to have the status of a Chinese province." "There is an impression that the Chinese are in control of all the key sectors of the economy."[31] From 2007 to 2011, China invested $515.9 million (including 64.8 million in direct investments).[32] A direct road linking the countries via Kulma was opened in 2004. The reconstruction of the road between Dushanbe and Chanak via Khujand is nearing completion, as are the Shakhristan and Shar-Shar auto tunnels. China is Tajikistan's largest investor.[33]

The Tajik-Chinese border spans 500 kilometers of mountainous terrain and has long impeded the development of trade relations, with goods coming from China to Tajikistan having to transit through Kazakhstan and Kyrgyzstan. With the opening of a direct road link to China (the first section of the Dushanbe-Dangara road was opened in 2011, with President Rahmon attending the ceremony), Chinese goods will flood into Tajikistan, which in light of the growing Chinese investment will indeed turn the country into an economic appendage of China. Of the total Chinese financial influx, 80 percent are loans ($640 million as of early 2009), which will leave Tajikistan totally mired in debt and unable to repay.[34] In 2011 alone, China provided $19 million in grants.

China has been investing in key sectors of the economy, including the electric power sector. Construction of the Lolazor-Khatlon and the South-North overhead power transmission lines, actively supported financially by China, was completed in 2009. China also participated in developing the design plans for the Zeravshan hydroelectric power plant project and has been eyeing the deposits of nonferrous metals (aluminum fluoride and cryolite in Khatlon Province) and gold (in Penjikent) since 2010–2012. In addition, China has been entering the agricultural sector of the economy.

Between 1992 and 2010, Tajik-Chinese trade expanded from $2.75 million to $1.5 billion and will probably soon exceed $2 billion.[35] Although trade turnover between the two countries increased fourteen-fold over the five-year period from 2006 to 2011, in actual fact it is greater by 45–50 percent than shown in the official Tajik statistics, which do not include the shuttle trade upon which thousands of families depend for survival. At the same time, Chinese traders have been trying to monopolize trade at the markets, and this has already led to a number of clashes between them and local businessmen at the Karvon and Sultan-Kabir bazaars in Dushanbe.

The Chinese presence in Tajikistan is evident even at the level of everyday life. China has been participating in the construction of buildings for the Ministry of Foreign Affairs, the National Library, and the State Museum. Since the work itself is often carried out by Chinese construction workers, this inevitably provokes the irritation of the local

population, which has suffered from unemployment; 82 percent of
Tajiks oppose allowing foreigners to work in the country.[36]

Beijing, following its usual practice, has refrained from becoming
involved in Tajikistan's domestic issues. Evidently, this approach comes
from the understandable and justifiable confidence that, no matter
who is in power, the Chinese presence in Tajikistan will continue over
the long term to be a durable factor and that relations between the two
countries will continue to develop.

RELATIONS WITH THE UNITED STATES

While China has formulated relations with Tajikistan strictly in economic terms, the most important issue for the United States is strategic political and military cooperation. Tajikistan borders Afghanistan,
and Tajik cooperation with the United States will become increasingly
important as a consequence of the planned withdrawal of coalition
forces from Afghanistan in 2014. U.S. politicians and military leaders
have long systematically developed acquaintanceships with their counterparts in Tajikistan, which some experts have linked with the accession
of Hamrokhon Zarifi to the position of Tajik foreign minister. Zarifi is
considered to be an advocate of pursuing active relations with the West.[37]

As the president of Tajikistan has stated repeatedly, it is prepared to
open its infrastructure (bridges and roads) for the use of military units
participating in the war in Afghanistan and to render assistance of any
kind in order to ensure the operation of sites for providing services to
the troops. The Americans consider Ayni Air Base to be a replacement
for Manas, where the use agreement is due to expire in 2014, though
U.S. politicians have stated repeatedly that the United States has no
plans to establish a military base in Tajikistan. In particular, this was
confirmed by Robert Blake, the assistant secretary of state for South
and Central Asian Affairs, during a meeting with Emomali Rahmon in
December 2011.[38] (That didn't stop developers of a game at the website
www.military.com called "Flash Point: Entry to Tajikistan," in which
the player can join an American special forces unit in Tajikistan as it
pursues terrorists who entered the country from Afghanistan.)

At the same time, in 2013 the United States plans to double, to $1.5 million, the military aid that it provides to Tajikistan under the framework of the Foreign Military Financing (FMF) program.[39] In 2011, the American embassy donated special equipment and uniforms valued at $115,000 to local border guards. Although such amounts clearly cannot compare to the resources that the United States has been allocating to many of the other Muslim countries, it would seem that American military and technical assistance to Tajikistan will only grow, since the conflict in Afghanistan is far from being resolved and the United States cannot ignore the fact that the situation in Tajikistan will affect the outcome.

Rahmon in turn has been capitalizing on U.S. interest in his country and demanding economic and financial aid in exchange for strategic cooperation. The total amount of U.S. investment in Tajikistan has already exceeded $1 billion, and the Americans are prepared to increase it.

In addition, the Tajik president is intending to weaken Russian influence as he develops cooperation with the United States. It was clearly no coincidence that NATO decided to increase the volume of its cargo passing through Tajikistan in 2007, at the same time that the country was involved in a dispute with Russia over construction of the Roghun dam.

However, it could hardly be said that Washington regards Emomali Rahmon as being an absolutely reliable partner. In the first place, his eagerness to develop relations with the United States has been induced by the deterioration of Tajik relations with Russia, against which Rahmon had occasionally made excessive demands. In spite of it all, Rahmon is not opposed to the Russian military presence and believes that Russia would support him fully should the domestic political situation in Tajikistan turn threatening. At the opening of the Dushanbe branch of the Moscow National University of Science and Technology of the Moscow Institute of Steel and Alloys (MISiS) in the spring of 2012, the president of Tajikistan stated reassuringly that he was "prepared to respect Moscow as a strategic partner," and that although he had been promised "mountains of gold" in exchange for opening foreign military bases in his country, "we did not even consider these proposals."[40] Second, Rahmon obviously does not always want to play "by

American rules." For example, he will never give up good relations with Iran. Third, the United States cannot expect with full confidence that Rahmon's regime will be stable over the long term, as events unfolding in the Middle East alone make Tajikistan's future unclear. The reliability of the regime as a predictable partner and its durability are viewed with a certain amount of doubt, a skepticism fully justified by the example of Kurmanbek Bakiyev, recently ousted as president of Kyrgyzstan.

REGIONAL RELATIONSHIPS

In the region itself, Tajikistan attaches the most significance to its relations with its eastern neighbor Uzbekistan, a relationship that has been marked by great and continuing tension. The underlying reason for the tendency toward conflict between the two states lies in the fact that as far back as the Soviet era, areas that the Tajiks continue to regard as centers of their culture and statehood, in particular Bukhara and Samarkand, were made part of the Uzbek Republic. The tension that existed between the two nationalities led to strained relations between the two independent states. Another reason was the problem of distributing water resources, which had become particularly acute following the construction of the Roghun hydroelectric power plant, with a tall dam that gives Tajikistan the ability to fully control water distribution throughout the southern part of the region and makes Uzbekistan reliant upon it.

Following the 1999 events in Batken, Uzbekistan laid land mines across a number of sections of the tortuous 1,200-kilometer Uzbek-Tajik border. By the end of 2011, these land mines had blown up about 90 citizens of Tajikistan and injured more than 150. No one knows how many kilometers of the border have actually been mined.[41]

In 2012, Uzbekistan raised tariffs by 32 percent on the transit of rail freight for Tajikistan, and in the same year it cut off supplies of gas with no notice. In 2010, under the pretext of a bridge explosion in the Uzbek portion of the Galaba-Amuzang railway, Uzbekistan blocked the road to Khatlon Province, effectively resulting in the economic blockade of an entire region. Over half of all rail freight to Tajikistan is shipped through Uzbekistan.[42] In 2011, the Uzbek administration demonstratively ignored the opening of the Patar customs post in Sughd Province, which is considered vital for Tajikistan. Tashkent and Dushanbe are not linked by any direct airline service.

In the spring of 2012, Uzbekistan cut off supplies of natural gas to Tajikistan, which dealt a severe blow to the Tajik economy. Major local enterprises were obliged to halt operations or significantly reduce their output. Aluminum producer Talco was able to operate at only 20 percent of capacity; Tajik Cement had to stop operations altogether. In addition, the Uzbek authorities began interfering with the supply of Turkmen gas to Tajikistan (the pipeline runs through Uzbek territory). Each side had its own explanations, some credible, as to why these conflict situations occur with such regularity. With all of that, Tajikistan is in much weaker economic shape than is Uzbekistan, and the Tajik regime is also much more vulnerable domestically than is the regime in Uzbekistan. It would be difficult to imagine a situation in which Dushanbe would be able to have an impact on events in any neighboring country. By contrast, there have been many known instances when Uzbekistan has exerted an influence beyond its borders. In 1999, for example, Tashkent supported Colonel Makhmud Khudoyberdiev, who had initiated an uprising in northern Tajikistan (Khudoyberdiev's fate remains unknown. According to some reports, he was killed in battle, while other sources say that he moved to Uzbekistan and even took part in crushing the Andijan revolt in 2005).

It is therefore natural that Tajikistan, as Russian expert Yefim Malitikov put it, "is obsessed with the Roghun dam—there is an element of wounded national pride, the desire to liberate itself from energy dependence, and a convenient political leverage over its neighbor in this project."[43]

Tajik expert Tahim Abduyev believes that "the renewal of Tajik-Uzbek relations can only be expected after the change of government in the neighboring country. People with a new mindset have to come into power."[44] This comment makes it clear that the ongoing tensions in the relations of the two countries have also been elevated by a lack of mutual understanding between the leaders and their incompatibility at a personal level.

CONCLUSION

Tajikistan will hold a presidential election in 2013. Exactly how it will turn out no one can yet say. Under the constitution, Rahmon cannot stand for another term in office, but the practice in the Central Asian countries has been for their rulers to get around this law by amending the constitution to allow them to stay in power. It is not yet known whether Rahmon will take this road. Whatever the circumstances, if he does decide to relinquish the presidency to someone else, he will demand from his successor firm guarantees of security for himself and his relatives.

Another possibility would be to implement a system of rotation, along the lines of Russia's "tandem" solution, with the next president merely filling the seat for Rahmon, who would then return to office after seven years. Such a scenario, however, is unlikely, since Tajikistan, already unstable, could experience events in coming years that would cut Rahmon and his clan out of power for good.

If, however, events do follow the constitution, then Tajikistan will have a new president, who will face the job of tackling the problems left by his predecessor and of making changes to the political system. It cannot yet be said whether the new president will continue to strengthen the authoritarian regime or will take the risk of at least partially drawing on Kyrgyzstan's reform experience.

According to Niyazi Aziz, "Tajikistan will need to take gradual and balanced steps in order to achieve quick socio-economic results. The faster it can beat poverty and misery, the faster the country will become stable."[45] The new president will need to act in two seemingly mutually exclusive directions: maintaining a fragile stability while simultaneously carrying out reforms and fighting corruption and drug trafficking. To simultaneously accomplish these two tasks successfully will be nearly impossible.

CHAPTER 7

TURKMENISTAN: NO LONGER EXOTIC, BUT STILL AUTHORITARIAN

Turkmenistan has several specific features that distinguish it from the other Central Asian countries. For one thing, Turkmen society is the most traditional. Nevertheless, there is a high degree of urbanization in the country, with 800,000 people of a total population of approximately 5 million living in Ashgabat, and a number of other cities also having populations that exceed 200,000. The Soviet period brought the development of the modern gas, construction, and textile industries, and what until recently had been a modern education system. Still, Turkmenistan remains a tribal-based society, with the corresponding hierarchy and even a kind of tribe-based "division of labor." Members of the largest and most influential tribe, the Akhal-Teke, for example, are given the most important government positions (the country's former and current presidents both belong to this tribe), while the technical intelligentsia, particularly within the gas industry, comes in large part from the Yomuds. The third largest tribe, the Ersari, forms an elite in the humanities. Turkmen scholar Shokhrat Kadyrov has called Turkmenistan "a nation of tribes,"[1] and with some justification. The republic's stability has depended upon the balance of power among these tribes and the clans they head, and it is easy to see why Turkmenistan's leaders have remained "intent on preserving patriarchal and clan relations"[2] throughout the Soviet epoch and even more so over the post-Soviet period.

Of course, this tribal structure should not be seen as an absolute. Saparmurat Niyazov, Turkmenistan's first president, owed his rise to power not only to his tribal identity but also to his work within the Soviet Communist Party apparatus, including its Central Committee. He never forgot his tribal identity, but to his credit, he did make efforts to mediate relations among the different tribes.

In describing the Turkmens, many experts and representatives of other nationalities living in Turkmenistan, including Russians, have noted both their good-hearted nature and restraint, and their passive attitude, tendency to close themselves off within their family circle, and lack of initiative. As one Russian resident of Ashgabat noted, the Turkmens are not inclined to get together in the evenings to discuss society's current problems, which sometimes leads people to conclude that Turkmen society is "infantile" and that the effects of external wars, drug trafficking, and rising terrorist activity will push it "to the brink of collapse."[3]

This hypertraditionalism and passivity of the population, combined with the fact that Turkmenistan's first president had been molded within the heart of the Soviet system, defined the nature of the political regime in post-Soviet Turkmenistan. Another circumstance that played a significant part was the fact that Soviet Turkmenistan had remained on the sidelines of "greater Soviet politics." No Turkmenistan Communist Party first secretary ever became a member, or even a candidate member, of the Politburo, meaning that none of them ever attained national political stature. Turkmenistan produced no charismatic leaders of the likes of Kazakhstan's Dinmukhammed Kunayev, Uzbekistan's Sharaf Rashidov, or Tajikistan's Babadzhan Gafurov, and the various clans represented in its elite never fell into behind-the-scenes confrontation. No influential intelligentsia class ever developed, nor even a hint of dissident activity. Turkmenistan was a trouble-free, "invisible" republic.

NIYAZOV'S ASCENDENCY

Niyazov began his political career as first secretary of the Ashgabat district party committee, went to Moscow in 1984 to work in the

Communist Party central apparatus, and in 1985 became first secretary of the Turkmenistan Communist Party Central Committee, replacing Mukhamed Gapurov, who left no lasting impression in any way. Above all, Niyazov owed his career ascendency to Moscow (he could not rely on clan or relatives for support, having lost his father at a young age and grown up an orphan), and he served Moscow loyally as a representative of the Communist Party organization. At the Congress of People's Deputies in 1989, he voted against abolishing Article 6 of the constitution (which proclaimed the Communist Party's leading role), and in 1991 he supported the coup plotters who were attempting to oust Mikhail Gorbachev from power.

Niyazov was the exemplary Soviet politician and standard-bearer of Soviet political culture while the society that he ruled remained quintessentially traditionalist. As a result, post-Soviet Turkmenistan became a symbiosis between Eastern despotism and totalitarianism. For the post-Soviet space, the term "totalitarianism" would be most appropriately applied only to Turkmenistan under the rule of Niyazov.

It was precisely the exceptional similarity between his regime and the Soviet system that made Niyazov try to distance himself in every way from it and to discredit any suggestion of continuity with the Soviet period. In 1998, at a meeting with a Russian State Duma delegation, Niyazov explained the situation thus: "Not a single person here expressed the desire to fight against the communist ideology. Nobody in Turkmenistan speaks the words 'communist' and 'communism.' These words have faded from our social lexicon all of their own accord."[4] In Kazakhstan and Kyrgyzstan, the two words have survived, as have the parties that these names represent, although without any real influence. Niyazov has turned out to be the most zealous guardian of Soviet communist tradition and has refused to allow any opposition at all to exist.

From the beginning of his presidency, Niyazov had had no serious rivals in Turkmenistan, having already forced them all aside during the Soviet period of his rule, and his regime subsequently retained a significant potential for him to maintain personal power. As far back as 2000, one of Niyazov's political rivals, M. Salamatov, speculating as to who might replace Saparmurat Niyazov in power, had evaluated the president's political supporters, the democratic opposition, the national patriots, and supporters of political Islam and concluded that none of these various forces would be strong enough.[5]

The only rough spot in Turkmenistan's post-Soviet history came on November 25, 2002, when an attempt was made to assassinate Niyazov in a deliberately staged auto accident. According to the official version of events, this assassination plot was to have been the beginning of a coup led by former foreign minister Boris Shikhmuradov and supported by foreign forces. Another version that circulated abroad speculated that there had been no accident at all, and that the whole thing had been staged by Niyazov as a means of crushing any hint of an emerging opposition. In any case, hundreds of people were imprisoned after the incident, and Niyazov was able to thoroughly purge the political arena.

"TURKMENBASHI" AND THE CULT OF PERSONALITY

When Niyazov assumed the title of "Turkmenbashi" ("Father of the Turkmens"), he was not simply expressing his ambitions.[6] He also was demonstrating his desire to transform the Turkmen people from a collection of tribes into a new Turkmen nation. Implicitly, such a nation had already begun to form during the Soviet period: The Turkmenistan Soviet Socialist Republic was established as the nucleus of Turkmen statehood in 1924. No one can deny that Niyazov-Turkmenbashi did make progress in this direction by transforming Turkmenistan into a nation-state with him as its unquestioned (if eccentric) leader.

Niyazov's cult of personality was so exotic that it was often seen through humorous eyes both at home and abroad. Cities, mountain peaks, businesses, and military units were given his name (a Soviet tradition that was already in practice). He had monuments erected to his relatives and renamed the months, with November becoming "Turkmenbashi." In 2004, people began calling him Allah's messenger. The work he wrote, *Ruhnama*, became compulsory reading in all universities (like the works of Lenin, Stalin, and later Brezhnev in the Soviet Union), and every morning before beginning work, the citizens of the country had to swear an oath of loyalty to Niyazov (reminiscent of the oath of loyalty to the Soviet Communist Party and its leaders). This personality cult reached its height with the erection in 1998 of a 12-meter-high gilded statue of Niyazov that rotated with the sun's movement (the entire 75-meter edifice was officially called the "Arch of Neutrality").

Under the constitution that was adopted in 1992 (and subsequently amended five times), the president also served simultaneously as prime minister and formed the government. The parliament was empowered only to examine candidates for the positions of interior minister and justice minister. In 1999, the country's highest representative body, the Halk Maslahata, authorized Niyazov to remain in office indefinitely. In 1994–1995, there had even been talk of establishing a hereditary monarchy, and members of Niyazov's entourage had been ready to make him shah and declare Turkmenistan his kingdom. Niyazov, no doubt anticipating the jeers from abroad, decided this was excessive. However, as discussions continued over this possibility, the word "republic" was dropped from the country's official name (the only such case in Central Asia), which left Niyazov some maneuvering room should he ever decide to take the title of monarch in the future.

TURKMENISTAN'S FOREIGN POLICY

Turkmenistan's foreign policy reflected its domestic policy. Neutrality was declared to be its guiding principle, and Turkmenistan remained as a member of only the CIS, in which in reality it took no real part. It has refrained from joining any of the organizations that Russia has established or hopes to establish. Consistent with its foreign policy, Turkmenistan has not joined the Shanghai Cooperation Organization. Niyazov attempted to limit any external influence in order to cement the status of Turkmenistan as an independent country, equally distant from all foreign groups and forces.

Like Louis XIV, Niyazov could declare quite sincerely, "I am the State." The extent to which the Turkmen people actually believed this will probably never be known. The king was played by the retinue. Even Niyazov himself occasionally criticized the gigantic proportions that his cult of personality had assumed, although at the same time he realized that not even he could stop the machine that he had set in motion. Like all dictators, the Turkmen leader gradually became more paranoid with age and began replacing members of his entourage. Some officials even went so far as to try to avoid being appointed to senior positions, knowing that the higher they might climb, the harder and more painfully they would surely fall. Niyazov's final victim was the loyal head of his National Security Committee, Colonel General Mukhammed Nazarov, who lost his position in 2002. According to people who worked with Niyazov, including government ministers, he never listened to advice from anyone and often made spur-of-the-moment decisions.

Niyazov died on December 21, 2006. His death continues to be a topic of debate to the present day, with some asserting that he had been poisoned by members of his own inner circle who were fed up with his unpredictability.

A NEW LEADER

Niyazov's death was followed by a period of a brief and fierce struggle for succession from which Gurbanguly Berdimuhamedov emerged as the country's new leader. Berdimuhamedov, a dentist by profession, had been Niyazov's personal doctor before serving as health minister from 1997 to 2001, and thereafter as deputy prime minister. Niyazov had not designated a successor, and in any case could not have done so, since his death had been so sudden.

Berdimuhamedov seemed an unexpected compromise figure, although history has seen "interim" leaders before who ended up having long-lasting careers at the political summit. Although no one really expected the new president to radically change the face of the country, there was nonetheless hope that he would make some changes.

Change did begin, most importantly in the form of a certain amount of liberalization. Moscow-based analyst Andrei Grozin has described the new regime as being "more vegetarian,"[7] while Sebastien Peyrouse called the reforms "cosmetic" and "illusions of a Khrushchevian thaw."[8] In reality, it was not so much that the changes made were half-measures as that they were purely formal in nature. Still, the regime has managed to change its image from being nearly totalitarian to being hard-line authoritarian, or, to put it another way, from being an exotic exception along the lines of North Korea to being a typical authoritarian regime.

However, progress toward liberalization has been only formal and has not changed the political system. In the Law on Political Parties that was passed on January 13, 2012, Berdimuhamedov approved the establishment of a multiparty system, calling it "relevant in terms of the significant changes taking place in state administration and in terms of modernizing political mechanisms and rethinking the role and place of the country's social and civil institutions."[9] There is, however, no one who really believes that the parties to emerge would be allowed to operate free of control by the authorities. Turkmenistan today has only one party, the Democratic Party, which in fact is the renamed Communist Party of Soviet-era Turkmenistan and is completely under presidential control.

Berdimuhamedov won his second presidential election in February 2012 with 97.14 percent of the vote. In 2007, he had received 89.2 percent of the vote against five "opponents," while in 2012 he had faced seven opponents[10] (actually, public groups and organizations had initially put forward a total of fifteen candidates). The public dubbed these candidates the "seven goats," implying that the role of wolf had already gone to Berdimuhamedov. In any event, these "opponents" succeeded in winning no more than between 0.16 and 1.07 percent of the vote each.[11] Borrowing an election campaign trick from Putin's book, Berdimuhamedov declined to take part in televised debates with his opponents, "giving" them his share of airtime.

The country closed its land borders to foreigners before the elections, and people arriving at the airport had the contents of their computers inspected. At the same time, security services blocked access to two opposition websites operating abroad.

In 2011, Berdimuhamedov announced that members of the opposition based abroad (meaning the Republican Party and the Vatan sociopolitical movement) would be allowed to participate in the election. This did not happen, however, first because the country lacked the conditions for holding free elections, and second because in order to participate in the election, the opposition politicians would have had to return home and run the risk of being arrested.

The Turkmenistan constitution contains the so-called Occupational Experience Requirements, stipulating that a would-be president must have worked in government agencies, public organizations, enterprises, or institutions, thus creating further obstructions for opposition candidates. Although no real opposition candidate would be possible in Turkmenistan, these requirements in themselves are very telling.

For the first time, Turkmenistan agreed to submit a report on the human rights situation to the UN Human Rights Committee and to release a number of politicians from prison, including the former speaker of parliament, Ovezgeldy Atayev,[12] and several of those who had been arrested in connection with the 2002 assassination plot. However, Boris Shikhmuradov, the main defendant in that case, remains in prison, his fate and the state of his health unknown.

Berdimuhamedov reinstated the ten-year school system in the country (under Niyazov it had been a nine-year school program), reopened the national Academy of Sciences, and the opera and ballet theater (which Niyazov had "abolished"), and allowed Internet cafes to open, although under strict control of the authorities.

In Berdimuhamedov's words, "We are reviving ancient democratic traditions that see democracy as a culture of thinking and behavior."[13] In this regard could be mentioned, paradoxically, Kyrgyzstan (which in comparison to other Central Asian countries is democratic), where the seeds of democracy have sometimes taken root in the nomadic "free-spirited" traditions of society. The Kyrgyz and the Turkmens do share similarities in terms of their history, but while the "nomad democracy" of the Kyrgyz may have been one of the factors that prevented authoritarianism from taking hold in that country, in Turkmenistan it was suppressed by the Soviet political culture. If in order to highlight its democratic nature their country is compared to Turkmenistan, the Kyrgyz frequently become entertainingly upset.

One of Berdimuhamedov's most notable steps was to eliminate the Turkmenbashi cult of personality, albeit not completely. In this respect, he can actually be compared somewhat to Nikita Khrushchev.

Berdimuhamedov released the Turkmen people from the need to participate in public morning readings and study of Niyazov's *Ruhnama*, which court intellectuals and politicians had likened to the Quran. Niyazov's name was removed from the national anthem, and the oath of loyalty to Turkmenbashi was dropped. The names of the months reverted to their old names under the Gregorian calendar, and the Arch of Neutrality on Ashgabat's main square was taken down.

However, this process of dismantling the cult of personality did not lead to fundamental change. Berdimuhamedov himself has never expressed doubt in his predecessor's greatness and has been cautious in this "de-Turkmenbashization," fully aware (as are the other politicians in the country) that to completely dismantle Niyazov's image would deal a blow both to him and to his colleagues. It would thus be naive to expect Berdimuhamedov to begin to seriously denounce the old regime and clear the way for genuine deep-reaching transformation to begin. The replacement of the Arch of Neutrality by a "Monument to Neutrality" on the southern outskirts of Ashgabat (topped by the same gilded statue of Turkmenbashi) is symbolic of the half-baked nature of the changes. The monument's "rebirth from the ashes" is indirect evidence that Berdimuhamedov is not about to renounce the political traditions that he inherited and is not averse to using them himself, if in a somewhat milder way.

At the same time, the attempt by Berdimuhamedov's son Serdar to seize business assets from Niyazov's son Murat, in particular the Nisa Hotel in central Ashgabat, can be seen as evidence of a "tangible" move away from the Niyazov cult of personality. Incidentally, Berdimuhamedov's sister Gulnabat has also engaged in business ventures (cigarette imports), as has her son (that is, nephew of the country's leader), who has dabbled in the construction of buildings for retail markets.[14]

Meanwhile, a "modest" cult of personality has gradually begun to develop around Berdimuhamedov himself. He has already acquired a title of his own: "Arkadag" (Protector), which is not quite so pretentious as "Father of the Turkmens."

EPOCH OF RENAISSANCE

The "Golden Age" proclaimed by Niyazov has given way to a more modest and realistic "Epoch of Renaissance." At the same time, an "era of strength and happiness" has been pronounced, with conferences conducted at universities and other public forums in the country dedicated to the theme of "Turkmenistan, my homeland, the land of health and happiness." A concrete "Path of Health" was laid in the Kopetdag Mountains eight kilometers from Ashgabat. Berdimuhamedov has been named "Hero of Turkmenistan" merely once, whereas Niyazov was a six-time recipient of the award, perhaps too closely reminiscent of the Brezhnev era in Soviet times.

Instead of Niyazov's *Ruhnama*, Turkmens now read the *Turkmennama* (Story of the Turkmens), which extols the glory of the Turkmen people rather than lecturing on morals. *Turkmennama* would be more typical within the context of a nationalist ideology written by scholars close to the authorities. Its distinctive feature is that it portrays the Turkmens as the chosen people, meaning that Noah from the Bible was to have landed in Turkmenistan, the Aztecs and the Vikings were descended from the Turkmens (as local academician Odek Odekov has asserted), Zarathustra had supposedly come from southern Turkmenistan,[15] and even Russian epic folk hero Ilya Muromets was said to be a Turkmen as well. Not that there was anything original in this; such legend-making has occurred before in many countries, especially in the post-Soviet space, where many nationalities have strived to enhance the "quality" of their national identity.

Rather than presuming to author any philosophical tomes, Berdimuhamedov composed a song about white roses (reminiscent of the late Soviet-era song "Millions of Red Roses" by Russian pop diva Alla Pugacheva),[16] which he sang to his own guitar accompaniment, wearing a white suit (which turns out to be his favorite color). It thereafter became a matter of good politics to dress in white, and when Berdimuhamedov travels around the country, crowds now greet him waving white balloons.

The country once again abounds in portraits of the president, which may surprise the casual observer who does not follow developments in

Turkmenistan: Berdimuhamedov closely resembles his predecessor (one legend even has it that he is Niyazov's illegitimate son), which reinforces the impression that for all these years the country has been headed by one and the same person.

In addition to the outward resemblance of the two men, they have undertaken similar actions. Berdimuhamedov, for example, named Interior Ministry Troops Unit 1001 for his father, who had served there before retiring, as Niyazov had also been inclined to name various organizations for his relatives.

There have also been differences, however. Niyazov did not go in for moving his relatives up the political ladder. His son Murat had been indifferent to politics and became involved in business instead, while Berdimuhamedov's son demonstrates his community involvement by taking part in various public events. In time, he could well be named to a ministerial post. Family involvement in politics would certainly be nothing new for Central Asia and eventually could make Turkmenistan appear no different than its neighbors in the region.

After Niyazov's death, power lost its sacred aspect. Berdimuhamedov does not have the same charisma, and people do not worship him the way they did Niyazov. His nickname, GB (begging association with the all-too-familiar abbreviation KGB), was born out of a sense of humor rather than of fear.

Berdimuhamedov probably realizes that he will not be a "second Turkmenbashi," and in any case has not been striving for this, preferring instead to present the image of a "liberal despot," which he has so far done successfully.

ROLE OF ISLAM

Turkmenistan is a Muslim society, though it is hard to say exactly what role Islam plays there. The nomads practiced a syncretic form of Islam, limited to influencing family relations and everyday behavior but not playing a major part in shaping politics. Turkmenistan's Islam was aptly characterized by the term "everyday Islam," widely used in Soviet literature in the 1970s and 1980s.

At the same time, despite its apolitical nature, even "everyday Islam" contributes to the overall worldview of Muslims, including their political perceptions. Moreover, "everyday Islam" is remarkably stable, having survived the Soviet period by adapting to its demands and coexisting with the state-imposed atheist education. Scholars conducting religious research during the Soviet period noted remnants of Sufi Islam, which had retained its position among the Turkmens.[17]

At first glance, little has changed with respect to Islam in post-Soviet Turkmenistan. Its influence has centered on family life and rituals, and it appears to be distant from public political life. The Islamic "renaissance" that began with the decline of the Soviet Union seems hardly to have affected Turkmenistan, and what Islam there is has not become politicized. Partly because of repression, no successful attempts were made to create an Islamic party or movement, as had taken place in neighboring republics. When the president of a certain Muslim country visited Turkmenistan in the early 1990s, police officers were stationed outside the homes of every member of the Islamic Party for the Renaissance of Turkmenistan (all four of them) to prevent them from leaving.

Niyazov at first paid no attention to Islam, seeing in it no threat to his authority. In 1992, he stated that "there is no reason to exaggerate the likelihood of Turkmenistan's Islamicization."[18] In keeping society and the state closed (Turkmenistan's "neutrality" was aimed at maintaining such isolation), Niyazov to some extent had followed the Soviet model, replacing the cult of Lenin with that of himself. By the mid-1990s, however, he concluded that Islam needed some kind of official recognition and that it could also be useful in helping to strengthen his regime. In addition, Niyazov wanted to expand contacts with Muslim countries, hoping to receive financial assistance from them.

The country thereupon embarked on a program of building mosques, and imams began to sing Niyazov's praises in their sermons, to the point that these sermons, as well as the religious literature and even official propaganda, transformed into a symbiosis of religion and idol worship. At the same time, Niyazov extended total control over Islam, not allowing the slightest hint of criticism of him by the Muslim clergy. Nasrulla ibn Ibadulla, the chief mufti of Turkmenistan (formerly imam of the

Tashauz mosque and kadi in the Mari region) and the country's most influential spiritual figure, who had attempted to initiate an Islamic revival in the late 1980s and early 1990s, was imprisoned for criticizing the excessive obsequiousness to Niyazov.

Niyazov "monopolized" Islam, and genuinely considered himself to be extremely knowledgeable about it. In this respect he can be likened to other post-Soviet politicians, such as Tajik President Emomali Rahmon and Ramzan Kadyrov, the leader of Chechnya. In 2000, Niyazov ordered that 40,000 copies of the Quran be burned because he disagreed with the way the holy book had been translated into Turkmen.

Berdimuhamedov has been indifferent to Islam, sticking to his previous conviction that politicization of Islam in Turkmenistan would not be possible. Talk of a potential religious political opposition emerging in the country has not yet been confirmed. At the same time, there is speculation about the existence of a "parallel Islam" with those who have left Turkmenistan saying that even in rural areas in the country, some villages have "two mosques each" (as one respondent phrased it), of which one would be an underground prayer house delivering sermons of protest.

Turkmenistan will not likely be able to completely isolate itself from the events taking place in the rest of the Muslim world; neither will it be able to erect any "Great Wall" along the borders with its Central Asian neighbors, where radical Islam has been growing in activity. Clearly, Berdimuhamedov will soon have to deal with a rise in Islamic protest sentiments, for which he is obviously ill-prepared.

ENERGY

Fossil fuels are the cornerstone of Turkmenistan's regime. Gas sales accounted for 70 percent of the country's GDP in 2009. The authorities use gas revenue to maintain a tolerable standard of living and put on a show of caring for the needs of the people. Gas ensures the regime's survival and the success of its populist ideology. When he came to power, Berdimuhamedov did not abolish the policy of providing gas, electricity, and also water and salt to the population free of charge. In fact, beginning in 2008 owners of private cars have been allocated 120 liters of gasoline free each year, bus owners receive 200 liters, and motorcycle owners get 40 liters.[19]

Amount of Reserves in Dispute

Turkmenistan is fourth in the world in terms of the size of its gas reserves, which continues to be debated in engineering, economic, and political circles. The Turkmenistan authorities claim that accessible reserves total 20 trillion cubic meters. Russia, which has the world's largest accessible gas reserves, has 44.8 trillion cubic meters. According to BP, proven reserves in Turkmenistan increased from 2.6 trillion cubic meters to only 8 trillion cubic meters between 2000 and 2011,[20] although accessible reserves total no more than 3 trillion cubic meters.[21] Although the authorities in Turkmenistan have estimated the reserves of the largest field, Yolotan, at 6 trillion cubic meters, in reality the amount is several times less than that. Moreover, Yolotan gas has a high content of hydrogen sulfide, which complicates extraction.

Turkmen authorities have always deliberately exaggerated the country's gas reserves and have offered large purchase contracts to numerous foreign buyers for shipment in a number of different directions at once (such as to China, Europe, Iran, and Russia) that frequently have turned out to be unrealistic. Such tactics, however, have maintained a high level of interest among potential buyers of Turkmenistan's gas, enabling Ashgabat to attract the investment needed to build the appropriate infrastructure.

To assess the actual level of gas production in Turkmenistan today is difficult in light of the numerous large fluctuations that have occurred over the past twenty years, due both to the global economic situation and to Turkmenistan's own technological capabilities. Although, for example, gas production increased from 42 billion cubic meters in 2000 to 66 billion in 2008, it dropped to 45 billion cubic meters in 2010,[22] and gas exports for the year totaled only 22.6 billion cubic meters. For 2012, gas production has been estimated at 66.5 billion cubic meters. Development of the Garabil and Gurrukbil fields, the Central Karakum, and the right bank of the Amu Darya River is under way.

Other Markets

Although Russia had been Turkmenistan's largest gas buyer for many years, relations between Moscow and Ashgabat began to sour in 2008, when Turkmenistan sold Gazprom 50 billion cubic meters for $7 billion. At the end of that year, due to the global crisis, Turkmenistan demanded a higher contract price for the gas, which Gazprom refused to pay. This provoked a dispute that finally led Gazprom head Alexei Miller to shut off the Russian supply route in 2009. At the same time, there was an explosion in the gas pipeline, which Gazprom claimed was caused by purely technical reasons, but Ashgabat argued it had been intentionally set off by Gazprom itself. As a result, Turkmenistan was left incapable of supplying gas to Russia until the end of 2009. Once sales resumed in 2010, they came to no more than 11 billion cubic meters. Moscow has refused to purchase the 40 billion cubic meters that remained from the previous contracts, and this has given it leverage to pressure authorities in Turkmenistan.

The European market no longer requires large quantities of gas from Turkmenistan, and Gazprom has been able to satisfy the European demand for gas with its own resources. This has kept Turkmen-Russian relations tense. Naturally, Ashgabat has responded by stepping up efforts to diversify its gas supply routes and has been providing gas to its neighbor, Iran, for the past few years, delivering between 8 billion and 14 billion cubic meters in 2011, based on various estimates. Iran has also proposed to Turkmenistan that a new gas pipeline be built to the Persian Gulf.

For a time, Turkmenistan showed some interest in the Nabucco project, but it would not be possible for Turkmenistan to join the project unless a 300-kilometer trans-Caspian gas pipeline is built. Russia has expressed objections to the construction of the pipeline, and India has also recently become unhappy with such a prospect. There are two proposed routes for the Nabucco project: the trans-Anatolian route or the trans-Adriatic (Turkey-Greece-Italy) route. This project is the main rival to the Southern Stream project, in which Moscow has placed great economic and political hope. It should also be noted that no investment has yet been offered to build the underwater pipeline. (Some think that if the situation really turned serious, Russia would be prepared to use any means, including its powerful Caspian military flotilla, to prevent construction of the trans-Caspian pipeline from proceeding.)

China is becoming the main purchaser of gas from Turkmenistan. The gas pipeline to China was opened in 2009, and by as early as 2010 Turkmenistan was already exporting about 5 billion cubic meters of gas to China at a price of $192 (or $170–$180) per cubic meter, while at the same time Gazprom was paying $240 per cubic meter. By 2012, exports to China could reach 15 billion or even 30 billion cubic meters, and by 2015 they could be around 65 billion cubic meters. Work has already begun on building a second pipeline to China.

The TAPI Project

Ashgabat places high hopes on the TAPI project, which envisages the construction of a 1,735-kilometer pipeline with a capacity of 30–33 billion cubic meters to supply gas to Turkmenistan, Afghanistan, Pakistan, and India. Along with the Chinese export routes, it has been seen as an alternative to cooperation with Russia.

The TAPI project agreement was signed in 2010. Although the project is expected to cost $7.6 billion, much higher figures (up to $12 billion) have also been cited.[23] Construction is scheduled to begin in 2013, and the pipeline is set to begin operation in 2017.

As Ashgabat sees it, TAPI may help to stabilize the situation in Afghanistan. At the same time, however, it cannot be ruled out that the gas pipeline (or more accurately, its security) might be used by Taliban groups as a means to pressure the Afghan authorities and extort money from the companies and countries that have an interest in the uninterrupted operation of the pipeline. Thus, the need to maintain the security of gas traffic over the pipeline could end up contributing to the growth of a radical opposition (as was the case in Russia during the Chechen wars).

Interest in TAPI has been expressed not only by countries seeking to buy Turkmen gas, but also by Gazprom, which has increasingly been attempting to take part in energy projects not directly related to Russian gas.

TAPI has faced a number of obstacles. First, Turkmenistan's partners continue to be nervous about its lack of suitable transparency in addressing financial matters. Since Niyazov's time, gas sales have remained under the direct and undisputed control of the president, with 80 percent of the revenue going into Berdimuhamedov's own pocket. By continuing the tradition begun by Niyazov, who controlled all energy sector contracts through special accounts, he has established one of the distinguishing features of Turkmenistan's shadow economy. Under the laws of Turkmenistan, only 20 percent of the revenue from oil and gas exports goes into the state budget.[24] Berdimuhamedov has merely developed these corrupt schemes further. A contract concluded between a foreign buyer and Turkmenistan essentially amounts to a contract with the country's president. Second, instability continues in Afghanistan, and third, the success of the project will depend upon the unpredictable relations between Pakistan and India.

Finally, the question remains as to whether Turkmenistan actually has enough gas for all of these ambitious projects. The country plans to increase its gas production to 230 billion cubic meters and its exports to 180 billion cubic meters by 2020. Of these exports, 65 billion cubic meters are slated to go to China, 33 billion to TAPI, 20 billion to Iran, 10 billion to Europe, and 42–52 billion to Russia.[25]

Ties to Uzbekistan?

Since 2009, Turkmenistan has been trying to establish its own ties with Ukraine (to put it in other terms, in selling its excess gas it would like to bypass Russia). While visiting Kiev in 2012, Berdimuhamedov suggested the idea of building a pipeline with a capacity of 25 billion cubic meters a year from Turkmenistan to Azerbaijan and Georgia, and from there to Ukraine. Although some cautious overtures were made to Chevron, ExxonMobil, and ConocoPhillips, none of them showed any particular interest in the concept.

Moscow, always highly sensitive to any "bypass" projects, simply laughed at this particular initiative. Vladimir Kornilov, director of the Ukrainian branch of the Institute for the CIS Countries, said that direct gas supplies from Turkmenistan to Ukraine would be possible "only by aircraft."[26] (What's more, Ukraine had hoped to buy gas from Turkmenistan for $200, in spite of the fact that Turkmenistan is selling its gas to Russia for $350 and to Ukraine at the European price of $420.[27])

Turkmenistan's economy will always be dependent upon sales of fuels, primarily gas. Although this makes it possible for Turkmenistan to maintain a stable minimum level of well-being for its people, it also removes any incentive for the ruling class to undertake real reform.

Following its dispute with Russia, Turkmenistan has been left the option of exporting its gas to its eastern neighbors (China, India, and Pakistan) and south to Iran. Gas exports to the West and to Russia will probably be of secondary importance, especially in light of the numerous competitors Turkmenistan would face in the European market.

BUSINESS AND FINANCE

Along with the ruling family's monopolization of big business must be considered the issue of basic honesty in business and finance in Turkmenistan, where foreign partners have from time to time been cheated. The Argentine company Bridas, for example, which invested more than $1 billion in designing the trans-Afghanistan gas pipeline, had its profits appropriated.

In 2010, the Russian telecommunications company MTS (with 2.4 million subscribers in Turkmenistan) was pushed out of the national market. The current local monopoly, Turkmenistan Online, charges $213 a month for the cheapest Internet connection with a speed of 64 kilobits per second, and $6,821 a month for a connection of up to 2,048 kilobits per second. This financial control goes hand in hand with a stringent political censorship, which has led Reporters Without Borders to put Turkmenistan Online on its blacklist. The quality of telecommunications is notably poor and has not improved in spite of attempts to do so using the state television company Altyn Asyr.

In 2011, forty Turkish companies accused the government of Turkmenistan of refusing to pay a billion dollars for contracts that had already been carried out. The situation remained unresolved even during Turkish President Abdullah Gul's visit to Ashgabat. Foreign businesspeople loudly complain about the corruption that stifles business life. The current regime, like its predecessor, continues to see Turkmenistan as an exception, where the authorities and their friends have license to break the rules of business. If during the first post-Soviet years people had been willing to tolerate such "naughty tricks" and saw them all as being part of the growing pains of the transition period, their behavior has now become an impediment to international relations and made the country less attractive in foreign investors' eyes. International financial organizations have become ever more reluctant to grant loans to Turkmenistan. On the list of the 210 least favorable countries in the world ranked according to the World Bank's Control of Corruption Index, Turkmenistan is at number six.

The lone exception has been China. Beijing loaned Ashgabat $4.1 billion in 2010 to develop the Southern Yolotan gas field. However, as is the case with Tajikistan, this has bound Turkmenistan so tightly to China that the country could be seen as turning into a "province of China."

ISSUE OF MINORITIES

The status of ethnic Russians remains a sensitive issue in relations between Turkmenistan and Russia. The exact number of ethnic Russians in the country is not known. The Russian Interior Ministry has put their number at 3.5 percent of the total population in 2005, while in 2001 Niyazov had said that they comprised 2 percent of the population. Most likely, the number of Russians fluctuates between 120,000 and 150,000 people.

Turkmenistan authorities have taken an ambiguous approach to the Russians. On the one hand, they form the highest-skilled portion of the country's technocracy and intelligentsia, and the regime cannot do without them. On the other hand, they do not fit into local traditions and are thus rejected (as are the Russian-speaking Turkmens drawn more to Russian culture). Turkmenistan's ruling elite also speaks Russian, but their Russian/Soviet upbringing and background are offset by their nationalist views.

The Russian cultural and language environment has been shrinking. The only Russian-language newspaper left in Turkmenistan is *Neytral'nyy Turkmenistan*, which contains little of interest and merely provides a dully symbolic presence of the Russian language in the press. The import and distribution of Russian newspapers was prohibited in 2002, and (supposedly for technical reasons) the Russian radio station Mayak, which had previously been broadcast in all of the former Soviet republics, had to cease activity, while the availability of Russian Public Television (ORT) was cut to two hours a day.

The Russian Community of Turkmenistan was closed at the end of the 1990s and its leaders (Nina Shmelyova, Vyacheslav Mamedov, and Anatoly Fomin) were given prison sentences and then were deported. It was a sharp contrast to other Central Asian republics, where Russian community organizations have at least some opportunity to pursue social activities and work to protect the rights of the local Russian population. In Turkmenistan, they were deprived of any such opportunity.

The Russians in Turkmenistan were abandoned to their fate by the Russian leadership, which before 2010 ignored them totally, seeing its interests solely in the realm of energy cooperation and gas purchases and transit, and giving all other issues only peripheral attention, if that.

Turkmenistan and Russia had signed an agreement to establish rules on dual citizenship as early as 1993, when Russians in Turkmenistan enjoyed equal rights to those of the ethnic Turkmens. In 2011, however, Ashgabat announced that dual citizens would no longer be allowed to leave the country unless they assumed Turkmen citizenship alone. Anyone who refused to renounce Russian citizenship would be forced to leave the country. Based upon the new law that came into effect on April 1, 2012, only bearers of the new foreign travel passport, which is not issued to dual citizens, are permitted to travel abroad.

Russia did not recognize Turkmenistan's withdrawal from the 1993 agreement as lawful but could do nothing to change the situation. Meanwhile, Russians in Turkmenistan now also found themselves unable to privatize their homes. The prices at which the Russians would be able to purchase these homes from the state are rumored to have been raised so high as to make doing so impossible.

Whether or not Russia will more energetically protect the rights of Russians in Turkmenistan is difficult to say. The case of the Russian pilot arrested in Tajikistan shows that when it wants to, Russia can stand up for the rights of its citizens, even to the extent of threatening political and economic sanctions. In Turkmenistan, however, as in the other Central Asian republics, a set of principles and an overall concept for protecting the rights of ethnic Russians needs to be developed and implemented. At the moment, however, as over past years, this matter is still not on the table for Russian strategy in the region.

CONCLUSION

Opinions are divided on Turkmenistan's future. One view, expressed in a report by the American organization Crude Accountability, suggests that sooner or later Berdimuhamedov's regime will encounter the same problems that have brought down regimes in the Middle East and North Africa. The question is whether events will follow the milder "Tunisian" scenario, or whether they will take the Libyan road and raise the specter of civil war.[28]

In contrast, journalist Arkady Dubnov, one of the top experts on Central Asia, thinks that "Berdimuhamedov's sun will continue to shine for a long time to come."[29] Dubnov's view is more likely the correct one, since the public in Turkmenistan is clearly not capable of any mass protest. In the way it is structured, society in Turkmenistan is indeed reminiscent of that of Libya, although Libyans occupy a completely different geopolitical environment than the Turkmens. Turkmenistan has for decades been on the edge of global political and cultural processes. It is too "sluggish," and even a hypothetical revolution would not radically change the dominant values and political culture there. This means that Berdimuhamedov's sun (and the "sun" of dictatorship in general) will indeed continue to shine for a long time to come.

Neither should any major changes be expected with respect to foreign policy. The regime is not about to renounce its declared policy of neutrality, from which it has already gained a fair number of advantages and which has been recognized by its international partners. Turkmenistan is hardly likely to allow any military bases to appear on its soil, and rumors that the United States has sought to take over the former Soviet Air Force base in Mary are groundless (although it is true that the base in Mary would be very convenient for launching airstrikes against Iran).

Turkmenistan's presence in the CIS is purely formal, and the fact that Ashgabat has never hosted a CIS summit is symbolic. Hints that Turkmenistan might join the Collective Security Treaty Organization are baseless. It certainly has no inclination to join the Customs Union, and even less so the Eurasian Union. The only organization that it might perhaps consider joining in the future (under special conditions) would be the Shanghai Cooperation Organization. But for it to take such a step would be predicated above all on the degree to which Ashgabat wishes to develop its relations with China.

CHAPTER 8

UZBEKISTAN: IS THERE A POTENTIAL FOR CHANGE?

Uzbekistan is one of the two key players in Central Asia. The other is Kazakhstan, which represents not only a slice of Central Asia, but also a significant portion of Eurasia itself. Although Central Asia could theoretically be considered without including Kazakhstan (which lies wedged between Russia and China), no serious study of the region would fail to analyze its dominant state, Uzbekistan, located at the very center of the Central Asian region. Its population of 28 million constitutes half of the total population of the region, including Kazakhstan.

In a geopolitical context, Uzbekistan sees itself as being a regional Central Asian power, with its regional influence likewise translating into geopolitical importance. Not to underappreciate the importance of other Central Asian states, but the situation in those countries is significantly influenced by the internal affairs of Uzbekistan. At the end of the 1990s, an interesting publication appeared in Kyrgyzstan that had the symbolic name "Kyrgyzstan and Uzbekistan: Weak Neighbor Survival Tactics."[1] Uzbekistan has been striving to maintain relations both with its neighbors and with outside powers (China, Europe, Russia, and the United States) exclusively from the standpoint of a regional leader.

This is clearly the reason for the outside world's interest in the internal political situation in Uzbekistan and in the changes anticipated in its ruling elite. The main, persistent mystery is how the transfer of authority will proceed and who will lead the country after Islam Karimov, its first president; answers to these questions remain unpredictable. This is the way things go whenever power has been concentrated in the hands of a single person. Over the twenty years since national independence, a rigid authoritarian regime has formed in Uzbekistan. In contrast to Kazakhstan, whose president allows independent, albeit loyal, political actors to participate in the public life of the country, Islam Karimov has eliminated any potential opposition, fearing the emergence of any distinctive individual who could oppose him. In Kazakhstan, one or two names are continuously discussed as potential successors; in Uzbekistan, no such rumors circulate.

MODERNITY AND TRADITION

The situation in Uzbekistan is shaped by two aspects: the modern and the traditional. Modern politics are represented by such institutions as the presidency, parliament, and political parties. The constitution, adopted in 1992, is reasonably democratic, based on global standards.

At the same time, these institutions have been formalized, with the modern aspect of political life being heavily image-based. The existing political parties in the country (the Justice Social Democratic Party of Uzbekistan "Adolat," the National Revival Democratic Party "Milliy Tiklanish," the Movement of Entrepreneurs and Businessmen—Liberal-Democratic Party, and the National Democratic Party "Fidokorlar") are typical political imitations. No "political competition and struggle for ideas" takes place among them, even if that is the way it is portrayed in official media publications.[2] Should it hypothetically ever turn out that parties can be freely formed in Uzbekistan, the new parties would be created on a qualitatively different basis, including according to region. The main presidential People's Democratic Party of Uzbekistan is also an imitation and de facto serves only as a tool for Islam Karimov. The same can be said about the Parliament, the Oliy Majlis, which unreservedly supports any initiatives that Karimov proposes.

The presidential administration (that is to say, Karimov himself) makes all of the key decisions, which are then discussed (or more precisely, endorsed) by the media and are not always fully understood by the public. The last such decision was the amendment of the constitution by the Uzbekistan Senate on December 5, 2011, to shorten the presidential term from seven years to five. On the sidelines of Tashkent politics and abroad, the amendment was seen as implying that Karimov would not run in the 2014 presidential election, while others argued that this amendment would on the contrary provide him with a legitimate constitutional basis to be elected to another term. There were also some who felt that by reducing the presidential term, he was hinting to future presidents that their terms would be for only five years and that they would not remain as heads of state for as long as the founder of independent Uzbekistan had done.

The shortening of the presidential term can also be regarded as a signal to the West that Karimov still has democratic leanings.[3] Indeed, speeches by him and high-ranking Uzbek officials contain many references to a respect for democratic values and human rights. From time to time the Uzbek leadership demonstrates mercy by releasing imprisoned opponents, usually during periods of improving relations with the West or on the eve of visits by high-ranking Americans. As U.S. Secretary of State Hillary Clinton was preparing to visit the country in October 2011, for example, the authorities released human rights activist Norboy Kholigitov and also investigative journalist Jamshid Karimov, who had been detained for five years and was being subjected to compulsory psychiatric treatment. During the summer of that same year, poet Yusuf Juma was released from the Jaslyk detention facility. Islam Karimov himself not only offered his guest his "personal and profound welcome," but also declared his willingness to take significant steps toward the liberalization of the political system so as to "leave this legacy to our children and grandchildren."[4]

Under the current president, however, there will be no significant liberalization. The political system is not competitive, there is no influx of any new ideas, and access to information is restricted. The opposition's foreign websites, the Uzbek BBC website, and the site of the influential Russian newspaper *Nezavisimaya Gazeta*, which publishes materials on Central Asia, are all blocked.[5]

After the Internet was used as a tool (albeit not the main one) to overthrow several Arab regimes, the government of Uzbekistan began to actively monitor Internet and social network activity. To what extent these fears about the Internet are justified is difficult to say. After all, it is well known that the 2005 events in Andijan took place without the Internet.

According to the results of research conducted by the American Pando Networks, the average speed of the Internet in Uzbekistan is 73 kilobytes per second (KBps).[6] In this respect Uzbekistan lags behind even Turkmenistan, where the average speed is 76 KBps. Internet connection speeds can reach 200 KBps in Kyrgyzstan and Tajikistan, 212 KBps in Kazakhstan, 325 KBps in Mongolia, and 790 KBps in Russia. With a total population in Uzbekistan of 28 million, the number of Internet users has reached 7.55 million, and there are 4.5 million mobile Internet users. However, Internet coverage does not extend to the whole country and is available only in the major cities: Tashkent, Samarkand, Bukhara, Navoiy, and Khiva. Small settlements and rural areas located only a few dozen kilometers away from these cities have no Internet access.

The International Crisis Group, in one of its reports, has described the political environment in Uzbekistan as "deteriorating,"[7] an assessment that is justified with respect to the activities of local parties, the insignificance of the Parliament, and the virtual lack of secular opposition. However, when the "traditional component" (inter-clan rivalry, power struggles in the president's inner circle, and illegal Islamist opposition) is taken into consideration, to say that political life in Uzbekistan is "dying out" would not be accurate.

Clans first began to form in Uzbekistan at the end of the nineteenth century based upon territorial communities reminiscent of Kazakhstan's hordes (or *jüz* in Kazakh), and were transformed relatively quickly into influential political institutions that de facto became recognized by the government of the Russian Empire and then by the Soviets. The clan system became integral to the Soviet administration, and Moscow gradually learned how to put them to use for controlling the local political situation.

There are a number of clans in Uzbekistan: the Samarkand (Samarkand-Bukhara), Tashkent, Ferghana, Karakalpakstan, Khiva, and Surkash (of Surkhandarya and Kashkadarya). The Tashkent and Samarkand clans are the most well positioned in the country; Islam Karimov himself has been thought to belong to first one, then the other of the two. However, it appears that Karimov's conduct has not been determined by his affiliation with one of the clans, but from the very beginning by his desire to position himself as a national leader. It is also important to remember that he rose to his position as leader of the country after beginning as the first secretary of the Communist Party of Uzbekistan. In modern terms, after the collapse of the Soviet Union, Uzbekistan underwent something of a "reformatting," and as a result the same person who had been leader continued as such and was considered by the majority of post-Soviet society to be a legitimate leader, although now one of a qualitatively different type: the leader of a national state.

Karimov has repeatedly had to defend and assert the leadership position he inherited from the Soviet era. As the new state formed, he was confronted by rivals from among both the secular opposition (which enjoyed a certain amount of popularity in society in the early 1990s) and the Islamists, as well as by continuing clan rivalry.

In 1992, the Tashkent clan, informally headed by Shukrullo Mirsaidov, vice president of Uzbekistan, attempted to weaken Karimov's grip on power or even dump him by using the opposition political parties that had emerged, Erk and Birlik. However, this excessively diverse coalition lost to Karimov (who had enjoyed the support of the Samarkand clan), and the leader of the Tashkent clan was arrested. The Samarkand clan dominated the political landscape in the country throughout the 1990s. The head of the clan, Ismoil Jurabekov, was not only named to the influential post of minister of agriculture (giving him control over the highly important cotton industry), but was also appointed deputy prime minister (giving him control over the budget, including foreign currency circulation). It appeared as though the Samarkand clan had gained complete control over the government.

In 1999, however, Jurabekov was suddenly sent into retirement and his supporters were dismissed from their posts. At the same time, the position of Timur Aliev, an adviser to Karimov who was affiliated with the Tashkent clan, was suddenly enhanced. In turn, Aliev saw to the appointment of a number of members of the Tashkent clan to political and administrative positions, including his relatives and friends (in particular, his relative Kadyr Gulyamov was appointed minister of defense). Simultaneously, Aliev included the previously peripheral Ferghana clan in the governance of the country. In recognition of his increased influence, he was even called by the title, "Timur the Great."

Each of the warring factions attempted to draw the president over to its own side, sometimes resorting to blackmail. The Tashkent clan had especially great ambitions and sought to bring the president under its control. Members of the clan threatened to expose Karimov's involvement in drug trafficking and in fact supported Emomali Rahmon's statement that Karimov had been behind a coup attempt in Tajikistan. In February 1999, terrorists carried out an attack directed against the president in Tashkent. Although it was officially attributed to Islamists, some rumors suggest that it had resulted from internal conflicts. Either way, Karimov again became more favorably inclined toward the Samarkand clan to rebalance his relations with the clans.

The factor of inter-clan tension dropped to secondary importance for politics in the country in the 2000s. Islam Karimov had finally consolidated his position as national leader, rendering speculation as to which clan the president belongs pointless (although by inertia he continues to be associated in the public consciousness with the Samarkand clan). Outside powers such as China, Russia, and the United States pay less and less attention to the clan factor, not believing that the ethnicity of politicians in Uzbekistan or which clan the next president of Uzbekistan represents is very important.

In this context, the way that the government reacted to the 2005 Andijan massacre is very revealing, in that responsibility was attached to politicians based not upon their clan affiliation, but upon their level of professionalism. Interior Minister Zakir Almatov, for example, was dismissed from his position in spite of being affiliated with the very influential Samarkand clan (although it must be noted that he was replaced by Bakhodir Matlubov, also a member of the Samarkand clan). The head of the National Security Service, Rustam Inoyatov, retained his position due not to his membership in the Tashkent clan, but because of his relatively high level of competence. Like Islam Karimov, Inoyatov has avoided positioning himself as a representative of the clan and instead has demonstrated his independence from them all (although he is occasionally accused of having too many Russians among his subordinates).

A number of interest groups created in the country allow representatives of different clans to cooperate actively with each other; at the same time, the clans themselves sometimes become involved in sharp disagreements.

With no secular government opposition in the country, the only available avenue for protest against the government is through Islam. At the very beginning of Uzbekistan's existence as an independent state, a solid Islamic opposition was formed. It encompassed numerous factions, the largest of which were Hizb ut-Tahrir al-Islami (HTI) and the Islamic Movement of Uzbekistan (IMU), with the Akramiya, Adolat Uushmasi, Islam Lashkari, Nur, Tovba, Izun Sokol, Ma'rifatchitlar, and Takfirshirlar movements also participating. The majority of the Islamic organizations consist of small groups, or even circles. However, according to opposition leaders, more than 100,000 of their supporters languish in prisons.[8] Although this number is undoubtedly greatly exaggerated, it nonetheless indicates the breadth of Islamist support.

Information that the IMU has nearly 3,000 armed fighters in its ranks seems dubious. In fact, they appear to number only a few hundred, including some based in Afghanistan. Moreover, the IMU has been less active since the early 2000s.

Most HTI factions are concentrated in the Ferghana Valley (the Namangan, Ferghana, and Andijan oblasts), with funding coming primarily from local sources. Some limited sums of money continue to be sent from abroad. There have been some indications that the Islamists have been receiving funds from Uzbek immigrants who have settled in other Muslim countries.

Although the Islamists have been working to create a supranational caliphate in Central Asia centered territorially in the Ferghana Valley, the pro-caliphate movement in essence stands primarily for fighting the regime and Islam Karimov, who has been characterized in HTI and IMU literature as the "devil incarnate," an ally of the West and of Zionism, and Moscow's accomplice in restoring the Soviet imperial space. One HTI leaflet said that "his soul is full of hatred ... to Islam ... he does not like Islam. He is an infidel who does not recognize Islam."[9]

These factions are primarily engaged in disseminating propaganda and recruiting new supporters. HTI's journals *Al-Wa'I* and *Al-Hadara* are distributed in mosques and universities and are handed out around public transportation sites; hundreds or thousands of such leaflets are regularly seized by the authorities. While in the Ferghana Valley in the early 2000s, I personally heard it joked that if you opened a window, an HTI leaflet would immediately fly in. Although the content of these leaflets and other such publications is primitive, it is accessible to the "average man," with an emphasis on egalitarian ideas and social justice and many references to the Quran and Hadith. The leaflets are printed in both the Uzbek and Russian languages, and in recent years an increasing number of Islamist materials have been appearing on the Internet, although such websites are blocked by the authorities and access to the Internet remains relatively limited. Whether the Islamist propaganda is effective is difficult to judge. In Uzbekistan, especially in the Ferghana Valley, information on HTI is passed along informally, by word of mouth.

Acts of terrorism committed by religious extremists provoke negative reactions among the Uzbek people and discredit the opposition in their eyes. The most famous such incident was the attempt on President Karimov's life in 1999,[10] and there were several terrorist attacks in 2004 in Tashkent, the Tashkent Oblast, and Bukhara (for which the organization Islamic Jihad claimed responsibility), and the act of terrorism in Khanabad that occurred a matter of days before the Andijan incident.[11]

The fact that the IMU proclaimed its noninvolvement in the events in Khanabad and Andijan (as Tohir Yo'ldosh, its head, reported immediately after the attacks) is very revealing. The IMU and its leaders have repeatedly emphasized that their party rejects terrorism as a means to pursue its goals. This creates an impression that the acts of terrorism are being carried out by marginal Islamist organizations or individual terrorists, or turn out to have been nothing other than provocation by the government or the aftermath of commercial conflicts.

In 2009, a number of attempts were made on the lives of some influential members of the loyal Muslim clergy. Shortly after an attack on Abror Abrorov, the deputy director of the Kukaldosh madrasa, was carried out, the chief imam of Tashkent, Anvar-qori Tursunov, and the imam of the largest mosque in the capital, Khoja Akhror Vali, were also attacked (according to one version of events, the attack had been business-related). The authorities reacted by arresting "individuals with a higher level of religiosity and the relatives of those previously convicted on religious grounds."[12]

INSTRUMENTALIZING ISLAM

In the context of Islam, the regime has concentrated its efforts in two directions. First, it seeks to "monopolize" Islam and use it as a tool to retain power and as a key component of official ideology. At the same time, Karimov has officially opposed Muslim xenophobia, emphasizing that "attempts to use the idea of Islamic exclusivity to consolidate the Muslim world against the United States, Western Europe, and other power centers in the modern world will go nowhere."[13]

Second, the regime has acted to suppress religious opposition. After having first experienced the power of the Islamists in 1991, Karimov has gained an abiding fear of them and considers them the main threat to his regime. In his domestic policy, he has elevated the conflict with them to the level of a cult. Karimov's critics believe that his excessively aggressive methods in combating the Islamic opposition have contributed to its increasing popularity, and that he has deliberately exaggerated the actual Islamic threat. As Nigara Khidoyatova, executive secretary of the Ozod Dekhonlar (Free Peasants) Party, has noted, "... look, there are Kyrgyzstan and Kazakhstan nearby and absolutely no one there is afraid of either Hizb ut-Tahrir or Wahhabism."[14] This comment also belies a certain polarity, though of a different aspect: In Kyrgyzstan and Kazakhstan (since 2011), Islamists are subjected to ever increasing government scrutiny. Even before that, the Kazakh secret service had repeatedly uncovered and eliminated Islamic factions in the south of the country that frequently were associated with the Uzbek underground.

In contrast to his post-Soviet neighbors, Islam Karimov has successfully merged nationalism and Islam into an official ideology and made it part of the political life of the country. Whether his successor will be able to maintain this balance, however, remains a question. According to Martha Brill Olcott, "Whether Uzbekistan will remain a secular state depends upon whether this generation—and more importantly, subsequent generations—works out the balance between religion and nationalism."[15]

There is a probability that the conflict will escalate during the transition of power. Should Karimov choose his own successor and remain for a period of time as patron, the transition will be relatively painless, since the second president's term will begin under the shadow of Karimov's authority. Should, however, Karimov not be involved in the decision to appoint a successor, then relations among the elite will be greatly complicated, with intensified rivalry among clans and individual politicians. Under such circumstances, the various interest groups may appeal to forces in the community that have not become involved in politics. In addition, the religious opposition could join in the power struggle as well.

At the same time, the Islamists in Uzbekistan will have no chance of succeeding on their own, at least for the foreseeable future. A solid opinion has emerged in the aftermath of the Andijan massacre that "had the conspirators won [meaning Akramiya], it is unlikely that we would have a secular regime in Uzbekistan today."[16] Neither Akramiya nor its members, however, had much support in other regions of the country, including the Ferghana Valley itself; moreover, the Andijan massacre had not simply been an "Islamic rebellion."

ECONOMIC CONDITIONS

The condition of the economy will also influence the transition of power. Since Uzbekistan has no large reserves of hydrocarbons, it has not needed to become a raw materials appendage to other more developed countries, as was the case with Turkmenistan. The country's reserves total a mere 100 million tons of oil and 1.6 trillion cubic meters of gas; in 2011, it produced 3.6 million tons of oil and 57 billion cubic meters of gas.[17] Uzbekistan is the world's sixth-largest producer of uranium (2,400 tons) and also produces around 90 tons of gold a year.

The country is in generally positive overall economic standing. The national economy is diversified, with 24 percent of the country's GDP coming from industry, 44 percent from services, 7 percent from construction, and 18 percent from agriculture (which is less than 20 percent devoted to the production of cotton). The World Bank feels that Karimov's government has managed to achieve macroeconomic stability and restrain inflation by pursuing tight credit and fiscal policy and gradually reducing the national debt.[18]

However, such economic success was possible largely due to increased state control, which in turn created barriers to the development of a free market, hindered necessary liberal economic reforms, and discouraged the emergence of small- and medium-size enterprises. This governmentalization of the economy inevitably also led to the proliferation of corruption. As a result, on a list of 183 states with the highest levels of corruption, the American publication *Daily Beast* ranked Uzbekistan 178.[19] The Uzbek shadow economy accounts for approximately 40–60 percent of GDP.

The country desperately needs foreign investment; however, the local bureaucratic system and the self-serving practices of its public servants have provoked skepticism among potential investors. Named as among the main obstacles to foreign investment are bureaucratic red tape and the illegal interference of government agencies in the affairs of enterprises that work with foreign investment. "Government policy in Uzbekistan has tended to be rather capricious, and strict foreign exchange controls have been imposed, making it difficult for foreign investors to transfer profits back to their home country."[20] It is very significant that this comment was made by analysts from China, which enjoys preferential treatment in Central Asia and is less dependent on the whims of local officials.

A presidential decree "On Additional Measures to Encourage Foreign Direct Investment" adopted in 2012 offered certain benefits to investors and indicated that the country generates more than $3 billion annually, which is 26.6 percent of the total investment amount. The new decree emphasizes that businesses that invest more than $5 million in the local economy will retain the same tax rates for ten years as applied at the time that the enterprise was registered and that companies that invest $50 million will be provided with the necessary engineering and communications infrastructure. The procedure for obtaining multiple-entry visas will also be simplified for investors.

Karimov had previously distributed personal benefits to foreign companies that made large investments: the Uzbek-American Zarafshan-Newmont gold mining company, the Uzbek-British Uz-Texaco, and the Uzbek-Russian Wimm-Bill-Dann Taskhent milk plant. However, most of these benefits were canceled in 2006 and were maintained only for Gazprom and Lukoil. Several enterprises were accused of tax evasion and retroactively fined. In the same year foreign companies were prohibited from petitioning foreign courts. This approach is reminiscent of the situation in Turkmenistan, where only the president himself and people close to him can give reliable guarantees to businesses.[21]

A most formidable problem for Uzbekistan remains unemployment, which according to data from the Ministry of Labor and Social Security amounted to 625,500 in 2012 (or 5 percent of the number of employable people).[22] In reality, it is a much greater number, estimated by the European Union to be as high as 35 percent.[23] It must be remembered that more than 1 million Uzbek migrant workers work in Russia every year, and they remit $4.3 billion a year to Uzbekistan[24] (other sources put this number at $5 billion in 2011). Prime Minister Shavkat Mirziyoyev's assertion that a million jobs are created in the country every year[25] is thus highly questionable.

The leaders of the country regard labor migration as an inevitable, long-term phenomenon, as evidenced at least by the fact that under the 2012 Year of the Strong Family Program, everyone who goes abroad to work is presented with a color booklet, paragraph 12 of which reminds them, "you are responsible for your family."[26] (It has become a tradition in Uzbekistan for each year to be devoted to a problem that the government considers to be particularly important. Before the Year of the Family, the country had already marked the Year of Human Interests, the Year of the Woman, the Year of the Healthy Generation, the Year of *Mahallas*, the Year of Kindness and Mercy, and the Year of the Harmoniously Developed Young Generation.)[27]

The demographic situation contributes to growing unemployment. The high birthrate and the continuous migration of young people from rural areas to the cities have given rise to persistently worsening social tensions, and for the near future it will not be possible to solve these problems. According to a forecast prepared by an international research center with the support of the Asian Development Bank and the UN Development Program, the population of Uzbekistan will reach an estimated 33.2 million in 2025, and 7 million will be unemployed.[28]

The general situation has been aggravated by environmental challenges: a shortage of water, reduction of arable land, and extreme soil salinization (more than 50 percent).

These and other issues will require attention from now on, and without outside assistance Uzbekistan will find it impossible to overcome them. That is why cooperation with foreign partners, above all China, Russia, and the United States, and more recently with Europe (especially with Germany), will become more and more imperative for Uzbekistan. Tashkent views such cooperation as one of the most important factors to ensure its stability and security.

RELATIONS WITH THE UNITED STATES AND RUSSIA

Uzbekistan's relations with Russia and the United States have been full of intrigue, which upon closer examination has a simple and understandable explanation. Since Russia and the United States have been competing for influence in Uzbekistan, Uzbekistan's multivectoral foreign policy largely reflects the rivalry between these two countries. Although Tashkent has alternated between strengthening and diminishing ties with each of them, the general trend has been toward greater rapprochement with Washington and a slow, careful retreat from the influence of Moscow. Over its entire twenty-year history, Uzbekistan (as well as the other former Soviet republics) has been engaged in a constant search for new partners to provide an alternative to Russia and free them from Russian dominance, yet not eliminate its economic and political support.

The United States: Closer Ties

Uzbekistan began its swing toward the United States following the events of September 11, 2011, when Karimov decided that he would become America's key Central Asian partner in the war on terrorism. However, the economic and political dividends from this turned out to be less impressive than Tashkent had anticipated: Not only was the money less by an order of magnitude, but the Americans also continued to criticize the regime for its human rights violations and lack of democracy. The United States remained suspicious of Uzbekistan and felt that it could quickly shift back to Russia. It was also important that "a central feature of U.S. global, political hegemony—democracy promotion—proved to be fundamentally incompatible with the interests of the government of Uzbekistan."[29] This dilemma, where security interests run counter to democratic norms in the political structure, has always been the "squaring the circle" challenge for U.S. policy in Central Asia.

If September 11 led to closer ties between the United States and Uzbekistan, the violent crackdown on protests in Andijan in 2005 alienated Tashkent from Washington. Western countries levied a series of sanctions on Uzbekistan, in particular a ban on the sale of weapons. Once again, Islam Karimov was subjected to severe criticism. Such measures, however, had no significant impact on the Uzbek regime, which did not intend to change its domestic policy and certainly had no remorse for the methods used to suppress the Andijan protest. The effect of sanctions in general, as evidenced by other experiences, tends to be minimal. With Russia as its ally, Uzbekistan did not need to worry about sanctions at all, especially since "Moscow with few scruples pronounced the uprising in fact a terrorist attack, and effectively shielded Karimov from international pressure."[30] (Interestingly, Moscow did not comment on the 2003 attempt to assassinate Saparmurat Niyazov, thus providing indirect evidence of its attitude toward the Turkmen regime at the time.)

Karimov adopted a wait-and-see attitude, since he was confident that sooner or later his actions would be forgotten and that the sanctions would be eased and eventually dropped altogether. Time has shown that his tactics were correct. The drama around Andijan became history relatively quickly, eclipsed by other events in Kyrgyzstan and the Middle

East. However, the main factor that caused the approach to Uzbekistan to change was Barack Obama's decision to withdraw U.S. troops from Afghanistan in 2014. This inevitably necessitated adjustments to U.S. policy in Central Asia, making it subordinate to the main mission in Afghanistan and demanding that the United States pay much greater attention to its relations with its regional partners. The United States has already been using Uzbekistan as a transit bridge for cargo shipped to the coalition forces, and some of the money paid for the NATO transit shipments ends up in the pockets of Uzbek officials.

On September 22, 2012, the U.S. Congress decided to resume arms supplies to Uzbekistan, lifting the ban that had been imposed in 2004. In order to determine the kinds of weapons that Uzbekistan needed, Secretary of the Navy Ray Mabus led a delegation to Tashkent. This visit resulted in the so-called Mabus list, which included devices for mine clearing, night vision, terrain scanning, and eavesdropping, as well as equipment to help control the Internet and break into social networking sites. Uzbekistan also expects to obtain body armor and all-terrain armored vehicles. Such weapons and equipment are all dual-purpose.[31] Since Uzbekistan will not face Taliban aggression for the foreseeable future, the regime will use the weapons it wants from the United States primarily for its own internal purposes, both to fight the armed Islamic radicals and to quell discontent and dissent. Finally, such weapons could be used on Uzbekistan's borders with its neighbors.

Washington has not formally set any conditions for providing military and technical assistance. Negotiations would hardly be able to address the compatibility of principles of behavior between political systems or the development of democracy. What is evident is something different: American assistance works to weaken the military and political cooperation between Uzbekistan and Russia. Karimov has undertaken these attempts to obtain weapons from the United States in order to demonstrate to Moscow that Uzbekistan can get along without the weapons that Russia has supplied to bind Uzbekistan to its orbit (although Russia clearly does not have enough of the modern electronic weapons to be able to "sponsor" them to its allies).

Karimov has been quite honest about this. In 2009, for example, at a meeting in Tashkent with William Burns, the deputy U.S. secretary of state, and Michael McFaul, who at the time was adviser to the president on Russia and Eurasia and was later appointed U.S. ambassador to Russia, Karimov argued that the Collective Security Treaty Organization (CSTO) had been created as a counterweight to NATO. The CSTO, he emphasized, has three goals: to promote Russian domination in the post-Soviet space; to provide multinational protection in the event of a Russian attack on such problematic countries as Georgia and Ukraine; and to station Russian troops in Central Asia on a permanent basis. Karimov even suggested that the attack on Andijan had been a signal to force Uzbekistan to join the Collective Rapid Reaction Force.[32]

The United States has repeatedly advised Uzbekistan to withdraw from the CSTO, declaring its willingness to provide military and technical assistance in return. Karimov, however, has continued to maneuver, refusing to let the American vector of his foreign policy act to the detriment of the Russian vector. Nevertheless, he did make a strategic turn in mid-2012, anticipating that Uzbekistan would eventually become the main U.S. partner in the region after the withdrawal of U.S. troops from Afghanistan.

One must remember that in 2001, hopes for such strategic partnership had been dashed. The antiterrorist coalition that emerged was too broad for anyone to claim an exclusive role within it, and the Afghan component of the overall war on terror was not clearly articulated, since when they began military operations in 2002 the Americans had clearly expected victory to be rapid. Aside from that, cooperation between the United States and Russia became a cornerstone in the global war against terrorism.

The coalition to combat terrorism turned out to be a myth; after a brief period when U.S.-Russian relations were "reset," the competition between Washington and Moscow in Central Asia has again intensified. Vladimir Putin's new course (which in fact is the same as before) to create Russian-sponsored international structures is being panned by the Central Asian countries, while Washington has increasingly been less concerned about democracy and human rights in its dealings with the regimes of the region. Pragmatic calculations have predominated. In such a context, there is optimism for improvement in U.S.-Uzbek relations. When Uzbekistan finally left the CSTO in 2012, its decision symbolized the change in relations between Tashkent and Washington.

The Arab Spring, which resulted in Islamists coming to power in a number of Muslim states, has contributed to improved relations between Uzbekistan and the United States. Washington as never before needs reliable partners in the Muslim world, which is the way Uzbekistan has recently been presenting itself. The regime in Uzbekistan has succeeded in convincing the United States of its stability. It has turned out to be more durable than the authoritarian regimes of Egypt, Libya, Tunisia, and Yemen. It is also important that the hypothetical alternative to the Uzbek regime is seen to be moderate Islamism as in Turkey, rather than religious radicalism.

Russia: Difficulties, But Still Cooperating Economically

At the same time, while embracing improved relations with the United States, Uzbekistan does not intend to end its relations with Russia. Islam Karimov has been able to accustom Moscow to the turns in his policies and pays no attention to the criticism it levels at him. It is worthy of note that high-level Russian politicians rarely express irritation with the escapades of the Uzbek leadership, while Karimov has criticized Russia sharply and quite frequently.

Against this backdrop of intense political emotion, Uzbek-Russian economic relations have continued to develop quite positively. According to the trade missions of both countries, trade between them reached the level of $6.7 billion in 2011, making Russia Uzbekistan's top trading partner, accounting for nearly a quarter of the country's total trade turnover in 2011.[33] Of Russia's CIS partners, Uzbekistan is number 4.

Uzbekistan provides Russia with natural gas, automobiles, and textiles. Gazprom purchases 13.5 billion cubic meters of gas annually,[34] and Soyuzneftegaz, Lukoil, and Transneftegaz also have projects in Uzbekistan.[35] Lukoil has been actively engaged in developing the Khauzak natural gas field, the potential size of which has been estimated at 12 billion cubic meters. Over the next seven years, Lukoil plans to invest $5.5 billion in the Uzbek economy.[36]

Of course, economic cooperation between Uzbekistan and Russia has presented challenges of its own. In particular, the matter of the former Chkalov aircraft manufacturing plant, which had been a leader in the Soviet aviation industry, remains unresolved. An agreement to establish a joint venture based on this plant was signed in 2007, including a contract to build four Ilyushin IL-114-100 aircraft. Three of them were built at the plant in 2010.[37] Nevertheless, the agreement was not implemented, and the Tashkent Aviation Plant (which had replaced the Chkalov factory) began to dismantle the equipment used to manufacture aircraft at the end of 2012 and will begin to produce construction materials, consumer products, and spare parts for agricultural machinery.

Another problem was the fact that Uzbekistan had agreed to assemble Korean Daewoo automobiles for subsequent sale in Russia at dumping prices, while impeding the import of Russian Lada cars into its market (even though the prices and maintenance costs for the Ladas would be quite suitable for the Uzbek population). This problem was later resolved: The Korean-Uzbek Daewoo cars failed to be in high demand in Russia, while Russian cars (including used ones) continue to be popular in Uzbekistan, especially in rural areas.

In 2012, Uzbek authorities pressured Russian Mobile TeleSystems (or more specifically, its subsidiary company Uzdunrobita), arresting and imprisoning the head of Uzdunrobita, Russian citizen Radik Dautov, and several other employees. MTS management asserts that the company broke no laws that would justify such actions. Dautov's wife wrote an open letter to Vladimir Putin asking for his support. The letter and other details of the case were covered in the Russian press, indicating that the Russian authorities were unhappy with the proceedings and were prepared to intervene (a rare occurrence).

In general, however, despite such difficulties, Uzbekistan and Russia both regard bilateral economic cooperation optimistically.

Although political relations between Tashkent and Moscow have been becoming more and more complex, it appears that both sides have become accustomed to this. Tashkent would prefer to structure purely bilateral relations with Russia and feels that joining international organizations created under Moscow's auspices could diminish its sovereignty. Uzbekistan has no intention of becoming bound by any other commitments. While Tashkent views the CIS as an inevitable and useless vestige of a bygone post-Soviet era, it regards the CSTO with suspicion and feels that Uzbekistan would have nothing whatsoever to gain from belonging to it.

Uzbekistan had already withdrawn from the CSTO once before, in 1999. At that time, the decision had been prompted by Moscow's refusal to help Tashkent to counter attacks by the Islamic Movement of Uzbekistan, which convinced Islam Karimov that the CSTO would be of no use to his country. After the Batken tragedy, two revolutions in Kyrgyzstan, and the 2010 Osh massacre, Karimov finally concluded that Moscow would not and could not come to the rescue of any regime that it considers fragile and unsustainable, and he no longer saw Moscow as an absolutely reliable guarantor of his personal power. Analyst Viktor Litovkin believes that Uzbekistan uses the CSTO as a means to achieve its goals,[38] apparently due to the CSTO's inaction and actual uselessness whenever extreme situations have arisen in the region.

In the summer of 2012, Tashkent announced that it would suspend its membership in the CSTO. Since the CSTO Charter does not provide for such a procedure, this will essentially be a withdrawal by Uzbekistan. The decision was not unexpected, since Uzbekistan had previously expressed disagreement with a number of CSTO decisions (in particular with having to commit its troops to resolve internal conflicts in other member states) and had refused to participate in the CRRF. Finally, Tashkent did not sign the agreement under which establishment of military bases by third countries within the borders of a CSTO member would be allowed only if approved by all of the organization's members.

Moscow's reaction to Tashkent's decision to withdraw from the CSTO proved to be moderate. Apparently, the Kremlin has either become accustomed to its ally's unstable behavior, or it has concluded that the CSTO can get along without Uzbekistan. Moscow is coming to realize that by constantly trying to draw Uzbekistan into the CSTO, it would eventually appear to be pleading for it to do so. At the same time, the situation has highlighted the CSTO's problems and made other members more critical of the organization.

In purely military terms, Uzbekistan's participation in the CSTO is formally of great (to a certain extent even crucial) importance: A number of military airfields are within its territory (in Khanabad, Chirchik, Tashkent, Bukhara, and other locations), and it has three military academies and the largest and probably the most powerful army in the region. However, its true potential is not in fact being realized, as the CSTO is not geared for conducting actual military operations. Once Uzbekistan withdrew from the CSTO, the very idea of presenting a collective defense against an external enemy that had existed mainly in the imagination of Russian military planners (do they themselves believe it?) evaporated.

Symbolically, the decision to leave the CSTO had been made just a few weeks after Vladimir Putin's visit to Tashkent, which had been intended for the purpose of engaging Uzbekistan in new Russian integration projects. In spite of the rumors emanating from Moscow that Uzbekistan had an interest in joining the Common Economic Space, its withdrawal from the CSTO unequivocally demonstrated that Tashkent will not only place priority on bilateral relations,[39] but will also be increasingly oriented toward the West.

RELATIONS WITH CHINA

Relations between Uzbekistan and China are less tense, inasmuch as their political component has been of lesser importance. In June 2012, Chinese leader Hu Jintao and Islam Karimov signed an announcement on the establishment of a strategic partnership. When Karimov visited China, 40 agreements were signed for a total of $5.2 billion. Among them are ones covering manufacturing, transportation, hydrocarbon processing, and chemical production, as well as information technology, communications, and pharmaceuticals, and confirming the bilateral intention to accelerate construction of the China-Kyrgyzstan-Uzbekistan railway,[40] which will be of great importance for the entire region.

Chinese investment in Uzbekistan totaled $4 billion in 2011. Trade between the two countries increased by 18.9 percent over the previous year, to a total of $2.6 billion.[41]

At the same time, Beijing has not been happy with Uzbekistan's hesitation to actively participate in the SCO, in particular its lack of participation in the development of a common strategy for the organization regarding Afghanistan. It is well known that Tashkent long refused to support the proposal of allowing Afghanistan into the SCO as an observer. However, China has traditionally been reluctant to pressure its partners, preferring instead the tactic of persuasion. Moreover, Uzbekistan has not been as obviously dependent upon China as are Tajikistan and Kyrgyzstan, and it has also actively demonstrated its interest in developing relations with the United States.

RELATIONS WITH NEIGHBORING STATES

Uzbekistan's relations with its neighbors have been complex and prone to conflict, for several reasons. First of all, there are "fears of possible Uzbek expansionism" among Uzbekistan's neighbors and apprehensions that since "ethnic Uzbeks live in all the other states, Uzbekistan could make irredentist claims on its neighbors."[42]

Uzbeks comprise the second-largest ethnic minority in Kyrgyzstan, Tajikistan, and Turkmenistan. However, despite sporadic friction with the so-called titular nationality, they do not act as a "fifth column" in favor of their historic motherland. Uzbekistan, in turn, has not been very keen on helping its former compatriots, and there are well-known differences in culture and mentality between Uzbeks living in the neighboring republics and Uzbeks living in Uzbekistan. The Kyrgyz Uzbeks, for example, especially women, enjoy a greater degree of freedom of behavior and thought than do their relatives in Uzbekistan. Incidentally, this is one of the reasons behind Tashkent's decision to have the Kyrgyz Uzbeks who had fled the country after the 2010 Osh massacre return to Kyrgyzstan as quickly as possible, since there was apprehension in Tashkent that they might have a negative influence upon the population in Uzbekistan, which has been accustomed to obedience.

In Tajikistan, local Uzbeks have become incorporated into political life and do not constitute an independent factor. Relations have been very cool between Tajikistan and Uzbekistan, and it is difficult to predict Uzbekistan's reaction should its neighbor's situation worsen, but clearly it would not be interested in seeing the country split along ethnic lines. Be that as it may, Tashkent would prefer to work with a more flexible leadership in Tajikistan that would be more willing to consider concessions.

Second, Uzbekistan's relations with its neighbors have been complicated even further by border disputes directly related to the alternating patterns of ethnic distribution in border areas. As a simple glance at a map shows, the borders in Central Asia were artificially drawn. Territorial disputes exist along all of Uzbekistan's borders. The overall situation is made even more difficult by the existence of ethnic enclaves within the borders of its neighbors: The villages of Sokh and Shakhimardan are the biggest Uzbek enclaves located in Kyrgyzstan, and the Kyrgyz village of Barak and the Tajik village of Sarvak are situated in the territory of Uzbekistan. The atmosphere in these enclaves remains tense, and the border is "flexible"—in other words, territory frequently—and illegally—changes hands from one country to another. Until 1951, for example, the village of Sarvak had belonged to the Tajik Soviet Socialist Republic. In 1995, the Uzbeks requested that the Tajik side allow their shepherds to pass through to their pasture lands, in 1996 they erected border posts at the entrance and exit to Sarvak, and in 1999 they planted mines that killed eight local residents and wounded six over the next six years. Uzbekistan has laid mines along several segments of its border with Tajikistan, leading to the deaths of 90 Tajik citizens and wounding 150 others over the past eleven years.

After the Batken crisis in 1999, Tashkent unilaterally introduced a visa regime and permanently concentrated Uzbek troops along the border. Kyrgyzstan has responded by repeatedly pointing out that in the border areas of Uzbekistan, "there are too many troops for peacetime and it is unclear why they have been deployed on the border with an allied state."[43]

On the one hand, the excessive reinforcement of border control and even the militarization of the border areas can be justified by pointing to the periodic domestic crises among its neighbors (Kyrgyzstan and Tajikistan). On the other hand, such measures work to restrict cooperation, including on a psychological level, and serve as a source of continuing mutual mistrust.

Several other recurrent issues in relations between Uzbekistan and its neighbors can be seen both as economic and political problems, key among which is the mutually irritating dispute with Tajikistan over the height of the Roghun dam, as described in chapter 6. Also unresolved is the dispute with Kyrgyzstan over ownership of the Arkyn and Burgandin oil and gas fields, with their 1.9 million tons of oil and 4.6 billion cubic meters of gas. The fields are currently de facto controlled by Uzbekistan, although the Kyrgyz parliament decided in 2012 to reconsider the issue of their ownership.

Against a backdrop of tense relationships with Kazakhstan, Kyrgyzstan, and Tajikistan, Uzbekistan's relations with Turkmenistan have improved markedly since Gurbanguly Berdimuhamedov came to power in 2008. The two countries signed a number of agreements on economic cooperation in 2009, and Turkmen gas is exported to China through Uzbekistan. This improvement is particularly striking given the fact that Ashgabat had openly accused Uzbekistan of being involved in a coup attempt in 2002.

CONCLUSION

The question of succession remains the key problem for domestic policy in Uzbekistan in the early 2010s, and, consequently, for its foreign policy as well. In all of the Central Asian countries, power is typically personified, and whoever succeeds Islam Karimov will have to serve as national leader and bear personal responsibility for the situation in the country. The option of establishing a parliamentary system in Uzbekistan as in Kyrgyzstan would not be feasible, and even if it were, it would serve only as cover for inter-clan conflicts (the Kyrgyzstan experience was in large measure responsible for discrediting the idea of establishing a parliamentary system).

Although the regime in Uzbekistan will remain authoritarian, its head will not have the kind of authority that Islam Karimov has enjoyed, and in the eyes of the elite and society he will likely appear to be something of an intermediate, compromise president. The new leader will need to follow the risky path of self-affirmation and win the right to lead the country, which will be accompanied by conflict within the elite that could affect the situation in the society at large. However, there will be no "Orange Revolution" (which in the Muslim world has come to be called "Midan Tahrir") during this transition of power.

External actors will have no significant impact upon the transition of power, with neither China, the United States, nor especially Russia expressing any preference for "their" candidates. Beijing, Washington, and Moscow will accept whomever the local elites choose (regardless of whether he has been "appointed" by Islam Karimov or selected by consensus). Moreover, there are no plans to seriously change the nature of the regime. The West has acknowledged that liberalization of the political system could work to strengthen the position of the Islamists, while Russia feels more comfortable and familiar dealing with any authoritarian regime than with those of a more liberal bent (as evidenced by the Russian criticism of parliamentarianism in Kyrgyzstan).

The new leader will continue to develop the strategic imperatives set by Karimov and will continue to pursue a multivectoral foreign policy, but with an even greater emphasis on the West. If the transition of power goes smoothly, Uzbekistan could experience a brief period of limited liberalization—yet another signal to the United States and Europe.

Russian influence will continue to decline, accompanied by assurances of friendship and cooperation, especially economic ones. With no unambiguously pro-Russian politicians remaining in Uzbekistan, there will be no one in the country to lobby for Russian interests.

The future of relations between Uzbekistan and the Muslim world will be intriguing. Tashkent will need to accept the fact that Islamists will come to power in many countries and that the Islamic factor will exert a greater impact on international politics. In that context, it cannot be ruled out that the government will need to modify its approach to the Islamist opposition, making it more pragmatic and recognizing the existence of the opposition's moderate wing.

WHO CHALLENGES RUSSIA IN CENTRAL ASIA?

Thousands of books and articles have been written about Russian rivalry and cooperation with other states. In the conclusion to this book, I prefer to avoid repeating the insights of my colleagues and—although this will definitely not be easy—will attempt to present some new ones.

What external challenges does Russia face in Central Asia? For the most part, there are three: China, the United States, and Islam.

EXTERNAL CHALLENGES

The Challenge From China

The challenge presented by China has formally been limited to its financial and economic penetration into the region, which has become a true expansion. China has helped to build ramified transportation and power distribution infrastructures in the area, thus binding Central Asia to China and expanding Chinese influence westward toward Europe. As Russia has worked to establish itself in the region by building regional infrastructure, China has been operating within the Russian sphere of interest. At the same time, while implementing these projects, China has succeeded in containing gang-style post-Soviet corruption, yet another example of the "Chinese miracle."

China's behavior has been like that of a new rich tenant who has moved into a house and is now gradually spreading to occupy the areas that are still partly controlled by previous tenants. It is true that China has viewed Russia with a certain amount of contempt. "Even though it is not being said openly, Russia is considered by China as a country that is going through a decline."[1] Although the older "Soviet" generation of the Chinese establishment continues to harbor some affinity toward Russia, a rising China will not need Russia as much as it did before. The younger generation in Beijing has hazy recollections of Sino-Soviet friendship and has never heard the popular 1950s song "Moscow-Beijing: Our Friendship Forever."

In response to the Chinese challenge, Russia has sought above all to maintain its economic influence by formalizing it through such multilaterally integrated projects as the Customs Union, the Common Economic Space, and the Eurasian Union (to come in 2015). Second, Russia has attempted to become involved in joint projects with China to the greatest possible extent. Since Beijing knows that it will always lead these projects unilaterally, it has agreed to include Russia in them. The Chinese economic expansion does not represent a political challenge to Russia, and in that respect there has been no difference of opinion between them. China has always positioned itself as a country that refrains from intruding into other countries' political matters, and it does not want to get involved. Its foreign policy has been shaped by the sheer size of the country, its economy, and its sudden (in historical terms) ascent as an emerging great power. Chinese activities in Central Asia represent only a fraction of its total multidirectional activity as it pursues a global economic expansion that no country would be able to sustain for long. This tectonic shift has transformed the global geopolitical context and will inevitably affect Russia, as well.

The Challenge From the United States

Although the challenge presented by the United States does contain an economic aspect (more precisely, an energy aspect), on the whole it has remained a primarily political (or military political) competition.

The overall U.S. approach to Central Asia was formulated in the 1990s, and considering its subsequent refinements has amounted to support for the sovereignty of the former Soviet republics, assistance as they democratize their political systems, and promotion of economic development and reform.[2] This policy was best described by Deputy Secretary of State Strobe Talbott in 1997. Divergent interests among different agencies within the U.S. government, however, have impeded its consistent implementation. In particular, the Department of State and such associated agencies as the U.S. Agency for International Development have focused on problems of democratization, while the Pentagon has concerned itself with military and strategic issues (which, as it turns out, have been easy to address when dealing with authoritarian rulers).

To a certain extent, the U.S. approach *can* be considered a threat to Russia. By supporting sovereignty, the United States has implicitly supported greater independence of Central Asian states from their former imperial ruler. Democratization in these countries will bring them closer to Western, as opposed to Russian, political norms. Reform will not be possible without financial and technical assistance from abroad. The United States has promised to help modernize the local economies, which Russia would be able to do only to a limited extent, since its own economy also requires modernization. With respect to the stability of these countries and the prevention of conflicts (which have occurred in Central Asia previously and may do so again), Washington has intimated that since Russia would be unable to guarantee stability on its own and would do so only at the cost of a partial loss of sovereignty by the Central Asian states, their governments should seek help from "outside third parties." Behind such moves can be seen a desire to diminish Russian influence or to exert pressure on Russia. The phrase "exert pressure" is more appropriate than "expel," which is the way Russian politicians most often put it. To expel Russia will not be possible over the medium term, and neither of the outside parties wants this to happen (nor do the Central Asian states themselves, which need Russia to maintain a balance among the outside players, while China and the United States have an interest in Russia's continuing to bear its share of responsibility for the situation in the region).

Although the amount of influence Moscow can exert on its southern neighbors is a function of their own domestic political situations, it nevertheless also depends upon the attractiveness of Russia as such and its strength politically.

Not all of the goals articulated under U.S. policy in Central Asia or posed by U.S. research organizations have been implemented. Some of them have been reconsidered. Not all of the challenges that Russia might have expected to face have materialized. No democracy has been established in any of the Central Asian states, not even on a rudimentary level. The opinion advanced by a number of experts that U.S. strategy in the early 2000s had been to "force regime change"[3] is not entirely convincing (if that had been the case, then this kind of activity would have enhanced the position of Russia, which supports the current regimes).

Nascent democracy in Kyrgyzstan continues to endure its test for survival. In my opinion, it was easy to see in advance how attempts to transform the countries to Russia's south into an area of Central Asian liberalism might end. As Canadian analyst Nicole J. Jackson has noted: "despite active, if unsystematic, Western promotion of democratization ... many semi-autocratic regimes not only persist, but are successfully adapting to new domestic and international ... realities.... All five regimes have continued and/or strengthened their autocracies."[4]

The current political stability in Central Asia can hardly be explained as resulting solely from the positive influence of the United States. The rigidity of the ruling regimes has served as their own best protection. If hypothetically an "Arab Spring" were to occur in the region, it will not have been instigated by the United States, nor would such a possible transformation represent a likely Russian response to the challenges it faces in Central Asia.

When Russia faced challenges in Ukraine and Georgia, the United States had supported the anti-Moscow side, going so far as to provide military and technical assistance. The Kremlin reacted poorly to such events: "In his first term, Putin's policy toward the Commonwealth of Independent States countries was passive.... In his second term, Russia's policy toward the CIS was dominated by the so-called colored revolutions in Georgia, Ukraine, and Kyrgyzstan, and gas trade."[5] Russia harshly opposed the color revolutions.

No broad opposition movements capable of overthrowing or replacing ruling authoritarian regimes have developed in any of the countries of Central Asia except Kyrgyzstan, and even the Kyrgyz revolutionaries sought to demonstrate their allegiance to Moscow immediately after achieving victory. Although some of them undoubtedly nurse a cautious hope that the West might provide their country with generous assistance, none have yet advertised this. The United States expressed satisfaction with the pace of democratization in Kyrgyzstan and, recognizing Russia's (and possibly Kazakhstan's) special interests in the country, assumed a passive stance. Moscow could gain some reassurance from the events in Kyrgyzstan, which served to demonstrate that not every revolution necessarily poses a threat to its policies in the post-Soviet space. However, since the last revolution, which occurred in 2010 and eventually transformed Kyrgyzstan into a parliamentary republic, relations between Moscow and Bishkek have deteriorated. Opinions are divided as to whether this indicates a fundamental shift in relations between the two countries or will prove to be only a temporary situation.

The U.S. failure to sow the seeds of democracy in Central Asia has inevitably prompted the conclusion that it must now foster relations with authoritarian regimes. This change can be seen as presenting yet another challenge to Moscow, which has always believed that its support for authoritarian leaders would guarantee the continuation of its influence in the region. Against a backdrop of halfhearted appeals to respect human rights and news conferences with the émigré opposition, the United States has sought to build constructive relations with Uzbekistan, Tajikistan, and Turkmenistan by advancing proposals to their dictators and promising to provide them with help. The dictators see that as a guarantee that, should revolutionary sentiment in Central Asia reach a certain level, they would be able to count on at least favorable neutrality from Washington. Under such conditions, the value of Russian support for the Central Asian regimes is diminished. There is a clash of promises between Russia and America that in large measure depends upon the location of the particular country. This juxtaposition can correctly be seen as a political competition, one in which Washington has not been as ambitious or as touchy as has Moscow. The United States views the

Arab world and the Middle East as being more important; Central Asia is important only to the extent that it relates to Afghanistan.

Until 2001, Washington had been building relations with the Central Asian states based upon two principles: "unilateral advantage" and "minimization of all costs."[6] After September 11, the United States shifted its main emphasis in the region to that of ensuring a military presence. This precipitated the entry of NATO into Afghanistan, which can be identified as being the U.S. reaction to the Taliban challenge. Not perceiving any threat in a U.S. military presence in Central Asia, Russia consented to it, although both Uzbekistan and Kyrgyzstan would most likely have offered their air bases to the U.S. Air Force even if Moscow had opposed it.

Russia itself has allowed its territory to be used for the transit of coalition cargo to Afghanistan. In 2012, agreement was reached to establish a "transit facility for non-military NATO goods to Afghanistan" in Ulyanovsk. (It is very revealing that Russian Deputy Prime Minister Dmitry Rogozin called those who believe that the facility established in Ulyanovsk is a NATO military base and thus support the idea of Russian-American military cooperation "idiots.")[7]

The challenges of China and the United States to a certain extent cancel each other out, and Russia has used that to its own advantage. This situation, however, will not last forever. As Chinese analyst Pan Guang has written, the Shanghai Cooperation Organization will cooperate with the United States, while in Central Asia China will establish dialogue directly with the United States, bypassing Russia entirely. In two decades, if not sooner, China and the United States will each view the other, and not Russia, as being major players in the region, which indeed is what has already been happening in the rest of the world.

The United States does not perceive Russian-Chinese solidarity as threatening, neither in Central Asia nor in the rest of the world. Sometimes it appears that China and Russia are pursuing their own individual goals, and any agreement between them on certain issues is purely accidental. Interestingly enough, Washington's assessments of those major issues where Russian and Chinese positions have converged (such as Iran, Libya, and Syria) address most (though not all) criticism at Moscow.

The security issue, considered to be the main topic in the Russian-Chinese-American trilateral exchange of opinions, is viewed differently in each of the three capitals. Russia seeks to maintain a security that depends upon continuing and reinforcing its exclusive influence, keeping local regimes loyal, as well as preventing (or at least limiting) the activities of third parties in the region. For example, the recent CSTO decision to allow third countries to operate military bases in the region only after consent has been obtained from all of the members directly confirms this policy. It is also revealing that the Russian interpretation of security does not necessarily mean that the Islamic radical opposition must be eradicated. By threatening the local regimes, this opposition has been driving them into even closer unions with Russia.

To implement Russia's essentially idealistic vision of security would be impossible, as policymakers in Moscow understand (or at least should understand). Therefore, as it seeks to diminish the role of external parties, the Kremlin has tried to find common ground with them (sometimes very inconsistently), while also attempting to set each of them against the other, to the extent that this is possible.

The U.S. view of security in Central Asia is based upon the premise that consensus will eventually be reached among the three major external actors (China, Russia, and the United States). Although Central Asia continues to be listed by the United States as an area of prime concern, it has obviously not held the same significance as the Middle East, Iran, and Afghanistan (although its importance to the United States has increased sharply as a result of the Afghan conflict, especially in light of the "Greater Central Asia" concept). Under this view, security in the region will depend upon U.S. success in Afghanistan (or more broadly, in Afghanistan and Pakistan).

As U.S. troops withdraw from Afghanistan, Central Asia will become even more important for U.S. strategy, inasmuch as Kyrgyzstan, Tajikistan, and Uzbekistan might consider allowing U.S. military bases to be established within their borders. Such bases would serve as observation points and help ensure stability in South Asia. According to Berlin-based security expert Jorg-Dietrich Nackmayer, "if the United States hopes to retain its status as a great world power, it will need to continue its presence in Afghanistan and Central Asia. Should the

United States leave the region, it will be the beginning of the end."[8] Although this statement may appear excessive, it must be admitted that the international prestige of the United States will inevitably depend upon the extent of its losses (or gains) from withdrawing from Afghanistan.

In order to establish military bases in Central Asia, the United States will need the consent of China and Russia. China has evinced little concern on the subject and has refrained from commenting on the questions of continuing operations at the U.S. air base at Manas (the Transit Center) and potentially establishing new bases at Chanabad and in Tajikistan. To a certain extent, Beijing has benefited from the U.S. presence, which has suppressed Islamist activities in both the Central Asian region and in the neighboring Uygur Autonomous Region of Xinjiang, China. The United States has every reason to expect that the Chinese will consent to its new military bases, even though Russian-Chinese relations will suffer when Russian politicians react to the U.S. military presence as being threatening.

Although China believes that all external actors will need to bear responsibility for maintaining security, it considers it the duty primarily of the United States and Russia. Under such conditions, China will need to refrain from participating in any war games and to rely upon its overall political and economic importance to guarantee that security is maintained.

Although Russia would not be directly threatened by U.S. military bases in Central Asia (the 2011 rumors that another American base would likely be established in Kazakhstan were quickly rebuffed), its influence as the guarantor of security would unquestionably be diminished. These bases therefore do not challenge Russia's security as much as they do its authority and prestige.

The Challenge From Muslim States

The activity of Muslim states in the region represents yet another external challenge facing Russia, although one that could also be considered a challenge domestically, considering the fact that the countries of Central Asia (notably Tajikistan and Uzbekistan) have been growing increasingly Islamicized under the influence of the rest of the Muslim world, which has promoted Islamic upbringing, subsidized the creation of a system of Islamic education, built mosques, and propagated a political ideology based upon religion. This ongoing process represents the restoration of that segment of the Islamic world that had been destroyed under the Soviets. Central Asia has now returned to the Muslim world and grown apart from Russia in social and cultural terms. For Russia, this need not be a challenge, but it should be taken as a signal for it to restructure its policies around the civilizational identity of the peoples inhabiting these countries.

The most active Muslim state in the Central Asian region has been Turkey. Pakistan is becoming more involved there, while Iran has traditionally had a strong influence in Tajikistan.

As it has pursued cooperation with Central Asia, Turkey has frequently emphasized its cultural and linguistic affiliation with the region. At the same time, Ankara has refrained from imposing pan-Turkism on the region, as it would not be popular in countries whose identity is based upon indigenous nationalism. In addition, Turkey has already gotten involved in conflicts in the Middle East and the Caucasus, and, as a consequence, it lacks the resources to pursue the "Turkization" of Central Asia. Pan-Turkism might be compared to eurasionism, which also failed to overcome the influence of local nationalism, especially in Tajikistan, Turkmenistan, and Uzbekistan. Tajik analysts Iskander Asadullaev and Bobokul Muminov believe this to be the case: "We do not need a Eurasian empire."[9]

The countries of the Arab world are mainly concerned with reviving Islam, building mosques, and developing Islamic education, and the Persian Gulf countries have actively pursued these goals. The emergence of small but ambitious Qatar (which is establishing cooperative initiatives with Kyrgyzstan and Tajikistan) has been particularly noteworthy. In a sense, the challenge that the Muslim countries present is to the United States.

PROBLEMATIC ISSUES
The Spread of Religious Radicalism

One immediate result of Islamization has been the spread of religious radicalism. This is a highly problematic issue, as it did not emanate from any individual parties or movements. Instead, Islamization was a consequence of the worldwide politicization and radicalization of Islam, and it affects the United States, Europe, China, the national regimes in Central Asia, and Russia as well. It presents a challenge both externally and domestically, inasmuch as international radical organizations have long been active in Central Asia. An Islamist opposition has formed along both sides of the Russian borders with Central Asia, and Russian citizens have been among the members of Islamist International in the region, working alongside their Central Asian colleagues. Hizb ut-Tahrir has grown strong in many regions in Russia and includes Central Asians among its members. Uzbeks, Tajiks, Kyrgyz, natives of the North Caucasus, and Tatars have been receiving military and ideological training in camps in Afghanistan.

The emergence of extremism and international terrorism,[10] which long since have changed from fitting the so-called nontraditional threat category to being of a more traditional kind, has been reinforced by the domestic problems within the states of Central Asia. Russia's experience in fighting terrorism has been impaired by its inability to resolve its own problems in the North Caucasus. Moreover, the kind of purely coercive methods that were used so widely in the North Caucasus would be of no use in Central Asia.

Trafficking in Narcotics

The second problematic issue is trafficking in narcotics, which can be likened to a global natural disaster forcing the international community to move toward consolidation and mutual assistance. "In 2012 Afghanistan maintained its position as the lead producer and cultivator of opium globally," despite that in this year the harvest of opium poppy was below its average.[11] Afghanistan and Central Asia now form a drug enclave divided between drug producers and traffickers. Although there is probably no government on earth that has not been engaged in its own battle to end drug trafficking, and countless international and national programs have addressed the issue, this zealous campaign has unfortunately yielded so few results to date as to compare to the global war on poverty. It sometimes appears as though the war is being fought mainly at a verbal level or is just being simulated. It is inconceivable that some kind of international supersystem, in which Russia, the United States, China, and the Central Asian countries would participate, could be created to counter drug trafficking. The war on drugs has in reality been nothing more than a demonstration of humanitarian cooperation. Even the most successful cases, readily reported by the media, represent only uncoordinated episodes.

Moreover, drug money is systematically being laundered and legalized by investment into legal forms of business in Central Asia, thereby making such resources a part of legal economic life in these countries. The war on drug trafficking has thus been rendered fruitless. Considering the fact that Russia has 3 million drug addicts (according to official data, which tend to understate the scale of the problem), the situation in Central Asia represents a risk for Russia as well. The problem will not be alleviated by reducing the production of drugs in Afghanistan and thereby cutting the amount of narcotics transiting through Central Asia; this would inevitably lead to an increase in the production of narcotics in Central Asia itself. The fact that many people depend upon the cultivation of narcotic plants for their existence is a factor that greatly complicates the war on drug trafficking.

The Transit of Energy-Related Products

Another challenge for Russia has been the attempts made to diminish its role in allowing the transit of energy-related products through its territory, a problem that extends far beyond the framework of Central Asia and, more broadly, the Caspian region.

Throughout the first half of the 2000s, Gazprom strove to retain its control over Russian and Central Asian gas exports as a way to keep these countries within the Russian sphere of influence. However, in the end, its effect was just the opposite. In December 2009, Chinese leader Hu Jintao presided over the opening of the world's longest gas pipeline, linking Turkmenistan to Xinjiang. That, according to English political scientist Adrian Pabst, "marked the end of Russia's monopoly on energy transmission in Central Asia."[12] The gas pipeline splits into several lines, every one of which bypasses Russia. The inevitable and predictable diversification of pipeline routes has already occurred, affected by the 2008–2009 Russian-Ukrainian gas dispute and the "mysterious" April 2009 explosion at a pipeline in Turkmenistan (as discussed in chapter 7, Ashgabat hinted that this blast had been arranged by Gazprom in order to secure the transit of Turkmen gas to Russia). Today, Russia's energy purchases in Central Asia have already been surpassed by those of China.

As early as the late 1990s, it had already been predicted that consumers of Russian energy, as well as consumers of gas supplied through Russian transit lines, would eventually begin to establish alternate routes. Some such projects had already been under consideration at the time (the main one being the Baku-Ceyhan pipeline). However, Russia's position in this arena was ultimately weakened by the centuries-old awkwardness of its policies, its urge to maintain its monopoly, and its inability to navigate quickly through changing circumstances. If Gazprom had been more flexible and willing to make some concessions, it would have been able to retain its influence. Eventually, Russia was pushed aside by the large-scale TAPI pipeline project, rated at a capacity of 30–33 billion cubic meters of gas, which will become a strategic route connecting Turkmenistan, Afghanistan, Pakistan, and India. Turkmenistan rejected Gazprom's offer of assistance in financing the project. Simultaneously, the Chinese National Petroleum Company announced that the amount of Turkmen gas to be supplied to China would increase from 13.5 billion cubic meters to 60 bcm by 2015. The Bank of China has granted Turkmenistan a loan for $4.1 billion. Although this situation may be seen as a challenge to Russia, it is also the result of Russia's own mistaken policies.

CONCLUSION

Strictly speaking, American and Chinese activities can hardly be considered as presenting strategic challenges to Russia. Such developments have been local, and only an equal or at least comparable opponent would be capable of presenting a strategic challenge. Russia cannot be compared to either the United States or China, as is evident from the GDPs of these countries ($15.2 trillion in the United States and $5.75 trillion in China, based on purchasing power parity, versus $1.88 trillion in Russia). The Russian political elite seems flattered if the Russian Central Asia policy has been discussed in the context of challenges and possible responses to them.

Russian influence continues to diminish. There is now nowhere in the world where Russia can act as the true successor to the Soviet Union, as is evident in the Arab East: Russian influence in Egypt, Iraq, and Libya is meager. Its impact on conflicts in the Middle East, if any, is insignificant. This is the reason that the Kremlin has been so tenacious regarding the conflict in Syria since 2011—its steadfast support for Bashar al-Assad has been based on the fact that he represents the last vestige of the Soviet presence in the region.

Although the Russian influence is undoubtedly vastly greater in Central Asia than in the Middle East or the Arab world, even there its influence is waning, and new forces have moved to fill the resulting void. As Igor Ivanov has written, "For the first time in several centuries, the continental environment of Russia in Eurasia (primarily China and India) has turned out to be more dynamic and more successful than Russia itself. The relative weakness of the foreign policy's material basis will have to be compensated for by building up advantages in 'nonmaterial' dimensions."[13]

At the regional level, the greatest challenge to Russia in the Central Asian countries may turn out to be regime change. In none of these countries will any unwavering pro-Russian politicians come to power. Moreover, in my opinion, Moscow has done little (or nothing at all) to create or enhance a pro-Russian lobby within the younger generation of politicians, thereby creating even greater problems for itself in the future. Another self-made Russian problem has resulted from the fact that its elite has long treated Central Asia with an old-fashioned, Soviet-style attitude. It was a long time before Russia began to realize that the former Soviet republics were becoming sovereign independent states. Apart from that, many of the local politicians had developed a certain pattern of dependency in their relations with Russia, which can be regarded as being a reaction to the memories of a common past that Moscow now cultivates.

It is unclear who in Moscow makes the final decision on Central Asian policy (and actually, not on the Central Asian policy alone). Political scientists and lobbyists are accustomed to referring to certain "Kremlin towers" that disagree with one another on strategy and tactics, similar to the way arguments arise between the U.S. Department of State and the Pentagon. A shortage of professional diplomats who are well versed in the intricacies of Central Asian politics (or at least who can speak the local languages) has created major political and diplomatic problems for Russia. By contrast, in the United States, a solid system is in place for preparing such professionals, which in this respect gives it an advantage over Russia.

Geopolitical shifts have forced Russia to assume a reactive, defensive stance. It would be difficult to assign blame for this situation, other than to blame the Soviet communists who let the Soviet Union collapse, thereby destroying the old international system and making Russia a hostage to its previous status. Still, Russia had begun to shift to a more defensive stance even before the collapse of the Soviet Union, following its outright defeat in the economic competition with the West.

Russia has no time to yearn for the past. It could transform its policy from a defensive to a more constructive "offensive" stance, in which case it would no longer feel obliged to respond to every challenge that confronts it. Russia needs to develop and present a new, alternative, dynamic policy, in other words, to present the world with a "new Russian challenge." Unless Russia addresses its domestic problems and implements a thorough political and economic modernization, however, this task will prove unfeasible, and Russia's economic weakness and the mental rigidity of its foreign policy will produce far greater negative consequences than any challenges that may be posed by outside actors.

NOTES

INTRODUCTION

1 The BRIC countries are Brazil, Russia, India, and China.

2 Zbigniew Brzezinski, *Velikaya shakhmatnaya doska* [The Great Chessboard] (Moscow: Mezhdunarodnuy otnosheniya, 1999), 170.

3 Marina Ottaway, *Democracy Challenged* (Washington, D.C.: Carnegie Endowment for International Peace, 2002), 3.

4 Evan Feigenbaum, "Shankhayskaya organizatsia sotrudnichestva i budushchee Tsentral'noy Azii" [The Shanghai Cooperation Organization and the Future of Central Asia], *Rossia v global'noy politike* [Russia in Global Affairs] (November/December 2007): 122.

CHAPTER I

1 Islam Karimov, *Uzbekistan na poroge XXI veka* [Uzbekistan on the Threshold of the XXI Century] (Tashkent: Uzbekiston, 1997), 306.

2 N. Kosolapov and M. Strezhneva, "Postsovetskoe prostranstvo: uslovnost' ili real'nost'" [The Post-Soviet Space: Convention or Reality], in *Transnatsional'noe politicheskoe sotrudnichestvo: novye real'nosti mezhdunarodnogo razvitia* [Transnational Political Cooperation: New Realities of International Development] (Moscow: IMEMO RAN, 2010), 49.

3 Nancy Lubin and Barnett R. Rubin, *Calming the Ferghana Valley: Development and Dialogue in the Heart of Central Asia*, report of the Ferghana Valley Working Group of the Center for Preventive Action sponsored by the Council on Foreign Relations and the Century Foundation (New York: Twentieth Century Fund, 2000), 130.

4 Francis Fukuyama, *Nashe postchelovecheskoe budushchee* [Our Posthuman Future] (Moscow: AST, Lyuks, 2008), 70.

5   "Yastrzhembsky prizyvaet uluchshat imidzh Rossii" [Yastrzhembsky Calls for Improving Russia's Image], *Izvestia*, January 30, 2007, http://izvestia.ru/news/392517.

6   A. Kiva, "Rossia: put' k katastrofe ili modernizatsii?" [Russia: The Road to Disaster or to Modernization?], *So Tsis: sotsiolog. issledovania* [Sociological Research], 11 (2010): 134.

7   *Integratsia v Evrazii: sotsiologicheskoe izmerenie* [Integration in Eurasia: the Sociological Dimension], issue 2 (2008): 11.

8   S. N. Abashin, "Tsentral'naya Azia: kakoy my yee vidim" [Central Asia: How We See It], in *Politicheskiy protsess v Tsentral'noy Azii* [The Political Process in Central Asia] (Moscow: IVRAN, TSSPI, 2011), 20–21.

9   M. Yusupova, "Zamki dlya granits" [Locks for the Borders], *Oazis*, no. 23 (163) (December 2011).

10 M. Rizoyev, "Kogda v sosedyakh Afganistan" (When Afghanistan Is Among Your Neighbors), *Oazis*, no. 19 (163) (October 2011): 4.

11 M. Suyunbayev, "Integratsia Tsentral'noy Evrazii: geopoliticheskie i geoekonomicheskie faktory" [Integration in Central Eurasia: Geopolitical and Geo-economic Factors], *Tsentral'naya Azia i Kavkaz* [Central Asia and the Caucasus] (Luleo, Sweden), no. 4 (16) (1998): 54.

12 A. Kazantsev, "Mnogovektornost' vneshnei politiki i geopoliticheskaya neopredelyonnost' v Tsentral'noy Azii" [Multi-vector Foreign Policy and Geopolitical Uncertainty in Central Asia], *Vestnik Instituta Kennana v Rossii* [Bulletin of the Kennan Institute in Russia], issue 19 (2011): 23.

13 E. Hatipoglu, "Regional Cooperation Between the Central Asian Republics and Integration Movements," *Eurasians Studies* (Ankara), no. 17 (Spring–Summer 2000): 64.

14 R. Abdullo, "Tajikistan i regional'naya integratsia v Tsentral'noy Azii" [Tajikistan and Regional Integration in Central Asia], *Tsentral'naya Azia i Kavkaz* [Central Asia and the Caucasus], no. 2 (50) (2007): 75.

15 S. Kushkumbayev, "Tsentral'noaziatskaya integratsia v kontekste istorii i geopolitiki" [Central Asian Integration in the Context of History and Geopolitics], *Tsentral'naya Azia*, no. 4 (16) (1998): 33.

16 A. Matveeva, "Russia's Policy in Central Asia," *International Spectator* (London), 42, no. 1 (March 2007): 45.

17 Anders Åslund, *Russia's Capitalist Revolution* (Washington, D.C.: Peterson Institute for International Economics, 2007), 181.

18 Ukaz prezidenta Rossiiskoi Federatsii "Ob utverzhdenii Strategicheskogo kursa Rossiyskoy Federatsii s gosudarstvami – uchastnikami SNG" ot 14 sentyabrya 1995 goda, no. 940 [Russian Presidential Decree "On Russia's Strategic Course With the CIS Member Countries" of September 14, 1995, no. 940].

19 M. Laruelle, *Russian Eurasianism: An Ideology of Empire* (Baltimore, Md.: John Hopkins University Press, 2008), 221.

20 A. Dugin, "Novyi tsentr: Yevraziiskoe delanie Rossii" [The New Center: Russia's Eurasian Opus], *Yevraziiskoe obozrenie* [Eurasian Review], Special issue (Moscow, year unknown).

21 N. Nazarbayev, *Bez pravykh i levykh* [Without Left or Right] (Moscow: Molodaya Gvardiya 1991), 244.

22 T. Mansurov, "Evraziisky Proekt Nursultana Nazarbayeva, Voploshchenny v Zhizn" [Nursultan Nazarbayev's Eurasian Project Becomes Reality] *Kazakhstankaya Pravda*, December 6, 2011, http://inkaraganda.kz/upload-files/pdf/archiv/2011/12/2011_12_13 /2011_12_13_4.pdf.

23 A. N. Vavilov, "Geopoliticheskie dominanty natsional'noy bezopasnosti Rossii v XXI veke i yevraziyskaya integratsia" [The Geopolitical Dominants in Russia's National Security in the XXI Century and Eurasian integration], in the Collection of Papers of the International Conference "*Yevraziystvo – budushchee Rossii: dialog kul'tur i tsivilizatsiy*" [Eurasianism—Russia's Future: Dialogue of Cultures and Civilizations] (Moscow: 2001), 201.

24 D. Mukhetdinov, "Islamskaya osnova dlya integratsii v stranakh SNG" [An Islamic Foundation for Integration in the CIS Countries], *Minaret* (Nizhny Novgorod), no. 1–2 (2009): 61–62.

25 I. Yakovenko, "Konechnaya ostanovka: 'Moskva – Tretiy Rim,'" [Last Stop: Moscow— the Third Rome], *Novaya Gazeta*, April 11, 2011.

26 R. Allison, "Virtual Regionalism, Regional Structures and Regime Security in Central Asia," *Central Asian Survey* 27, no. 2 (June, 2008): 186.

27 B. Nemtsov, *Ispoved buntarya* [Confession of a Rebel] (Moscow: Partizan, 2007), 62.

28 I. Iskanderov, "Amir Temur i sozvuchie vremyon" [Amir Temur in Accord With the Times] (Tezisy mezhdunarodnoy konferentsii "Amir Temur i ego mesto v mirovoy istorii") [Theses of the international conference "Amir Timur and His Place in World History"] (Tashkent: 1996), 40.

29 V. Panfilova, "Washington gotovit puti otkhoda iz Afganistana" [Washington Is Preparing for Its Retreat From Afghanistan], *Nezavisimaya Gazeta*, October 24, 2011, www.ng.ru/cis/2011-10-24/7_tashkent.html.

30 D. Malysheva, *Respublika Uzbekistan: Politika* [The Republic of Uzbekistan: Politics], 371.

31 A. Kurtov, "Mezhdunarodnaya zhizn" [International Life], in *Tsentral'naya Evrazia: Analiticheskiy ezhegodnik* [Central Eurasia: Analytical Yearbook], [S. l.] (Luleå, Sweden: CA&CC Press, 2009), 352.

32 A. Akhmedov, *Spetsifika razvitia mnogopartiynosti v Tsentral'noy Azii i ee vliyanie na politicheskuyu kul'turu (na primere Respubliki Tajikistan)* [The Specific Features of Multiparty System Development in Central Asia and Its Influence on Political Culture (Based on the Example of Tajikistan)] (Dushanbe, year unknown), 47.

33 I. Zvyagelskaya, *Stanovlenie gosudarstv Tsentral'noy Azii* [The Formation of the States of Central Asia] (Moscow: Aspekt-Press, 2009), 50.

34 V. Surkov, *Teksty 97–07* [Texts 97–07] (Moscow: Evropa, 2008), 122.

35 M. Akayeva, *U nadezhdy ne byvaet nochi* [Hope Knows No Night] (Moscow: Voskresen'ye, 2003), 258.

36 A. Karavayev, "Vremya Medvedeva i resursy Putina" [Medvedev's Era and Putin's Resources], *NG-Dipkur'er*, March 28, 2011.

37 Y. Tregubova, *Baiki kremlyovskogo diggera* [Tales of a Kremlin Digger] (Moscow: Ad Marginem, 2003), 289.

38 Martha Brill Olcott, "Kazakhstan at 20: Commentary," Carnegie Endowment for International Peace, December 12, 2011.

39 M. V. Starchak, "Rossiyskoe obrazovanie na russkom yazyke kak faktor vliyania Rossii v Tsentral'noy Azii: chto proiskhodit i chto delat'?" [Russian Education in the Russian Language as a Factor of Russia's Influence in Central Asia: What Is Happening and What Should Be Done?], www.fondedin.ru/dok/starchak.pdf.

40 A. Dzhumayev, "K istoriko-kul'turnym osnovaniyam blizosti Sredney Azii i Rossii: vzglyad iz Uzbekistana" [The Historical-Cultural Basis for the Closeness of Central Asia and Russia: The View From Uzbekistan], *Druzhba narodov* [Friendship of Peoples], no. 7 (2010): 157.

41 "Uzbekistan: v Tashkente lomayut memorial pamyati pogibshikh v Velikoy Otechestvennoy voine rabotnikov zavoda Tashselmash" [Uzbekistan: In Tashkent They Are Demolishing the Memorial to the Tashselmash Plant Workers Killed During the Great Patriotic War], www.fer05ananews.com/article.phpid=6888.

42 Kosolapov and Strezhneva, "The Post-Soviet Space," 47.

43 V. Panfilova, "Rossiyskie gazety doydut do Turkmenii" [Russian Newspapers Will Reach Turkmenistan], *Nezavisimaya Gazeta*, June 15, 2011.

44 A. Shustov, "Russkie shkoly vytesnyayutsya turetskimi" [Turkish Schools Are Squeezing Out Russian Schools], www.centrasia.ru/newsA.php?st=1263385020.

45 "Russkoyazychnye v Tsentralnoy Azii: Sotsial'nyi portret" [Russian Speakers in Central Asia: a Social Portrait] (Fond "Russkiy Mir," April 9, 2010), www.russkiymir.ru/russkiymir/ru/news/fund/news0274.html?print=true.

46 "V postsovetskoy Tsentral'noy Azii russkiy yazyk ukhodit na vtoroy plan" [Russian Language on the Decline in Central Asia], http://www.centrasia.ru/newsA.php?st=1317414420.

47 A. Shustov, "Skol'ko russkikh ostalos' v Tsentral'noy Azii?" [How Many Russians Are There Left in Central Asia?], *Russkaya narodnaya linia: Informatsionno-analiticheskaya sluzhba* [Russian People's Line: Informational/Analytical Service], November 20, 2007.

48 A. Dubnov, "Berdimuhamedov stanet ottsom vsekh Turkmen" [Berdimuhamedov to Become Father of All the Turkmen], *Moskovskie novosti*, December 14, 2011.

49 V. Panfilova, "Ne po dobroy vole" [Not by Good Will], *Nezavisimaya Gazeta*, September 7, 2011.

50 "Chto budet v Turkmenistane?" [What Will Happen in Turkmenistan?], working paper based on a roundtable of the Religion, Society, and Security Program, January 23, 2007, Carnegie Moscow Center, 1 (2007): 6.

51 L. Jonson, "The Tajik War: A Challenge to Russia Policy," Discussion Paper, Royal Institute of International Affairs, 74, [S. l.] (1998): 5.

52 D. Furman, "Zamknuty Krug: Popytka Vykhoda" [Trying to Break a Vicious Cycle], *Nezavisimaya Gazeta*, September 22, 2010, www.ng.ru/ideas/2010-09-22/5_kirgizia.html.

53 Starchak, "Russian Education in the Russian Language," 9.

54 Allison, "Virtual Regionalism," 194.

55 "Akezhan Kazhegeldin gotov sostavit' konkurentsiyu Nursultanu Nazarbayevu" [Akezhan Kazhegeldin Is Ready to Compete Against Nursultan Nazarbayev], *Segodnya*, October 31, 1998.

56 V. Ponomaryov, "Istoria odnoy poezdki, ili kak menya vysylali iz Ashkhabada" [Story of a Journey, or How I Got Deported From Ashgabat], *Indeks/Dos'e na tsenzuru* [Index/ Dossier on Censorship], no. 4–5, (1998): 270–78.

57 R. Zhangozha, "Russia and the Newly Independent States of Central Asia: Relations Transformed," in *Russia: The Challenges of Transformation*, ed. P. Dutkiewicz, [S. l.] (New York: New York University Press, 2011), 395.

58 A. Bolshakov, "Vneshnyaya politika Kyrgyzii v kontekste izmenenia konfliktnosti na postsovetskom prostranstve" [Kyrgyzstan's Foreign Policy in the Context of the Changing Nature of Conflict in the Post-Soviet Space], *Politeks: Politicheskaya ekspertiza* 6, no. 2 (2010): 111.

59 N. F. Reimers, "'Proekt veka' protivorechit nauchnym zakonam razvitia mira" [The "Project of the Century" Goes Against the Scientific Laws of the World's Development], *Nauka i zhizn'* [Science and Life], no. 12 (1987), no. 8 (1988).

60 B. Atchabarov and T. Sharmanov, "Voda dlya regiona" [Water for the Region], *Zvezda Vostoka* [Star of the East], no. 4 (1990): 117.

61 G. Chufrin, *Rossia v Tsentral'noy Azii* [Russia in Central Asia] (Almaty: Kazakhstansky Institut Strategicheskikh Issledovaniy Pri Prezidente RK, 2010), 95.

62 N. Rogozhina, "Vodnye resursy v stranakh Tsentral'noy Azii: Interesy Rossii" [Water Resources in Central Asia: Russia's Interests] in *Novye tendentsii vo vneshney politike Rossii v Tsentral'noy Azii i na Kavkaze* [New Trends in Russia's Foreign Policy in Central Asia and the Caucasus] (Moscow: Russian Academy of Sciences Institute of World Economy and International Relations, 2008), 111–26.

63 T. U. Usubaliev, *Voda —dorozhe zolota* [Water Is Worth More Than Gold] (Bishkek: 1998), 29.

64 I. Kirsanov, "Bitva za vodu v Tsentral'noy Azii" [The Battle for Water in Central Asia] *Nezavisimyi obozrevatel' stran Sodruzhestva* [Independent Reviewer of the Commonwealth Countries] no. 12 (2006), www.fundeh.org/publications/articles/48.

65 Evan Feigenbaum, "Shankhaiskaya organizatsiya sotrudnichestva i budushchee Tsentral'noy Azii" [The Shanghai Cooperation Organization and Central Asia's Future], *Rossia v global'noy politike* (November-December 2007): 123.

66 Jos Boonstra, "Is the EU-Central Asia Strategy Running Out of Steam?" EUCAM Policy Brief 17, May 2011, 4, www.fride.org/download/PB_17_EUCAM.pdf.

67 V. Panfilova, "Medvedev i Karimov poobshchalis' v blits-rezhime" [Brief Talks Between Medvedev and Karimov], *Nezavisimaya Gazeta*, June 15, 2011.

68 Y. Luzhkov, *Voda i Mir* [Water and Peace] (Moscow: Moskovskie uchebniki i kartolitografia, 2008).

69 See "Povorot Sibirskikh Rek" [Northern River Reversal], http://ru.wikipedia.org/wiki/
%D0%9F%D0%BE%D0%B2%D0%BE%D1%80%D0%BE%D1%82_%D1%81%D
0%B8%D0%B1%D0%B8%D1%80%D1%81%D0%BA%D0%B8%D1%85_%D1%8
0%D0%B5%D0%BA (Russian); http://en.wikipedia.org/wiki/Northern_river_reversal
(English). See also A. Volosevich, "V Tashkente Predstavili Proekt Superkanala:
Ot Karskogo Morya do Persidskogo Zaliva" [In Tashkent Plans Were Presented for
Building the Kara Sea–Persian Gulf Grand Canal], Fergana News, November 25,
2008, www.fergananews.com/article.php?id=5971.

CHAPTER 2

1 *Obzor vneshney politiki Rossiyskoy Federatsii* [Review of Russian Foreign Policy],
Russian Foreign Ministry, www.mid.ru/brp_4.nsf/sps/3647DA97748A106BC
32572AB002AC4DD.

2 R. Allison, "Virtual Regionalism, Regional Structures and Regime Security in Central
Asia," *Central Asian Survey* 27, no. 2 (June 2008): 190.

3 "Popytka dominirovania ostanovit integratsiyu: Pervyi vitse-prem'era Kazakhstana
o Yevraziyskom soyuze" [Attempts to Dominate Will Put a Stop to Integration:
Kazakhstan's Deputy Prime Minister on the Eurasian Union], *Kommersant*, November
23, 2011, http://kommersant.ru/doc/1822396.

4 O. Sapozhkov, "Komissary Yevrazii" [The Commissars of Eurasia], *Kommersant*,
October 31, 2011, http://kommersant.ru/doc/1807225.

5 "Attempts to Dominate."

6 "Ekspert: Tamozhennyy soyuz—eto vyzov na vyzhivanie" [The Customs Union Is a
Challenge for Survival—Expert], www.regnum.ru/news/1479510.html.

7 Ending customs formalities at internal borders has caused passengers considerable
difficulties. The separate "collection areas" set up at airports for people heading for
Customs Union countries are typically filled with crowds of irate people, who have
no snack bars or restaurants to provide them with service and are not even able to buy
things at the duty-free shops.

8 "Tol'ko integratsia mozhet spasti postsovetskie respubliki – sovetnik Nazarbayeva"
[Aide to Nazarbayev: Only Integration Can Save the Post-Soviet Republics],
www.islamsng.com/kaz/news/3546.

9 O. Khe and E. Korabaeva, "Sploshnye pryaniki" [Carrots Only], *Biznes & Vlast*
(Almaty), October 21, 2011, www.and.kz/peredovica/315-sploshnye-pryaniki.html.

10 I. V. Zadorin, ed., *Integratsia v Yevrazii: sotsiologicheskoe izmerenie* [Integration in
Eurasia: the Sociological Dimension] (Moscow: Institut Ekonomicheskikh strategiy,
2008), 74.

11 A. Olshevsky, "500 dnei posle soyuza" [500 Days After the Union], *Nezavisimaya
Gazeta*, September 30, 2011.

12 V. Putin, "Novyi integratsionnyi proekt dlya Yevrazii—budushchee, kotoroe rozhdaetsya segodnya" [A New Integration Project for Eurasia—a Future Born Today], *Izvestia*, October 4, 2011.

13 S. Shiptenko, "Yevraziyskiy soyuz: Vozrozhdenie na geopoliticheskom pepelishche" [The Eurasian Union: Rebirth From the Geopolitical Ashes], http://regnum.ru/news/1474084.html.

14 G. Abishev, "Ne rubl' ediny" [It Is Not Only an Issue of Money], *Kursiv*, November 24, 2011, www.kursiv.kz/news/details/vlast1/ne-rubl-edinyj.

15 See, for example, the interview with Igor Panarin, www.youtube.com/watch&v= XveMNQnGuWa.

16 S. Tostov, "Perspektivy Yevraziyskogo integratsionnogo proekta" [Outlook for the Eurasian Integration Project], *Nezavisimaya Gazeta*, October 31, 2011.

17 G. Abishev and K. Satpayev, "Kyrgyzstan vzyali v TS" [Kyrgyzstan Accepted Into the Customs Union], *Kursiv* (Almaty), October 20, 2011.

18 B. Toktarov, "Cherez Tamozhenniy Soyuz—v Evraziiskiy" [From Customs Union to a Eurasian One], *Biznes & Vlast* (Almaty), October 21, 2011, www.and.kz/peredovica/319-cherez-tamozhennyy-soyuz-v-evraziyskiy.html.

19 V. Panfilova, "Otlozhennaya partia Islama Karimova" [Islam Karimov's Postponed Match], *Nezavisimaya Gazeta*, December 7, 2011.

20 Vladimir V. Putin, "Annual Address to the Federal Assembly of the Russian Federation," April 25, 2005.

21 A. Nikitin, "Skol'ko pridetsya zaplatit' Rossii za vosstanovlenie SSSR?" [How Much Will It Cost Russia to Rebuild the USSR?], *Itogi* (October 24, 2011): 29.

22 Sapozhkov, "Commissars of Eurasia."

23 Putin, "A New Integration Project."

24 A. Khodasevich, "Bonus dlya Lukashenko" [A Bonus for Lukashenko], *Nezavisimaya Gazeta*, April 17, 2012.

25 Z. Kanafina, "Nerushimye nashi soyuzy" [Our Unbreakable Unions], *Karavan* (Almaty), November 25, 2011.

26 "Brzezinski: Ideya Putina o Evraziiskom Soyuze absurdna" [Putin's Eurasian Union Proposal Is Absurd, Brzezinski], October 21, 2011, www.newsland.ru/news/detail/id/807276.

27 "Ne rubl' yediny" [It Is Not Only an Issue of Money], *Kursiv*, November 24, 2011, www.kursiv.kz/print:page,1,1195216394-ne-rubl-edijnij.html.

28 "Nazarbaev: Rubl' Ne Gotov Stat' Edinoy Valyutoy Evraziyskogo Soyuza" [Ruble Is Not Ready to Become the Common Currency for the Eurasian Union—Nazarbayev], ibra.com.ua, November 28, 2011, http://ibra.com.ua/valyuta/34073-nazarbaev-the-rubl-is-not-ready-to-become-the-co.

29 Kanafina, "Our Unbreakable Unions."

30 Allison, "Virtual Regionalism," 192.

31 Data from the CIS Statistics Committee. See T. Mansurov, "Yevraziyskiy proekt Nursultana Nazarbayeva, voploshchennyy v zhizn'" [Nursultan Nazarbayev's Eurasian Project Becomes a Reality], *Kazakhstanskaya Pravda*, December 6, 2011.

32 V. Panfilova, "Moskva daet Bishkeku shans" [Moscow Gives Bishkek a Chance], *Nezavisimaya Gazeta*, February 20, 2012.

33 *Yevraziyskoe ekonomicheskoe soobshchestvo: sbornik bazovykh dokumentov* [The Eurasian Economic Community: A Collection of Basic Documents] (Moscow: Russkiy raritet, 2008), 23.

34 *Ustav Organizatsii Dogovora o kollektivnoy bezopasnosti* [Charter of the Collective Security Treaty Organization], www.dkb.gov.ru/b/azg.htm.

35 A. Tsyganok, *Rossia na Yuzhnom Kavkaze* [Russia in the Southern Caucasus] (Moscow: AIRO-XXI, 2010), 217.

36 *Arkhiv zayavleniy, vystupleniy, statyey drugikh chlenov SKB vklyuchaya general'nogo sekretarya SKB, predstaviteley gosudarstv-uchastnikov* [Archive of Statements, Presentations, and Articles by Other Collective Security Council Members, Including the Council's Secretary General and Member States' Representatives], www.dkb.gov.ru/d//aa.htm.

37 G. Chufrin, *Rossia v Tsentral'noy Azii* [Russia in Central Asia] (Almaty, 2010), 37.

38 A. Matveeva, "Russia's Policy in Central Asia," *International Spectator* 42, no. 1 (March 2007): 47.

39 I. Y. Yurgens, ed., *ODKB: otvetstvennaya bezopasnost'* [The CSTO: Responsible Security], (Moscow: Institute of Contemporary Development, 2011), 9, www.insor-russia.ru/files/ODKB.pdf.

40 V. Litovkin, "ODKB nastraivayut protiv tsvetnykh revolyutsiy" [The CSTO Is Being Set Against Color Revolutions], *Nezavisimaya Gazeta,* August 9, 2011.

41 "Raschety po privatizatsii 'Gazprom' 'Kyrgyzgaza' budut gotovy v fevrale 2012 goda (Kirgiziya)" [Estimates on Kyrgyzgaz Privatization by Gazprom Will Be Ready in February 2012 (Kyrgyzstan)], Regnum, December 20, 2011, www.regnum.ru/news/1481716.html.

42 Charter of the Collective Security Treaty Organization.

43 V. Panfilova, "V ODKB sozdayutsya edinye mirotvorcheskie sily" [CSTO Creates a Unified Peacekeeping Force], *NG-Dipkurier*, November 24, 2008, www.ng.ru/dipkurer/2008-11-24/13_odkb.html.

44 Speech by Hu Jintao at SCO Anniversary Summit, Regnum, June 15, 2011, www.regnum.ru/news/1415752.html?forprint.

45 B. Tsarev, "10 let posle Shankhaya" [10 Years After Shanghai], *Nezavisimaya Gazeta*, June 15, 2011.

46 E. Marat, "Afghanistan: NATO Out, SCO In?" *Eurasia Daily Monitor* 8, issue 98 (2011).

47 A. Dubnov, "Shankhayskaya organizatsia stala po-nastoyashchemu kitayskoy" [The Shanghai Organization Has Become Genuinely Chinese], *Moskovskie Novosti*, June 16, 2011.

48 "15 iyunya otmechaetsya desyatiletiye obrazovaniya Shankhaiskoy Organizatsii Sotrudnichestva. V svyazi s etim v kazakhstanskoy slolitse Astane proydet yubileyny sammit organizatsii" [The Shanghai Cooperation Organization Is Celebrating Its Tenth Anniversary on June 15. Kazakhstan's Capital Astana Will Host the Organization's Tenth Anniversary Summit], infoshos.ru, June 14, 2011, www.infoshos.ru/ru/print.php?idn= 8364.

49 A. Gabuyev, "Khod slonom" [Bishop's Move], *Kommersant*, June 15, 2011.

50 "Kazakhstan: v Astane proshel yubileynyy sammit ShOS" [Kazakhstan: SCO Held Its Anniversary Summit in Astana], Fergana News, June 15, 2011, www.fergananews.com/ news.phd?id=16876&print=1.

51 V. Kuzmin, "Shosse dlinoyu v desyat' let" [The 10-Year-Long Freeway], *Rossiyskaya Gazeta*, June 16, 2011, www.rg.ru/2011/06/15/prezident-site.html.

52 "Nadnatsional'naya Valyuta i Bor'ba s Internetom: Rech' Nursultana Nazarbayeva na Sammite ShOS" [The National Currency and the Struggle Against the Internet], Nursultan Nazarbayev's Speech at the SCO Summit, Regnum, June 15, 2011, www.regnum.ru/news/1415835.html?forptint.

53 George Perkovich, *Toward Realistic U.S.-India Relations* (Washington D.C.: Carnegie Endowment for International Peace, 2010), 24.

54 Nivedita Das Kundu, "SCO a Catalyst for Afghan Stability," *Russia & India Report*, October 31, 2011, http://indrus.in/articles/2011/10/31/sco_a_catalyst_for_afghan_ stability_13186.html.

55 T. Kosobokova, "India i Pakistan vynuzhdayut ShOS prevratit'sya v voennyy blok" [India and Pakistan Are Forcing the SCO to Become a Military Bloc], www.rbcdaily.ru/2011/ 06/16/focus/562949980438431/print.

56 Li Sheng, ed., *Xinjiang, Chinese Land: Past and Present* (Urumqi, Xinjiang: People's Publishing House, 2006), 338.

57 J. Chan, "SCO Summit Points to Deepening Global Tensions," World Socialist Site, June 22, 2011, www.wsws.org/articles/2011/jun2011shan-l22.shtml.

58 "Gensek ShOS: Afganistan ostaetsya istochnikom ugroz bezopasnosti regiona" [Afghanistan Continues to Pose Security Threats to the Region, SCO Secretary General], Novosti-Kazakhstan, June 1, 2011, www.newskaz.ru/politics/20110601/ 1532852-print.html.

59 Speech by Dmitry Medvedev at SCO Summit, *Regnum*, June 15, 2011, www.regnum.ru/ news/1415741.html?forprint.

60 "Prezident Kyrgyzii vyskazalas' za sozdanie 'poyasov bezopasnosti' na granitse s Afganistanom" [President of Kyrgyzstan Supports Creation of "Security Belts" on the Border With Afghanistan], *Regnum*, June 15, 2011, www.regnum.ru/news/1415698.html ?forprint.

61 P. Goncharov, "Afganistan vstupaet v ShOS: komu eto vygodno?" [Afghanistan's Accession to the SCO: Who Benefits?], www.infoshos.ru/ru/print.php?idn=8366.

62 Zhang Haizhou, "SCO Can Play 'Bigger Role' in Afghanistan," *China Daily*, January 27, 2012.

63 J. P. Panda, "China or the SCO: Who Will Supervise Afghanistan?" *China Brief* 11, issue 15 (2011).

64 Allison, "Virtual Regionalism," 196.

65 Goncharov, "Afghanistan's Accession to the SCO."

66 Kosobokova, "India and Pakistan Are Forcing the SCO."

67 "Ekspert: Turtsiya mozhet vstupit' v Shankhayskuyu Organizatsiyu Sotrydnichestva" [Turkey May Join Shanghai Cooperation Organization], Regnum, May 23, 2011, www.regnum.ru/news/1407750.html.

68 Yu. Solozobov, "ShOS – eto kitayskaya otmychka dlya Tsentral'noy Azii" [The SCO Is a Chinese Master Key to Central Asia], IA REX, June 2, 2011, www.iarex.ru/print/16020.html.

69 Pan Guang, "China and the USA in Central Asia: Role of the SCO and Possibility of Cooperation in Afghanistan," *China and US Focus*, September 7, 2011.

70 N. Belonogova, "ShOS: vzglyad molodezhi" [The SCO: Youth's Viewpoint], Portal InfoShOS, May 30, 2011), www.infoshos.ru/ru/?idn=8286.

71 A. Kizekova, "The Shanghai Cooperation Organization: Challenges in Cyberspace," Commentary 033, S. Rajaratnam School of International Studies, Singapore, 2012.

72 Ekspert: Rossii vygodno ob'edinit ShOS I ODKB [It Is Advantageous for Russia to Unite the SCO and CSTO], Regnum, May 24, 2011, www.regnum.ru/news/1407769.html ?forprint.

73 A. Grozin, "Postsovetskaya Tsentral'naya Azia: novye geopoliticheskie tendentsii i rossiyskie interesy" [Post-Soviet Central Asia: New Geopolitical Trends and Russian Interests], *Tsentral'naya Azia i Kavkaz* [Central Asia and the Caucasus] (Luleo, Sweden), no. 5 (2007): 57.

CHAPTER 3

1 Official website of the Government of Kyrgyzstan, www.gov.kg.

2 "Kyrgyzstan dolzhen poyti po puti Turtsii, kotoraya platit zarabotnuyu platu imamam—Atambaev" [Kyrgyzstan Should Follow Turkey by Paying Imams' Salaries, Atambayev], Islam v SNG, September 12, 2011, www.islamsng.com/kgz/news/2723.

3 A. Grozin, "Postsovetskaya Tsentral'naya Azia: novye geopoliticheskie tendentsii i rossiyskie interesy" [Post-Soviet Central Asia: New Geopolitical Trends and Russian Interests], Tsentral'naya Azia i Kavkaz [Central Asia and the Caucasus], no. 5 (2007): 57.

4 Marfua Tokhtakhodzhaeva, *Utomlennye proshlym* [Exhausted by the Past] (Vienna, Tashkent: Regional Program Office, 2001), 20.

5 Islam Karimov, *Uzbekistan na poroge XXI veka: ugrozy bezopasnosti, uslovia i garantii progressa* [Uzbekistan on the Threshold of the XXI Century: Threats to Security, Conditions and Guarantees of Progress] (Moscow: Drofa, 1997), 43.

6 Radio Liberty, October 25, 2004, www.rferl.org/newsline/2004/10/251004.asp.

7   The role of women is covered in detail in the above-mentioned book by Marfua Tochtachodzhaeva.

8   Nancy Lubin and Barnett R. Rubin, *Calming the Ferghana Valley: Development and Dialogue in the Heart of Central Asia*, report of the Ferghana Valley Working Group of the Center for Preventive Action sponsored by the Council on Foreign Relations and the Twentieth Century Fund (New York: Twentieth Century Fund, 2000), 101.

9   "Simpozium, posvyashchennyy naslediu Abu Hanify, proshel v Tajikistane" [Symposium, Dedicated to the Legacy of Imam Abu Hanifa, Was Held in Tajikistan], Central Asia Online, August 10, 2009, http://centralasiaonline.com/ru/articles/caii/features/2009/10/08/feature-03.

10 J. Schoeberlein, "Islam in the Ferghana Valley," in *Islam in Politics in Russia and Central Asia, Early Eighteenth to Late Twentieth Centuries*, eds. S. Dudoignon and H. Komatsu (London: Kegan Paul, 2001), 338.

11 A. Zelkina, "Islam and Security in the New States of Central Asia: How Genuine Is the Islamic Threat?" *Religion, State and Society* 27, no. 3/4 (1999): 370.

12 Martha Brill Olcott, "Roots of Radical Islam in Central Asia," Carnegie Paper, Carnegie Endowment for International Peace, January 2007, 35.

13 H. Carrère d'Encausse, *L'Empire* éclaté [Broken Empire] (Paris: Flammarion, 1978), 260–70.

14 A. Khalid, *Islam After Communism* (Berkeley and Los Angeles: University of California Press, 2006).

15 B. Lewis, *The Assassins: A Radical Sect in Islam* (New York: Basic Books, 2003), 21.

16 "Glava gosudarstva posetil v Karagande novuyu sobornuyu mechet'" [The Head of State Visited New Cathedral Mosque in Karaganda], *KAZINFORM*, November 21, 2011.

17 Remarks by H. E. Nursultan Nazarbayev, President of the Republic of Kazakhstan at the 7th World Islamic Economic Forum, Astana (Kazakhstan), June 8, 2011, http://kazakhstanun.org/Remarks%20Nazarbayev%207%20%20Islamic%20Economic%20Forum.htm.

18 "Tyurki posovetovalis' v Alma-Ate" [The Turkomans Have Held Consultations in Almaty], *NG-Dipkurier*, October 31, 2011.

19 Address by the President of the Republic of Kazakhstan, Leader of the Nation, N. Nazarbayev "Strategy Kazakhstan-2050": New Political Course of the Established State," December 14, 2012, www.akorda.kz/en/page/page_poslanie-prezidenta-respubliki-kazakhstan-n-nazarbaeva-narodu-kazakhstana-14-dekabrya-2012-g_1357813742.

20 *Sovremennyy terrorizm: vzglyad iz Tsentral'noy Azii* [Modern Terrorism: A View From Central Asia] (Almaty: Friedrich-Ebert-Stiftung, 2002), 140.

21 S. Balmasov, "Vakhkhabitskaya ugroza Rossii iz Kazakhstana" [Wahhabi Threat to Russia Originating From Kazakhstan], *Komsomolskaya Pravda*, August 5, 2011, http://Pravda.ru/world/formerussr/other/05-08-2011/1086689-wahhab-0.

22 Zara Ibragimova, "Otechestvennyy terror-produkt" [Domestic Sources of Terrorism], *Oazis* (Almaty) 22, no. 162 (November 2011): 2.

23 O. Roy, "The Foreign Policy of the Central Asian Islamic Renaissance Party," paper from the Muslim Politics Project, New York, 1999, 26.

24 A. Rashid, *Jihad: The Rise of Militant Islam in Central Asia* (New Haven, Conn.: Yale University Press, 2002), 231.

25 Evgeniy Abdullaev and L. Kolesnikov, "Islam v sovremennom Uzbekistane" [Islam in Modern Uzbekistan], in *Uzbekistan: obretenie novogo oblika* [Uzbekistan: The Acquisition of a New Image] vol. 1 (Moscow: Rossiiskiy Institut strategicheskikh Issledovaniy, 1998), 253.

26 Dina Malysheva, "Tsentral'naya Azia v kontekste afganskoy situatsii" [Central Asia in the Context of the Situation in Afghanistan], *Mirovaya ekonomika i mezhdunarodnye otnoshenia* [Global Economics and International Relations] 5 (2011): 3–16.

27 Gilles Dorronsoro, "Afghanistan: The Impossible Transition" Carnegie Papers, Carnegie Endowment for International Peace, June 2011, 1.

28 "Reintegration, Reconstruction, and Reconciliation: Recommendations From the Region" (Regional Network of Strategic Studies Centers Working Group on Reintegration, Reconstitution, and Reconciliation in Afghanistan, Kabul, October 2011).

29 Malysheva, "Central Asia in the Context of the Situation," 3–16.

30 Rashid, *Jihad: The Rise of Militant Islam*, 198.

31 T. Dzhumanaliev, "Grozyat li nam taliby?" [Does the Taliban Pose a Threat to Us?], *Nasha gazeta* (Bishkek), July 4, 1997.

32 Quoted from: Elena Sadovskaya, "Kazakhstan v Tsentral'noaziatskoy migratsionnoy subsisteme" [Kazakhstan in the Central Asian Migration Subsystem], in *Postsovetskie transformatsii: otrazhenie v migratsiyakh* [Post-Soviet Transformations: A Reflection in Migrations], ed. Zhanna Zajonchkovskaja and Galina Vitkovskaja (Moscow: Adamant, 2009), 21.

33 Ibid., 290.

34 K. Rogov, "Simmetrichnye zalozhniki" [Symmetrical Hostages], *Novaya Gazeta*, November 14, 2011, www.novayagazeta.ru/comments/49437.html.

35 Estimated using "World Population Data Sheet: 2010," Population Reference Bureau, www.prb.org.

36 As was mentioned by Elena Sadovskaya at the "Zakat trudovoy migratsii" [The Decline of Labor Migration] seminar in Bishkek on May 18–19, 2009.

37 Nikita Sergeev, "Tadjikskaya isteria: uroki na budushchee" [The Tajik Hysteria: Lessons for the Future], *Nezavisimaya Gazeta,* November 30, 2011.

38 "Gastarbaytery uvelichili perevody v Tadzhikistan do 3 milliardov dollarov" [Home Remittances From Tajik Guest Workers Reach 3 Billion Dollars], Lenta.ru, January 19, 2012, http://lenta.ru/news/2012/01/19/migrants.

39 Galina Kozhevnikova, "Under the Sign of Political Terror," in *Xenophobia, Freedom of Consciousness and Anti-Extremism in Russia in 2009* (Moscow: Sova, 2010), www.sova-center.ru/en/xenophobia/reports-analyses/2010/03/d18151.

40 Emil Pain, "Predvaritel'nye itogi evolyutsii natsional'nogo voprosa v Rossii" [Preliminary Results of the National Question's Evolution in Russia], in *Rossia*

1992–2008: itogi transformatsii [Russia 1992–2008: Results of Transformation] (Moscow: Altayskiy Forum, 2009), 133.

41 As was noted by Elena Sadovskaya at the "Zakat trudovoy migratsii" [The Decline of Labor Migration] seminar in Bishkek, May 18–19, 2009.

42 Alexandra Samarina, "Gastarbaytery ne podelili rabochie mesta" [Guest Workers Quarrel Over Employment], *Nezavisimaya Gazeta,* July 25, 2011.

43 Lyudmila Maksakova, "Uzbekistan v sisteme mezhdunarodnykh otnosheniy" [Uzbekistan in the System of International Relations], *Demoskop weekly*, no. 415–16 (March 22–April 4, 2010), www.demoscope.ru/weekly/2010/0415/analit03.php.

44 Sergeev, "The Tajik hysteria."

45 "Svoy sredi chuzhikh: Intervyu Konstantina Romodanovskogo Dmitriyu Serkovu" [At Home Among Strangers: Konstantin Romodanovsky's Interview by Dmitri Serkov], *Itogi* (October 24, 2011): 37.

46 Marina Lemutkina, "Zakon dlya santekhnikov" [Law for Plumbers], *Moskovskiy Komsomolets*, November 23, 2011.

47 Maksim Cherepanov, "Musul'manskoe soobshchestvo v politicheskom pole regiona: strukturno-geneticheskiy analiz strategiy aktivistov" [Muslim Community in the Region's Political System: A Structural and Genetic Analysis of Activists' Strategies] (Abstract of Candidate of Sciences' dissertation, Perm, 2010).

48 "V Rossii zaderjany dva terrorista iz zapreshchennoy gruppirovki 'Hizb ut-Takhrir'" [Two Hizb ut-Tahrir Terrorists Are Detained in Russia], Newsru.com, November 30, 2004, http://newsru.com/arch/russia/30nov2004/tahtir.html.

49 "Terror i otvetnye deystvia: analiz i monitoring" [Terrorism and Responses to It: Analysis and Monitoring], Agentura.ru Research Center, www.agentura.ru/?col=118id=1114442640.

50 "V Tatarstane budut primenyat' zhestkie mery k banditsko-salafitskim gruppirovkam" [Severe Measures Will Be Taken Against Salafi Gangs in Tatarstan], Interfax, January 25, 2012, www.interfax-religion.ru/islam/?act=news&div=43924.

51 "Uspekh zavisit ot kazhdogo: Intervyu nachal'nika Upravleniya FSB Rossii po Orenburgskoy oblasti Kharuna Karchaeva" [Success Depends on Each Person: Head of the Orenburg FSB Branch Kharun Karchaev's Interview], *Pervaya Redaktsia* (Orenburg), March 8–14, 2008.

52 "Zayavka o prevalirovanii v rossiyskikh mechetyakh imamov-tadjikov—dezinformatsiua" [The Statement That the Majority of Russian Imams Come From Tajikistan Is False], IslamRF.ru, October 11, 2011, www.islamrf.ru/news/russia/rusnews/18306. It must be noted that in an interview on Ozodi (Liberty) Radio, the head of the Union of Tajik Youth in Russia, Izzat Amon, talked about 80 percent of imams being Tajiks. This figure is not accurate.

53 Omar Nasiri, a member of the Taliban from Morocco, gives a detailed account of his experience with the "Islamic international" in the Taliban camps that he passed through. See Omar Nasiri, *Inside Jihad: My Life With Al Qaeda: A Spy's Story* (New York: Basic Books, 2006).

54 Martin Schuler, "Migration Patterns of the Population in Kyrgyzstan," *Espace Populations Sociétés*, 1 (2007): 73–89, http://eps.revues.org/1967.

55 In 2011, the dilapidated old Moscow mosque that had been built in 1905 was demolished by the order of Ravil Gaynutdin, the chairman of Russia's Muftis' Council. Believers still pray at the site of the old mosque while the new one is being built.

56 Author's recording of the Public Chamber's meeting on November 17, 2011.

57 "Muftiy Gainutdin vidit prichinu aktivnogo pritoka migrantov v Rossiyu v moral'nom razlozhenii korennogo naseleniya" [Mufti Gaynetdin Blames Mass Migration to Russia on Moral Corruption of the Locals], Interfax-Religion, December 16, 2010, www.interfax-religion.ru/?act=news&div=38749.

58 "Tadjikskie migranty postroili vo Vladivostoke mechet" [Tajik Migrants Have Built a Mosque in Vladivostok] Ozodi Radio, August 26, 2011, http://rus.ozodi.org/content/article/24308514.html.

59 Andrey Melnikov, "Migratsia politicheskogo islama" [Migration of Political Islam], *NG-Religii*, May 10, 2011.

60 Sergeev, "The Tajik Hysteria."

61 Ahmet Yarlikapov has repeatedly explained this process at conferences as well as to me in private conversations.

62 "Text: Obama' Speech in Cairo," *New York Times*, June 4, 2009, www.nytimes.com/2009/06/04/us/politics/04obama.text.html?pagewanted=all&_r=0.

CHAPTER 4

1 Charles Fairbanks, C. Richard Nelson, S. Frederic Starr, and Kenneth Weisbrode, *Strategic Assessment of Central Asia* (Washington, D.C.: Atlantic Council of the United States and Central Asia-Caucasus Institute, January 2001), 33.

2 Zhanaozen is considered the most ecologically dangerous and the most expensive city in Kazakhstan. The people who live there say that "Rather than going to hell, sinners from Zhanaozen have to return to Zhanaozen." See E. Kostyuchenko, "Zhanaozen," *Novaya Gazeta* 143, December 21, 2011, www.novayagazeta.ru/politics/50191.html.

3 E. Kostyuchenko, "Yurta – znak bedy" [Yurta—A Sign of Trouble], *Novaya Gazeta* 16, February 15, 2012, www.novayagazeta.ru/society/51048.html.

4 Konstantin Syroezhkin, "Sotsial'no-politicheskiy protsess v Kazakhstane (opyt rekonstruktsii)" [Social and Political Developments in Kazakhstan (An Attempt to Reconstruct Events)], in *Politicheskiy protsess v Tsentral'noy Azii* [The Political Process in Central Asia] (Moscow: IV RAN [Institute of Oriental Studies, Russian Academy of Sciences], Center for Strategic & Political Studies, 2011), 161.

5 Almaz Rysaliev, "Rost ugrozy islamizma v Kazakhstane" [The Growing Islamist Threat in Kazakhstan], IWPR (Institute for War & Peace Reporting), RCA Issue 662, November 14, 2011, http://iwpr.net/report-news/does-kazakhstan-attack-reflect-rising-militancy.

6   Dosym Satpayev, "Kazakhstan khotyat prevratit' v tylovuyu bazu dzhikhada" [They Want to Turn Kazakhstan Into the Jihad's Rear Base], http://svpressa.ru/politic/article/38858.

7   Rysaliev, "The Growing Islamist Threat in Kazakhstan."

8   Almaz Rysaliev, "Uzhestozhenie politiki kazakhstanskikh vlastey v otnoshenii religii" [The Toughening Stance of the Kazakhstan Government Toward Religion], IWPR (Institute for War & Peace Reporting), November 8, 2011.

9   Nurtai Mustafaev, "Politika i obshchestvo" [Politics and Society], January 13, 2012, www.dialog.kz.

10 Zhanbolat Mamyshev, "Pervyi kanal 'Evrazia'" [First Channel "Eurasia"], January 27, 2012.

11 Alexandra Kazakova, "Kazakhstan v ozhidanii peremen" [Kazakhstan in Anticipation of Changes], Tsentral'naya Azia [Central Asia], RCA issue 665 (January 11, 2012), http://red001.mail.microsoftonline.com/owa/?ae=Item&t=IPM.Note&id=RgAAAAC11S.

12 Syroezhkin, "Social and Political Developments in Kazakhstan," 114.

13 "Vybory v Kazakhstane ne sootvetstvuyut fundamental'nym demokraticheskim standartam" [Elections in Kazakhstan Do Not Meet Fundamental Democratic Principles], January 16, 2012, AII (Agency of International Information) Novosti-Kazakhstan, http://newskaz.ru/politics/20120116/2512816.html; "Kazakhstan's Parliamentary Vote, Though Well Administered, Did Not Meet Key Democratic Principles," OSCE Press release, January 15, 2012, www.osce.org/odihr/elections/86984.

14 Nikolai Kuzmin, "My izmenilis'" [We Have Changed], Ekspert Kazakhstana, January 2012.

15 Martha Brill Olcott, "Kazakhstan's Political (R)evolution," Commentary, Carnegie Endowment for International Peace, January 27, 2012), 1.

16 Rustem Falyakhov, "'Nam ne nado nichego risovat' i priukrashivat." Masimov rasskazal Gazete.Ru o rassledovanii v Zhanaozene" ["We Do Not Have to Embellish Anything." Masimov Spoke to Gazeta.ru About the Investigation of Events in Zhanaozen], Gazeta.ru, January 23, 2012, www.gazeta.ru/business/2012/01/23/3971289.shtml.

17 Roza Kudabaeva, "Sovetnik Nazarbayeva: chto izmenitsya posle Zhanaozena" [Nazarbayev's Advisor: What Will Change After Zhanaozen], BBC News, January 13, 2012, www.bbc.co.uk/russian/international/2012/01/120112_kazakh_president_advisor_zhanaozen.shtml

18 Andrej Loginov, "Chyi ushi torchat za sobytiyami v Zhanaozene?" [Whose Fingerprints Are All Over the Events in Zhanaozen?], Politika i obshchestvo [Politics and Society], January 13, 2012.

19 Murat Kabdenov, "Shok i trepet. Vol'gotnoe sushchestvovanie na zagranichnykh khlebakh dlya kazakhstanskoy oppozitsii zakanchivaetsya" [Shock and Awe. Kazakh Opposition's Comfortable Life on Foreign Money Comes to an End], January 24, 2012, www.centrasia.ru/newsA.php?st=1327431960.

20 "V 2011 godu inflyatsiya v Kazakhstane sostavila 7,4%" [Inflation in Kazakhstan Reached 7.4% in 2011], *Kazakhstanskaya Pravda*, January 10, 2012, www.kazpravda.kz/ c/1326179367.

21 Kazakova, "Kazakhstan in Anticipation of Changes."

22 Alisher Sagadiev, "Zagadochnaya zhiznestoikost' pravitel'stva" [The Mysterious Resilience of the Government] spik.kz, January 22, 2012, www.spik.kz/?lan=ru&id= 102&pub=2270&hil=алишер.

23 R. Amanova, "Neftegazovaya otrasl': strategiya ustoichivogo rosta. Ot eksporta syr'ya – do glubokoy pererabotki" [Oil and Gas Industry: A Sustained Growth Strategy. From Raw Material Exports to Deep Processing], *Kazakhstankaya Pravda*, December 30, 2011, www.kazpravda.kz/c/1325210464.

24 The structure of Kazakhstan's exports by major commodity groups.

25 Edward C. Chow, Leigh E. Hendrix, Mikkal E. Herberg, Shoichi Bo Kong, Marie Lall, and Paul Stevens, "Pipeline Politics in Asia: The Intersection of Demand, Energy Markets, and Supply Routes," NBR Special Report no. 23, National Bureau of Asian Research, September 2010, 10.

26 "Prezident Kazakhstana sformiruet novoe pravitel'stvo s uchetom 'faktora Zhanaozena'" [The President of Kazakhstan Will Form a New Government With the "Zhanaozen Factor" in Mind], *Politika i obshchestvo*, January 16, 2012, http://newskaz.ru/regions/ 20120113/2486301.html.

27 Daniil Kislov, "Zachem Nazarbayevu mnogopartiynyi parlament?" [Why Does Nazarbayev Want a Multi-Party Parliament?], slon.ru, January 16, 2011, http://slon.ru/ world/vybory_v_kazakhstane-731008.xhtml.

28 Syroezhkin, "Social and Political Developments in Kazakhstan," 150.

29 Vystuplenie Prezidenta RK Nursultana Nazarbayeva na otkrytii pervoy sessii Parlamenta 3-go sozyva [President Nursultan Nazarbayev's speech at the opening of the first session of the third convocation of Kazakhstan's Parliament], Astana, November 3, 2004, www.parlam.kz/ru/presidend-speech/5.

30 The author of this paper had the opportunity to attend this election as an observer. I remember how surprised all of my colleagues and I were by the official results. According to exit poll results released on election night and unofficial information from Nazarbayev's headquarters, less than 80 percent of the voters had voted for him. Why this result had to be adjusted upward remains unclear.

31 Syroezhkin, "Social and Political Developments in Kazakhstan," 153.

32 "'Vtoraya volna krizisa neizbezhna.' Premier Kazakhstana o programme novogo pravitel'stva" ["A New Wave of the Financial Crisis Is Inevitable." Kazakhstan's Prime Minister on the New Government's Program], *Kommersant*, January 23, 2012.

33 Makhmud Kasymbekov, "Rabochiy grafik prezidenta: osnovnye itogi 2011 goda" [The President's Working Schedule: Main Results of 2011], *Kazakhstanskaya Pravda*, January 10, 2012.

34 "Kazakhstan's GDP Grew by 5% in 2012," Forbes.kz, February 14, 2013, http://forbes.kz/ news/2013/02/14/newsid_19018.

35 Address by the President of the Republic of Kazakhstan, Leader of the Nation, N. Nazarbayev, "Strategy Kazakhstan-2050: New Political Course of the Established State," December 14, 2012, Official Site of the President of the Republic of Kazakhstan, www.akorda.kz/en/page/page_poslanie-prezidenta-respubliki-kazakhstan-n-nazarbaeva-narodu-kazakhstana-14-dekabrya-2012-g_1357813742.

36 Kazakhgate refers to the bribery scandal involving American businessman James Giffen, a former Nazarbayev adviser, who is accused of paying bribes to Nazarbayev and his prime minister in exchange for lucrative oilfield contracts.

37 "The President of Kazakhstan Will Form a New Government With the 'Zhanaozen factor' in Mind."

38 Dariga is Nazarbayev's adopted daughter. Her mother was his first wife.

39 "The President of Kazakhstan Will Form a New Government With the 'Zhanaozen factor' in Mind."

40 Martha Brill Olcott, *Kazakhstan: Unfulfilled Promise* (Washington, D.C.: Carnegie Endowment for International Peace, 2002), 220.

41 Falyakhov, "'We Do Not Have to Embellish Anything.' Masimov Spoke to Gazeta.ru."

42 "Pobeda partii Nazarbayeva obespechit kurs na postroenie Evraziyskogo soyuza— glava komiteta Gosdumy RF" [Nazarbaev Party Victory Will Shore Up the Plans for the Eurasian Union—the Duma Committee Chair] Regnum, January 16, 2012, www.regnum.ru/news/1488620.html.

43 "Kazakhstan dolzhen gotovit'sya k unifikatsii tarifov estestvennykh monopoly v ramkakh EEP—Masimov" [Kazakhstan Must Prepare for Tariff Unification for Natural Monopolies Under the Common Economic Space Framework—Masimov], AMN Novosti-Kazakhstan, January 21, 2010, www.newskaz.ru/economy/20100121/426055-print.html.

CHAPTER 5

1 Dmitry Medvedev's Meeting With Leading Russian and Foreign Political Analysts, transcript, September 10, 2010, http://eng.kremlin.ru/transcripts/919.

2 Ekaterina Ionova, "Itogi prezidentskikh vyborov v Kyrgyzii i perspektivy vstupleniya v TS" [The Results of the Presidential Election in Kyrgyzstan and the Prospects for the Country's Accession to the Customs Union], *Rossia i novye gosudarstva Evrazii* [Russia and the New States of Eurasia], IV (XIII) (2011): 75.

3 "Kyrgyzstan: U Novoy Vlasti Poyavilas' Ob'edinennaya Oppozitisiya" [Kyrgyzstan: The New Regime Now Has a Consolidated Opposition], Fergana International News Agency, February 4, 2012, www.fergananews.com/news.php?id=18087.

4 Aida Salyanova, "Pravda prevyshe vsego" [Truth Is Above All Else], Report.kg, www.report.kg/governance/8727.

5 "VVP Stran Posle Raspada SSSR" [The GDP of the Former Soviet Republics After the Collapse of the Soviet Union], trinixy.ru, November 18, 2011, http://trinixy.ru/64256-vvp-stran-posle-razvala-sssr-16-foto.html.

6 "Gosudarstvenny Dolg Kyrgyzstana Priblizhaetsya k Otmetke v $3 mlrd" [Kyrgyzstan's National Debt Is Nearing 3 Billion Dollars], Kant.kg, November 24, 2011, www.kant.kg./2011-11-24/gosudarstvennyj-dolg-kyrgyzstana.

7 Viktoriya Panfilova, "Moskva dast Bishkeku Shans" [Moscow Will Give Bishkek a Chance], Nezavisimaya Gazeta, February 20, 2012, www.ng.ru/cis/2012-02-20/6_bishkek.html.

8 Nur Omarov, "Kyrgyzskaya respublika. Iskhodnye uslovia transformatsii" [The Kyrgyz Republic. Initial Conditions for Transformation], in Politicheskiy protsess v Tsentral'noy Azii: Rezul'taty, Problemy, Perspektivy [The Political Process in Central Asia] (Moscow: IVRAN, TSSPI, 2011), 214.

9 Materialy obshchestvennogo obsuzhdenia "Bezrabotitsa v Kyrgyzskoy Respublike: ugrozy i puti ikh preodolenia" [Materials From the "Unemployment in Kyrgyzstan: Threats and Ways to Overcome Them" (public discussion)] in "Bezraboitsa—Eto Simptom Bolezni Pod Nazvaniem 'Slabost' Mestnogo Samoupravlenia'" [Unemployment Is a Symptom of a Disease Called "Weak Local Self-Government"], Development Policy Institute, April 18, 2011, www.dpi.kg/ru/news/full/239.html.

10 E. Ivashchenko, "OON: Okolo Milliona Kyrgyzstantsev Krugly God Ispytyvayut Nedostatok V Prodovol'stvii" [About a Million Kyrgyzstan Residents Experience Food Shortages All Year Long, the UN], Fergana International News Agency, January 31, 2012, www.fergananews.com/news.php?id=18060&mode=snews.

11 Kirgiziya v Reytinge Indeksa Razvitiya Chelovecheskogo Potentsiala – 2011 Zanyala 126-e Mesto" [Kyrgyzstan Is 126th According to the 2011 Human Development Index Data], Regnum, February 2, 2012, www.regnum.ru/news/1495006.html.

12 "Prezident Kirgizii Sokratit Raskhody Svoego Apparata Na 200 mln Somov" [Kyrgyzstan's President Is to Cut His Administration Expenses by 200 Million Som], Regnum, December 28, 2011, www.regnum.ru/news/1484464.html.

13 A. Hedfors, interview with Johan Engvall, Korruptsiya v Kirgizii—Ne Prosto Odna Iz Problem Gosudarstva. Korrutsiya I Est' Gosudarstvo!" [Corruption in Kyrgyzstan Is Not Simply One of the State's Problems. Corruption Is Essentially the State!], December 28, 2011, www.fergananews.com/article.php?id=7227.

14 I. Donis, Almazbek Atambayev:"U Kirgizii Net Drugogo Puti Krome Vkhozhdeniya v Tamozhenny Soyuz" [Kyrgyzstan Has No Other Way But to Enter the Customs Union, Almazbek Atambayev], News-Asia, December 29, 2011, www.news-asia.ru/view/ks/Press%20centre%20Russia/2290.

15 D. Denisenko, "Natsstatkom: V 2011 Godu Rost VVP Kyrgyzstana Sostavil 5,7%" [Kyrgyzstan's GDP Has Grown 5.7% in 2011, the National Statistics Committee], Vecherniy Bishkek, January 15, 2012, www.vb.kg/doc/175306_nacstatkom:_v_2011_gody_rost_vvp_kyrgyzstana_sostavil_57.html.

16 "Prezident Kirgizii Sokratit Raskhody Svoego Apparata Na 200 mln Somov" [Kyrgyzstan's President Is to Cut His Administration Expenses by 200 million som], Regnum, December 28, 2011, www.regnum.ru/news/1484464.html

17 The immediate cause of the conflict that led to ethnic clashes was the problem of the allocation of land for housing.

18 Ekaterina Ivashchenko, "Kyrgyzstan: deputaty ostalis' nedovol'ny, kak vypolnyayutsya ikh postanovlenia po iyun'skim sobytiyam" [Kyrgyzstan: The Deputies Are Not Satisfied With How Their Decrees With Regard to the June Events Are Being Fulfilled], Fergana International News Agency, February 2, 2012, www.fergananews.com/news.php?id= 18080.

19 E. Ivashchenko, "Natsional'naya Politika v Kyrgyzstane: Ot Bratskikh Narodov k Vrazhduyushchim Plemenam" [Kyrgyzstan's Ethnic Politics: From Brotherly Peoples to Warring Tribes], interview with Tatyana Vygovskaya, Fergana International News Agency, January 27, 2012, www.fergananews.com/articles/7255.

20 "Kyrgyzstan: Uzbeki, Torguyushchie na Rynke v Kara-Suu, Pozhalovalis' Prezidentu Na Vymogatel'stvo" [Kyrgyzstan: Uzbek Merchants at the Kara-Suu Market Complained of Extortion to the President], Fergana International News Agency, February 6, 2012, www.fergananews.com/news.php?id=18101.

21 Ekaterina Ivashchenko, "Kyrgyzstan: deputaty ostalis' nedovol'ny, kak vypolnyayutsya ikh postanovlenia po iyun'skim sobytiyam" [Kyrgyzstan: The Deputies Are Not Satisfied With How Their Decrees with Regard to the June Events Are Being Fulfilled], Fergana International News Agency, February 2, 2012, www.fergananews.com/news.php?id= 18080.

22 Ivashchenko, "Kyrgyzstan: Lawyers Are Beaten While the Supreme Court Pretends Nothing Is Happening."

23 "Kandidat v Prezidenty Kirgizii Prizyvaet Narod Otomstit' Russkim za 1916 God" [A Candidate for Kyrgyz Presidency Urges People to Take Revenge on the Russians for the Events of 1916], August 22, 2011, Rosbalt, www.rosbalt.ru/exussr/2011/ 08/22/881864.html.

24 "Grazhdanstvo Rossii v 2011 Godu Poluchili Bolee 37 Tysyach Grazhdan Kirgizii. Za Poslednie 20 Let – 485 Tysyach Chelovek" [Over 37,000 Kyrgyz Citizens Received Russian Citizenship in 2011. More Than 485,000 Became Citizens in the Last 20 Years], Fergana International News Agency, January 15, 2012, www.fergananews.com/ news.php?id=17941.

25 E. Ivashchenko, "Kirgizskiy Uchi, Tebe Govoryat!" [Learn Kyrgyz, I Am Telling You!], Fergana International News Agency, January 23, 2012, www.fergananews.com/ articles/7249.

26 Ibid.

27 "Prezident Kirgizii: Mne Obidno, Chto v Sostave Pravitel'stva Net Ni Odnogo Russkogo" [I Am Upset That There Is Not a Single Russian in the Government—Kyrgyzstan's President], Regnum, December 30, 2011, www.regnum.ru/news/1485285.html.

28 E. Ivashchenko, "V Kyrgyzstane Obsudili Opasnost' Netraditsionnykh Religiy" [Danger Posed by Non-traditional Religions Was Discussed in Kyrgyzstan], Fergana International News Agency, December 15, 2011, www.fergananews.com/articles/7209.

29 Subsequently coordination of actions aimed at repelling the militants was criticized by both sides.

30 "V Kirgizii Monitoryat Natsional'nuyu Set' Interneta Na Predmet Ekstremizma" [Kyrgyzstan Is Monitoring Its Internet for Extremism], *Nezavisimaya Gazeta*, April 18, 2012, www.ng.ru/cis/2012-04-18/7_kirgizia.html.

31 Vitaly Naumkin, *Radical Islam in Central Asia* (Lanham, Md.: Rowman & Littlefield Publishers, 2005), 178.

32 Leonid Vasiliev, "Osobennosti bor'by s terrorizmom v Tsentral'noy Azii v sovremennykh usloviyakh" [The Peculiarities of Fighting Terrorism in Modern Central Asia], in *Mirovye derzhavy v Tsentral'noy Azii* [Global Powers in Central Asia], Sergey Luzyanin, ed. (Moscow: Institute of Far Eastern Studies, RAS, 2011), 190.

33 Nur Omarov, *Kyrgyzstan—2025: obrazy politicheskogo budushchego; Kyrgyzstan—2025: Strategii i stsenarii razvitiya* [Kyrgyzstan—2025: Possible Political Outcomes; Kyrgyzstan—2025: Strategies and Development Scenarios] (Bishkek: International Institute for Strategic Studies Under the President of Kyrgyzstan, Friedrich Ebert Stiftung, 2005), 54, http://kak.znate.ru/pars_docs/refs/10/9096/9096.pdf.

34 E. Ivashchenko, "Kyrgyzstan: Atambayev Obeshchaet Reshat' Problemy Yazyka, Korruptsii I Prisutstviya SShA" [Kyrgyzstan: Atambayev Promises to Solve Problems of Language, Corruption, and the U.S. Presence], Fergana International News Agency, December 29, 2011, www.fergananews.com/news.php?id=17877.

35 "Rossiysko-kyrgyzstanskoe sotrudnichestvo" [Russian-Kyrgyz Cooperation], *Novosti Sodruzhestva nezavisimykh gosudarstv* [News of the Commonwealth of Independent States], www.cisnews.org/analytics/1810-rossiysko-kyrgyzskoe-sotrudnichestvo.html.

36 Russian Trade Mission in Kyrgyzstan, http://torgpredkg.ru/index.php?option=com_content&view=article&id=1607Itemid=64.

37 "Rossiya Podarila Pogranichnikam Kyrgyzstana Komplekt Voennoy Tekhniki na Summu v Polmilliarda Rubley" [Russia Has Given the Kyrgyz Border Troops Military Hardware Worth 500,000 Million Rubles], Fergana International News Agency, January 18, 2012, www.fergananews.com/news.php?id=17976.

38 K. Latukhina, "Troystvenny vizit" [A Tripartite Visit], *Rossiyskaya Gazeta*, March 22, 2012, www.rg.ru/2012/03/21/putin.html.

39 T. Sulaimanov, "Chemodan bez ruchki" [Hand Luggage Without a Handle], February 16, 2012, www.gezitter.org/politic/8917.

40 "Putin i Nazarbayev 'prigrozili' kyrgyzskomu pravitel'stvu" [Putin and Nazarbayev Have "Threatened" the Kyrgyz Government], Gezitter.org, August 18, 2011, www.gezitter.org/politic/4376.

41 Grigorii Mikhailov, "Bilbordy s Putinym v Kyrgyzii zapreshcheny" [Billboards With Putin Are Prohibited in Kyrgyzstan], *Nezavisimaya Gazeta*, July 27, 2011, 6.

42 G. Turdaliyev, "Melis Myrzakmatov, mer goroda Osh: 'Ya Ne Khotel Predat' Kyrgyzskiy Narod I Uiti V Samoe Tragicheskoe , Slozhnoe Vremya Istorii'" ["I Did Not Want to Betray the Kyrgyz People and Leave in the Most Tragic and Hardest Moment in History," Osh Mayor Melis Myrzakmatov], Maidan.kg, no.1, 2, 5, February 1, 2012, www.gezitter.org/politic/8648_melis_myirzakmatov_mer_goroda_osh_ya_ne_hotel_predat_kyirgyizskiy_narod_i_uyti_v_samoe_tragicheskoe_slojnoe_vremya_istorii.

43 "Kyrgyzstan: Atambayev obeshchaet reshat' problemy yazyka, korruptsii i prisutstvia SShA" [Atambayev Promises to Solve Problems of Language, Corruption, and the U.S. Presence], Fergana International News Agency, February 1, 2012.

44 Alexander Knyazev, "Bishkek menyaet napravlenie" [Bishkek Is Changing Direction], interview to the Voice of Russia Radio, https://red001.mail.microsoftonline.com/owa?ae=Item&t=IPM.Note&id=AAAACIIS.

45 Grigorii Mikhailov, "Snachala 'Dastan,' potom – kredit" ["Dastan" First, Then a Loan], *Nezavisimaya Gazeta,* March 21, 2011, 7.

46 "Bazu VVS SShA vyvedem v 2014 godu" [We Will Remove the U.S. Air Base in 2014], Rosbalt, www.rosbalt.ru/exussr/2011/08/12/878759.html.

47 "Reshayushchiy khod vo vneshney politike" [The Decisive Move in Foreign Policy], Geziter.org, February 22, 2012, www.gezitter.org/politic/9121.

48 "Kyrgyzstan poluchil ot voennykh SShA $1,4 mlrd za 10 let prebyvaniya na baze "Manas" [Kyrgyzstan Received $1.4 Billion From the U.S. Military for Its Presence at Manas Air Base], Fergana International News Agency, December 21, 2011, www.fergananews.com/news.php?id=17840.

49 Chris Rickleton, "Kyrgyzstan: China's Economic Influence Fostering Resentment," Eurasianet, www.eurasianet.org/node/63383.

50 "Zhoomart Otorbayev: Intellektual'ny Kapital—Budushchee Kyrgyzstana" [Intellectual Capital Is Kyrgyzstan's Future—Zhoomart Otorbayev], "Azzatyk" radio, April 17, 2011, http://rus.azattyk.org/content/kyrgyzstan_economy_otorbaev/3444399.html.

51 O. Sidorov, "Geopoliticheskie Interesy Kitaya v Tsentral'noy Azii" [China's Geopolitical Interests in Central Asia], Gazeta.kz, December 13, 2004, http://articles.gazeta.kz/art.asp?aid=53686.

52 "V Kyrgyzstane Otkroyut Tsentr Po Obucheniyu I Orientirovaniyu Spetsialistov, Zhelayushchikh Rabotat' v Katare" [A Center That Will Prepare Specialists Willing to Work in Qatar Is to Open in Kyrgyzstan], Kabar.kg, March 6, 2012, www.kabar.kg/rus/society/full/29053.

53 "Prezidenty Kyrgyzstana I Turzii Podpisali Deklaratsiyu o Novom Istoricheskom Etape vo Vzaimootnosheniyakh" [Kyrgyz and Turkish Presidents Sign a Declaration on the New Historic Stage in Bilateral Relations], Fergana International News Agency, January 13, 2012, www.fergananews.com/news.php?id=17925.

54 "Dvustoronnie Otnosheniya Kirgizii i Kazakhstana Obsudili v Bishkeke Premiery Stran" [Kyrgyz and Kazakh Prime Ministers Discuss Bilateral Relations in Bishkek], Information Agency "News-Kazakhstan," September 16, 2011, www.newskaz.ru/economy/20110916/1900430.html.

55 N. Asanbaev, "Babanova Astana vstretila tsvetami, a Atambayeva kto vstretil?"
    [Astana Met Babanov With Flowers But Who Met Atambayev?] *ZhanyOrdo*, no. 6,
    March 2, 2012, www.gezitter.org/politic/9393_babanova_astana_vstretila_s_
    tsvetami_a_atambaeva_kto_vstretil.

56 Isak Karachev, "Premier Prizval Narod k Edinstvu" [The Prime Minister Urges People
    to Unite], kerege.kg, no.5, February 29, 2012, 3, www.gezitter.org/politic/9272_
    premer_prizval_narod_k_edinstvu.

57 A. Hedfors, "Korruptsiya v Kirgizii—ne prosto odna iz problem gosudarstva.
    Korruptsiya i est' gosudarstvo!" [Corruption in Kyrgyzstan Is Not Simply One of the
    State's Problems. Corruption Is Essentially the State!], Fergana International News
    Agency, December 28, 2011, www.fergananews.com/article.php?id=7227.

CHAPTER 6

1   "Demograficheskie posledstvia etnicheskikh i regional'nykh konfliktov v SNG" [The
    Demographic Consequences of Ethnic and Regional Conflicts in the CIS], *Naselenie
    i obshchestvo* [Population and Society], 27 (April 1997); A. Niyazi, "Tajikistan:
    Regional'nye aspekty konflikta (1990-e gg.)" [Tajikistan: Regional Aspects of the
    Conflict (1990s)], in *Etnicheskie i regional'nye konflikty v Evrazii*, Kniga 1, *Tsentral'naya
    Azia i Kavkaz* [Ethnic and Regional Conflicts in Eurasia, Book 1: Central Asia and the
    Caucasus] (Moscow: Ves Mir, 1997), 52.

2   A. Lyakhovsky and V. Nekrasov, *Grazhdanin, politik, voin* [Citizen, Politician, Soldier]
    (Moscow, 2007), 270.

3   Zakon Respubliki Tajikistan "Ob uporiadochenii traditsiy, torzhestv i obriadov v
    Respublike Tajikistan" [The Law of the Republic of Tajikistan on the Streamlining
    of Traditions, Celebrations, and Ceremonies in the Republic of Tajikistan], http://cis-
    legislation.com/document.fwx?rgn=17482.

4   M. Yanovskaya, "Tajikistan: v chest' 100-letia pechati zhurnalistov reshili ne sazhat'"
    [Tajikistan: 100th Anniversary of the Press Gets Journalists Let Off Going to Prison],
    Fergana International News Agency, November 3, 2012, www.fergananews.com/
    article.php?id=7308&print=1.

5   S. Shermatova, "Chto proiskhodit v Tajikistane i kak k etomu sleduyet otnositsya?"
    [What is Happening in Tajikistan and How Should We View It?], Fergana International
    News Agency, November 17, 2010, www.fergananews.com/article.php?id=6801.

6   Tilav Rasul-zade, "Tajikistan: Verbovka Molodykh Smertnikov Prodolzhaetsya"
    [Tajikistan: The Recruitment of Young Suicide Attackers Continues], Fergana
    International News Agency, November 3, 2010, www.fergananews.com/article.php?id=
    6787.

7   Ibid.

8   Farukh Ismanov, "Vernut' migrantov" [Return the Migrants], *Oazis*, no. 1 (165) (January 2012).

9   Reference to founder of the Hanafi school, 8–9th century theologian and jurist Abu Hanifah.

10 Some mosques were closed for purely economic reasons as well, when some communities, especially those in rural areas, could not raise the funds needed for their upkeep.

11 A. Dubnov, "Tajikistan: Novaya oppozitsia staromu prezidentu" [Tajikistan: A New Opposition for an Old President], *Rossia v globalnoy politike* [Russia in Global Politics], no. 2 (March-April 2011): 134–37.

12 D. Sariyev, "Stabil'naya nestabilnost'" [Stable Instability] *Oazis*, no. 24 (164) (December, 2011).

13 Nikolay Luchinsky, "Rogun, Korruptsiya … I Drugie Bedy Tajikskogo Naroda" [Rogun, Corruption … and Other Woes of the Tajik People], tjknews.com, June 8, 2012, http://tjknews.com/?p=1497.

14 From http://tjknews.com/?p=2060; the article and comments have since been deleted.

15 Shermatova, "What Is Happening?"

16 *Tajikistan Country Report*, www.gfmag.com/gdp-data-country-reports/165-tajikistan-gdp-country-report.html#axzz1qsiT82UH.

17 One reason for the brutality of the civil war was the shortage of land. Whole families were slaughtered, and their plots of land taken over by new owners.

18 "Tajikistan: Rogunskuyu GES Poatroyat Na Den'gi Nishchayushchego Naseleniya?" [Tajikistan: Will Tajikistan's Poverty-Stricken Population Pay for Building Rogun Hydroelectric Power Plant?], Fergana International News Agency, November 13, 2009, www.fergananews.com/news.php?id=13429.

19 Viktoriya Panfilova, "Dushanbe oboshel Tashkent na afganskom povorote" [Tashkent Bypassed Dushanbe at the Afghan Turn], *Nezavisimaya Gazeta*, August 4, 2011, 6.

20 "Macroeconomic Digest," Eurasian Development Bank, January 12–18, 2012, www.eabr.ru/general//upload/docs/publication/digest/macroeconomic/2012/macroeconomic_digest_20120118.pdf.

21 Payrav Chorshanbiyev, "Zolotovalyutny Zapas Tajikistana Sostavlyaet $801.6 mln" [Tajikistan's Gold and Foreign Currency Reserves Are $801.6 Million], January 19, 2012, http://news.tj/ru/news/zolotovalyutnyi-zapas-tadzhikistana-sostavlyaet-8016-mln.

22 Mariya Yanovskya, Dododzhon Atovulloyev: "Ya Ushel iz Sklifa—Tam Bylo Nebezopasno" [I Left Sklif (the Sklifosovsky Medical Facility)—It Wasn't Safe There], Fergana International News Agency, January 31, 2012, www.fergananews.com/article.php?id=7260.

23 Maxim Gusarov, "Sindrom priobretennogo tajikidefitsita" [Acquired Tajik-Deficiency Syndrome], Eurasia Center, February 23, 2011.

24 Rakhim Masov, *Aktual'nye problemy istoriografii i istorii tajikskogo naroda* [Current Issues in the Historiography and History of the Tajik People] (Dushanbe, 2005), 227.

25 Vladimir Georgiev, "Tajikistan: Rossiyskoe oruzhie sdelaet rezhim Rahmonova bolee deesposobnym" [Tajikistan: Russian Arms Will Make the Rahmonov Regime More Functional], Fergana International News Agency, November 10, 2007, www.fergananews.com/article.php?id=5396.

26 Andrey Kazantsev, "Rossiyskaya voennaya baza v Tajikistane nuzhna dlya obespechenia bezopasnosti prezhde vsego samogo Tajikistana" [The Russian Military Base in Tajikistan Will Contribute, Above All, to the Security of the Country Itself], Russian International Affairs Council, http://russiancouncil.ru/?id4=234.

27 "Ne stoit otnosit'sya k FMS kak k silovomu vedomstvu. Interv'yu glavy FMS Konstantina Romodanovskogo" [The Federal Migration Service Should Not Be Treated as a Law Enforcement Agency. Interview with the Head of the FMS Konstantin Romodanovsky], *Novaya Gazeta*, April 11, 2012.

28 Cross-Media, March 29, 2012. According to other sources, the Tajiks send from $3.5 billion to $4 billion home, which accounts to 30–35 percent of the country's GDP. A Euromoney Institutional Company.

29 Saodat Olimova and Muzaffar Olimov, "Migranty iz Tajikistana na fone krizisa" [Migrants From Tajikistan Against the Background of the Crisis], *Druzhba Narodov* [The Peoples' Friendship] (Moscow), no. 7 (2010): 156; (RiMM 109 no. 11 [2010]).

30 D. Sariyev, "Vse vozmozhnye soyuzy" [All Possible Alliances], *Oazis*, 23 (163) (December 2011).

31 Gusarov, "Acquired Tajik-Deficiency Syndrome."

32 "Kuda idut kitajskie investitsii?" [Where Do Chinese Investments Go?], *Nezavisimoe Mnenie*, December 29, 2011, http://nm.tj/economy/1339-kuda-idut-kitayskie-investicii.html.

33 "Kitay Vydelil Tadzhikistanu $19 mln Bezvozmezdnoy Pomoshchi" [China Grants Tajikistan $19 Million of Non-Repayable Aid], Regnum, June 16, 2011, www.regnum.ru/news/1415638.html.

34 V. Paramonov, A. Strokov, and O. Stolpovskii, "Ekonomicheskoe prisutstvie Kitaya v Tajikistane" [China's Economic Presence in Tajikistan], in *Vremya Vostoka*, June 18, 2009, available at www.centrasia.ru/news.php?st=1245820920.

35 Ibid.

36 "Rahmon I Hu Jintao Obmenyalis' Poslaniyami: Pogloshchaet li Kitay Tajikistan?" [Rahmon and Hu Jintao Exchange Messages: Is China Devouring Tajikistan?], Regnum, January 5, 2012, www.regnum.ru/news/fd-abroad/polit/1485894.html.

37 Marat Laumulin, "SShA ukreplyayut svoi pozitsii v Turkmenistane i Tajikistane" [The U.S. Is Strengthening Its Positions in Turkmenistan and Tajikistan], *Tsentral'naya Azia i Kavkaz* [Central Asia and the Caucasus] (Luleå, Sweden) vol.13, Issue 4 (2010): 57.

38 "Blake: SShA Ne Planiruyut Otkryvat' Bazy v Tsentral'noy Azii" [Blake: The U.S Is Not Planning to Open Military Bases in Central Asia], Asia-Plus, December 3, 2011, http://news.tj/ru/news/bleik-ssha-ne-planiruyut-otkryvat-bazy-v-tsentralnoi-azii.

39 "SShA Mozhet Vdvoye Uvelichit' Voennuyu Pomoshch' Tajikistanu" [The U.S. May Double Its Military Aid to Tajikistan] Asia-Plus, February 15, 2012, http://news.tj/ru/news/ssha-mozhet-vdvoe-uvelichit-voennuyu-pomoshch-tadzhikistanu.

40 Arkadij Dubnov, "Byt' so svoim partnerom" [To Be With Your Own Partner], *Moskovskie novosti*, April 18, 2012.

41 Tilav Rasul-zade, "Uzbekistan Proignoriroval Otkrytie Tamozhennogo Posta "Patar" Na Granitse s Tajikistanom" [Uzbekistan Ignores the Opening of Patar Customs Checkpoint at the Tajik Border], Fergana International News Agency, July 4, 2011, www.fergananews.com/article.php?id=7007.

42 Sorbon Turaev, "Kak god nachnesh'..." [The Way You Start a Year...] *Oazis*, 02 (January 2012).

43 Efim Malitikov, "Epokha utopicheskikh proektov kanula v letu" [The Era of Utopian Projects Has Passed], *Federal'naya gazeta* (Moscow), no. 06–07 (157–158) (July 2011).

44 Rasul-zade, "Uzbekistan Has Ignored the Opening of the 'Patar' Border Crossing Point with Tajikistan."

45 Niyazi Aziz, "Tajikistan: sovremennye tendentsii razvitia (politika, ekonomika, kul'tura)" [Tajikistan: Current Development Tendencies (Politics, Economics, and Culture)], in *Sotsial'naya spetsifika razvitia politicheskoy kul'tury v Tsentral'noy Azii* [Political Culture in Central Asia: The Social Dimension], eds. P. Linke and V. V. Naumkin (Moscow: TSSPI, 2009), 80.

CHAPTER 7

1 Shokhrat Kadyrov, *Natsia plemen* [Nation of Tribes] (Moscow: Centre for Civilizational and Regional Studies of the Russian Academy of Sciences, 2003).

2 Paul Kubicek, "Regionalism, Nationalism and Realpolitik in Central Asia," *Europe-Asia Studies* 49, 4 (1997): 644.

3 "Kaspiyskiy Tupik" [Caspian Dead-End], www.gundogar.org/?0212051210300000000000013000000.

4 *Vneshnyaya politika neytral'nogo Turkmenistana. Rechi, interv'yu prezidenta Turkmenistana Saparmurata Turkmenbashi* [Neutral Turkmenistan's Foreign Policy: Speeches and Interviews With President of Turkmenistan Saparmurat Turkmenbashi] (Ashgabat: 1999), 140.

5 M. Salamatov, "Kto khozyain v Turkmenistane?" [Who's the Boss in Turkmenistan?], *Erkin Turkmenistan,* (Moscow), no. 4 (May 2000): 34–36.

6 The opposition and the media reacted to the "Turkmenbashi" title by coming up with the term "bashism" as a definition for the semi-oriental, semi-communist regime.

7 Vadim Trukhachev, "Turkmeniya: Mif o Perestroyke Razveyan" [Turkmenistan: Perestroika Myth Debunked], Pravda.ru, February 13, 2012, www.pravda.ru/world/formerussr/other/13-02-2012/1107865-turkmen-0.

8 Sebastien Peyrouse, *Turkmenistan. Strategies of Power, Dilemmas of Development* (Armonk, NY and London: M. E. Sharpe, 2012), 108, 114.

9 "Zakon Turkmenistana O Politicheskikh Partiyakh" [Turkmenistan's Law on Political Parties], www.turkmenistan.gov.tm/?id=764.

10 One view is that his opponents in the elections were chosen from among representatives of the country's main economic sectors and some of its regions.

11 "Turkmeniya Vozvrashchaetsya Vo Vremena Niyazova, Schitayut Eksperty" [Turkmenistan Is Back to Niyazov's Times, Experts], RIA Novosti, February 13, 2012, http://ria.ru/world/20120213/564571584.html.

12 Atayev was arrested on charges of inciting inter-clan hostility and in connection with murky circumstances in his family life. In reality, under the constitution, after Niyazov's death Atayev should have been acting president until the election. This would have made him Berdimuhamedov's rival, and thus he had to be removed from political competition.

13 "Vystuplenie Prezidenta Gurbanguly Berdimuhamedova na Vstreche s Deputatami Medzhlisa Turkmenistana" [President Gurbangula Berdimuhamedov Speaks at the Meeting With Turkmenistan's Mejlis], *Turkmenistan—Zolotoy Vek*, January 11, 2012, www.turkmenistan.gov.tm/?id=550.

14 "Berdimuhamedov-mladshiy Pytaetsya Otobrat' Biznes, Prinadlezhashchiy Synu Pokoinogo Turkmenbashi" [Berdimuhamedov Junior Is Trying to Take Away the Business Belonging to the Son of the Late Turkmenbashi], centrasia.ru, May 11, 2012, www.centrasia.ru/newsA.php?st=1336715700.

15 "Turkmenskiy akademik dokazyval aziatskoe proiskhozhdenie atstekov i vikingov" [Turkmen Academic Tried to Prove the Asian Origins of the Aztecs and Vikings], *Khronika Turkmenistana* [Turkmenistan Chronicle] (Published by the Turkmenistan Initiative for Human Rights), www.chrono-tm.org/2012/05aziatskoe-proishozhdenie-atstekov-i-vikingov.

16 Rumor has it that the song was written by someone else.

17 S. M. Demidov, *Sufizm v Turkmenistane* [Sufism in Turkmenistan] (Ashgabat: Ilym, 1978), 157.

18 *Islam i politicheskaya bor'ba v stranakh SNG* [Islam and Political Struggles in the CIS Countries], ed. Alexander Verkhovsky (Moscow: August, 1992), 29.

19 V. A. Kulagin, "Neftegazovyi kompleks Turkmenistana" [Turkmenistan's Oil and Gas Sector], *Gazovaya Promyshlennost'* 667, December 2011, www.gas-journal-ru/gij_detailed_work_php?GIJ_ELEMENT_ID=43398&W.

20 "Turkmenistan's Oil and Gas Sector," *Gas Industry Journal*, January 13, 2012.

21 Innokenty Adyasov, "Konets turkmenskogo gazovogo blefa" [The End of Turkmenistan's Gas Bluff], *INFOLine—Natural gas*.

22 "Turkmenistan's Oil and Gas Sector."

23 "India poluchila dostup k turkmenskomu gazu" [India Gets Access to Turkmenistan's Gas], *Izvestia*, May 24, 2012.

24 "The Private Pocket of the President (Berdymukhamedov): Oil, Gas and the Law," Crude Accountability, October 2011, http://crudeaccountability.org/wp-content/uploads/2012/04/20111016-PrivatePocketPresidentBerdymukhamedov.pdf.

25 Oleg Lukin, "Turkmenistan: Strana, Gde Otmenen Sever" [Turkmenistan: The Country Where North Is Abolished], Neftegazovaya Vertikal 3, 2012, www.ngv.ru/upload/iblock/1da/1daee8f5344f297a8d4b9441a43564cf.pdf.

26 Mikhail Sheinkman, "Gaz dovel Ashgabat do Kieva" [Gas Takes Ashgabat to Kiev], www.gundogar.org/?021205122540000000000013000000.

27 If the Southern Stream project goes into operation, Ukraine's importance as a transit country for Russia would diminish, and gas prices could drop.

28 "The Private Pocket of the President (Berdymukhamedov): Oil, Gas and the Law," Crude Accountability, October 2011, http://crudeaccountability.org/wp-content/uploads/2012/04/20111016-PrivatePocketPresidentBerdymukhamedov.pdf.

29 Pavel Lobkov, "Zhurnalist Arkady Dubnov: Solntse Berdimuhamedova Budet Svetit' Dolgo" [Berdimuhamedov's Sun Will Be Shining for a Long Time—Journalist Arkady Dubnov], Gundogar, February 12, 2012, www.gundogar.org/?02340512166000000000000013000000.

CHAPTER 8

1 "Kyrgyzstan i Uzbekistan: taktika vyzhivania dlya slabogo soseda" [Kyrgyzstan and Uzbekistan: The Tactics of Survival for the Weak Neighbor], AKI Press Special Report, April 1999.

2 See Politicheskie partii I Dvizheniya Uzbekistana [Political Parties and Movements of Uzbekistan] (Tashkent: Jahon Information Agency, 1997), 194.

3 Yadgor Norbutaev, "Uzbekistan: Chto pod naperstkami u Islama Karimova?" [Uzbekistan: What Does Islam Karimova Have Under the Shells of His Shell Game?], Fergana International News Agency, December 8, 2011, www.fergananews.com/article.php?id=7203.

4 Yadgor Norbutaev, "SShA-Uzbekistan: Islam Karimov skazal imenno to, chto khotela uslyschat' Hillari Klinton" [Uzbekistan: Islam Karimov Said Exactly What Hillary Clinton Wanted to Hear], Fergana International News Agency, October 23, 2011, www.fergananews.com/article.php?id=7143.

5 Timur Yusupov, "Ne vremya dlya Demokratii. Pochemu v Tsentralnoy Azii vryad li poyavitsya svoy Navalnyy" [Not the Time for Democracy. Why Central Asia Will Not Get Its Own Navalny], Oazis 166, no. 2 (January 2012).

6 See "Global Download Study," ChartsBin, http://chartsbin.com/view/2484.

7 International Crisis Group, The Failure of Reform in Uzbekistan: Ways Forward for the International Community, International Crisis Group Asia Report, no. 76, March 11, 2004, 5, www.crisisgroup.rg/en/regions/asia/central-asia/uzbekistan/076-the-failure-of-reform-in-uzbekistan-ways-forward-for-the-international-community.aspx.

8 Sultan Khamadov, "Ot togo, kak budut stroit' v Uzbekistane otnoshenia s oppozitsiey, zavisit situatsia v regione" [The Situation in the Region Will Depend on How Relations With the Opposition in Uzbekistan Will Be Built], *Biznes & Politika* (Dushanbe), September 15, 2000.

9 "Deyania praviteley v Uzbekistane" [The Actions of the Rulers in Uzbekistan]. Quoted from: Vitaliy Ponomaryov, *Islam Karimov protiv Hizb Ut-Tahrir* [Islam Karimov vs. Hizb ut-Tahrir] (Moscow: Pravozashchitny Zentr "Memorial," 1999), 39.

10 There are different versions of the reasons for the attack. Version one is that it was a consequence of inter-clan strife, and version two is that it helped further strengthen the power of the president.

11 The Union of Islamic Jihad, formerly known as the Islam Jihad, took responsibility for the act.

12 Kamoliddin Rabbimov, "Respublika Uzbekistan. Religia" [The Republic of Uzbekistan. Religion], in *Tsentral'naya Evrazia. 2009. Analiticheskiy Ezhegodnik* [Central Eurasia. 2009. Analytical Yearbook] (Sweden: CA&CC, 2010), 395.

13 Islam Karimov, *Uzbekistan na poroge 21 veka: ugrozy bezopasnosti, uslovia i garantii progressa* [Uzbekistan on the Threshold of the 21st Century: Threats to Security, the Conditions and Guarantees of Progress] (Tashkent: Uzbekiston, 1997), 47.

14 *Srednyaya Azia: andijanskiy stsenariy* [Central Asia: The Andijan Scenario] (Moscow: Europe Publishers, 2005), 108.

15 Martha Brill Olcott, *In the Whirlwind of Jihad* (Washington, D.C.: Carnegie Endowment for International Peace, 2012), 305.

16 Central Asia: The Andijan Scenario, 8.

17 "Podtverzhdennye Zapasy Nefti Uzbekistana po Itogam 2011 Goda Otsenivayutsya v Razmere 0,1 mlrd tonn (0,6 mlrd barelley) I Gaza – 1,6 mlrd kubicheskikh metrov" [Uzbekistan's Confirmed 2011 Oil Reserves Are Estimated to Be 0.1 Billion Tons (0.6 Billion Barrels). The Country's Gas Reserves Amount to 1.6 Billion Cubic Meters], OLAM.uz, June 18, 2012, http://news.olam.uz/economica/10180.html.

18 Ulugbek Olimov, Yadgar Fayzullaev, "Assessing Development Strategies to Achieve the MDGs in the Republic of Uzbekistan," Country Study, United Nations Department for Social and Economic Affairs, March 2011, www.un.org/en/development/desa/policy/capacity/output_studies/roa87_study_uzb.pdf.

19 "Uzbekistan Vozglavil Reyting Samykh Korrumpirovannykh Stran" [Uzbekistan Tops the Most Corrupt Countries List], Lenta.ru, February 14, 2012, lenta.ru/news/2012/02/14/corruption. Another source suggests that Uzbekistan is 151 out of 164 countries in terms of corruption. See Kathleen Collins, "Economic and Security Regionalism Among Patrimonial Authoritarian Regimes: The Case of Central Asia," *Europe-Asia Studies* [Glasgow] 61, no. 2 (March 2009): 263.

20 Hsiu-Ling Wu & Chien-Hsun Chen, "The Prospects for Regional Economic Integration Between China and the Five Central Asian Countries," *Europe-Asia Studies* 56, no. 7b (November 2004): 1074.

21 Daniil Kislov, "Uzbekistan: president Karimov vydal vizu inostrannym investoram" [Uzbekistan: President Karimov Issued a Visa to Foreign Investors], Fergana News, www.fergananews.com/article.php?id=7332.

22 "Uroven' Bezrabotitsy v Uzbekistane Sostavlyaet 5%" [Unemployment Is at 5% in Uzbeskistan], UzDaily.uz, www.uzdaily.uz/articles-id-11007.htm.

23 Mikhail Bushuev, "Kazhdiy Tretiy v Uzbekistane Bez Raboty" [Every Third Person Is Unemployed in Uzbekistan], Uzbekinfo.org, April 23, 2006, http://rus.at.ua/news/2006-04-23-45.

24 A. Gevorkyan, "Sosedyam Na Zhizn' i Detyam Na Uchebu" [For Neighbors' Living Expenses and Children's Tuition], *Novye Izvestiya*, June 8, 2012, www.newizv.ru/economics/2012-06-08/164704-sosedjam-na-zhizn-i-detjam-na-uchebu.html.

25 Abdul Salimov, "Vmesto ottepeli—merzlota" [Instead of a Thaw, Frozen Ground], *Oazis* 164, no. 24 (December 2011).

26 Maksim Beylis, "Uzbekistan: god krepkoy yacheiki" [Uzbekistan: The Year of a Strong Family], June 5, 2012, www.centrasia.ru/newsA.php?st=1338879120.

27 Ibid.

28 "Uzbekistanu grozyat golod i bezrabotitsa?" [Is Uzbekistan Threatened by Hunger and Unemployment?], SNGdaily, http://Sngdaily.ru/2011/11/22/uzbekistanu-groziat-golod-bezrabotica.html.

29 Ruth Deyeremond, "Matrioshka Hegemony? Multi-leveled Hegemonic Competition and Security in Post-Soviet Central Asia," *Review of International Studies* 35 (2009): 168.

30 Pavel K. Baev, "Turning Counter-Terrorism Into Counter-Revolution," in *European Security* (Oslo: International Peace Research Institute, 2006), 7.

31 Yadgor Norbutaev, "Bronezhilet dlya Karimova" [A "Bullet-Proof Vest" for Karimov], Fergana News, www.fergananews.com/article.php?id=7116.

32 "Iz teksta sekretnoy depeshi v Washington" [From the Text of a Secret Dispatch to Washington] 05 Tashkent 001271, July 22, 2009, *Komsomol'skaya Pravda*, September 29, 2011.

33 A. Knyazev, "Dorozhnaya Karta Putina: Vperedi Tashkent" [Putin's Road Map: Tashkent Is Ahead], RIA Novosti, June 4, 2012, www.ria.ru/analytics/20120604/664520104-print.html.

34 "Tashkent stal blizhe" [Tashkent Has Gotten Closer], *Rossiyskaya Gazeta*, June 19, 2012.

35 Elena Ionova, "Razvitie rossiysko-uzbekskikh otnosheniy" [The Development of Russian-Uzbek Relations], *Rossia i novye gosudarstva Evrazii* [Russia and the New States of Eurasia] (Moscow), no. 3 (2011): 82.

36 "Lukoil Investiruyet v Uzbekistan Okolo $5,5 mlrd—Putin" [Lukoil Invests Around $5.5 Billion in Uzbekistan—Putin], June 5, 2012, http://uzdaily.uz/articles-id-11300.htm.

37 Omar Sharifov, "Myortvaya Petlya Dlya TAPOiCh" [Vertical Loop for Tashkent Aviation Production Association (TAPOiCH)], Fergana International News Agency, November 15, 2010, www.fergananews.com/articles/6798.

38 Viktor Litovkin, "ODKB dlya Tashkenta—prokhodnoy dvor" [The CSTO Is a Revolving Door for Tashkent], *Nezavisimaya Gazeta*, July 2, 2012.

39 It is very revealing that on the eve of withdrawal from the CSTO, Uzbekistan refused to allow military equipment to pass through its territory from Kazakhstan for participation in the SCO's "Mission of Peace—2012" military exercise (the equipment was finally sent to Tajikistan through Kyrgyzstan, bypassing Uzbekistan), underscoring Uzbekistan's reluctance to participate in multilateral cooperation.

40 "Islam Karimov v Kitae Podpisal Bolee 40 Kontraktov na Obshchuyu Summu $5,2 milliarda" [Islam Karimov Signed More Than 40 Contracts Worth $5.2 Billion in China], Regnum, June 8, 2012, www.regnum.ru/news/1539966.html.

41 "Ob'yom Kitayskikh Investitsiy v Uzbekistan Prevyshayet $4 mlrd" [Chinese Investments in Uzbekistan Exceed $4 Billion], Rosbalt News, July 30, 2012, www.rosbalt.ru/exussr/2012/07/30/1016790.html.

42 Paul Kubicek, "Regionalism, Nationalism and Realpolitik in Central Asia," *Europe-Asia Studies* (Glasgow) 49, no. 4 (1997): 639.

43 "Kyrgyzstan and Uzbekistan: The Tactics of Survival," 5.

CONCLUSION

1 Dmitri Trenin, *True Partners? How Russia and China See Each Other* (Moscow: Centre for European Reform and Carnegie Moscow Center, 2012), 29.

2 A. Cranston, "Out of Focus: US Policy Toward Central Asia," *Harvard International Review* 15, no. 3 (1993); G. E. Fuller, "Central Asia: The New Geopolitics: Prepared for the Under Secretary of Defense for Policy" (Santa Monica: Rand Corporation, 1992); N. Lubin, "Dangers and Dilemmas: The Need for Precedent Policy Toward Central Asia," *Harvard International Review* 15, no. 3 (1993); N. MacFarlane, *Western Engagement in the Caucasus and Central Asia* (London: The Royal Institute of International Affairs, 1999); *Central Asia and the New Global Economy*, ed. B. Rumer (New York: M.E. Sharpe, Inc., 2000); *Thinking Strategically: The Major Powers, Kazakhstan and the Central Asian Nexus*, ed. R. Legvold (Cambridge Mass.: American Academy of Arts and Sciences, 2003).

3 Murat Laumulin, *Tsentral'naya Azia v zarubezhnoy politologii i mirovoy politike* [Central Asia in International Political Science and Global Policy], vol. 2 (Almaty: Kazakstan Institute for Strategic Studies (KISI), 2006), 276; Mekhman Gafarly, "Gosdep SShA initsiiruet 'smenu vlasti' v Kyrgyzii i Kazakhstane" [U.S. State Department Initiates a Regime Change in Kyrgyzstan and Kazakhstan], *Novye Izvestia*, March 11, 2003; Aleksandr Knyazev, *Vektory i paradigmy kyrgyzskoy nezavisimosti* [The Directions and Paradigms of Kyrgyzstan's Independence] (Bishkek: Obshchestvenny Fond Aleksandra Knyazeva, 2012), 155.

4   N. J. Jackson, "The Role of External Factors in Advancing Non-liberal Democratic Forms of Political Rule: A Case Study of Russia's Influence on Central Asia," *Contemporary Politics* 16, no. 1 (March 2010): 101.

5   Anders Åslund, *Russia's Capitalist Revolution: Why Market Reform Succeeded and Democracy Failed* (Washington, D.C.: Peterson Institute for International Economics, 2007), 264–65.

6   Andrey Grozin, "Postsovetskaya Tsentral'naya Azia: novye geopoliticheskie tendentsii i rossiyskie interesy" [Post-Soviet Central Asia: New Geopolitical Tendencies and Russia's Interests], *Tsentral'naya Azia i Kavkaz*, no. 5 (2007): 59.

7   "Rogozin otvetil golodayushchim v Ulyanovske: 'Net nikakoy bazy NATO. Pro neyo govoryat provokatory i idioty'" [Rogozin Has Replied to the Hunger-Strike Participants in Ulyanovsk: "There Is No NATO Base. The Only People Talking About It Are Provocateurs and Idiots"], Newsru.com, April 10, 2012, www.newsru.com/russia/10apr2012/ulianov.html.

8   Quoted from Muzafar Rizoev, "Kogda v sosedyakh Afghanistan" [When Afghanistan Is Among Your Neighbors], *Oazis*, no. 19, 159 (October 2011): 4.

9   Iskander Asadullaev and Bobokul Muminov, "Neoyevraziystvo—vzglyad iz Tajikistana" [Neo-Eurasianism—A View From Tajikistan] in *Problemy modernizatsii i bezopasnosti gosudarstv Tsentral'noy Azii i Rossiyskoy Federatsii v novykh geopoliticheskikh usloviyakh* [Modernization and Security Issues for the Central Asian States and the Russian Federation Under New Geopolitical Conditions] (Dushanbe: 2011), 179.

10 Gennadiy Chufrin, *Rossia v Tsentral'noy Azii* [Russia in Central Asia] (Almaty: 2010), 13.

11 United Nations Office on Drugs and Crime, *World Drug Report 2013*, May 2013, 30–31, www.unodc.org/unodc/secured/wdr/wdr2013/World_Drug_Report_2013.pdf.

12 Adrian Pabst, "Novaya bol'shaya igra v Tsentral'noy Azii" [The New Great Game in Central Asia], *Mir peremen* [World of Changes], no. 3 (2010): 165.

13 Igor Ivanov, "What Diplomacy Does Russia Need in the 21st Century?" *Russia in Global Affairs*, no. 4 (October/December 2011).

INDEX

between Uzbekistan
and Russia, 210
economic recession, in
Tajikistan, 156–160
economic situation, in
Kyrgyzstan, 129–131
energy, abundance in
Kazakhstan, 112–114
energy prices, 46
energy reserves
in Turkmenistan, 184
of Uzbekistan, 202
energy resources, in
Turkmenistan, 183–188
energy transit routes, Central
Asia providing for Russia, 1
energy transit sector, not possible to
continue with the status quo in, 5
energy-related products,
transit of, 227–228
Engvall, Johan, 129–130, 147
environmental challenges,
in Uzbekistan, 205
"Epoch of Renaissance," in
Turkmenistan, 180
ethnic and linguistic exception,
Tajikistan as, 149–150
ethnic enclaves, within the borders
of Uzbekistan's neighbors, 214
ethnic groups, principle of
coexistence among, 132
ethnic nationalism, factor potentially
leading to destabilization, 134
ethnic nationalism and religion,
in Kazakhstan, 108–109
ethnic Russians, Moscow unable
to protect interests of, 3
Eurasian Commission,
supranational, 122

Eurasian Economic Commission, 51
Eurasian Economic Community
(EurAsEC), 40, 43, 53–55, 60, 73
Eurasian Integration Project, 48–49
Eurasian Party of Russia, 18
Eurasian Union, 2, 44, 218
benefiting Russia most of all, 50–51
compared to EurAsEC, 53–54
establishment of, 17, 49
expanding, 50
as it exists today, 49
Kazakhstan's stance
remaining pragmatic, 122
not having much impact at
the regional level, 50
positive view of by Kyrgyzstan, 137
pursuing integration, 121
Russia actively promoting, 162
Eurasian vision, 16, 17
Eurasianism
compared to Pan-Turkism, 225
convenient ideology for Russia
and Kazakhstan, 17–18, 121
recurrent discussion about, 101
Europe, visions of Central Asia, 101
European countries, in a
dialogue with Islamists, 85
European Union, 40, 89
external challenges, faced by
Russia in Central Asia, 217
external parties, Russia seeking
to diminishing, 223
extremism
emergence of, 226
facing various forms of, 111
migration's role in
spreading, 91–100
extremist organizations,
adherents to, 135

no chance of succeeding
in Uzbekistan, 202
not destabilizing political
situation in Russia, 91
posing a threat to Russia's
allies, 85–86
presence and increasing
influence of, 82
Islamization
intensifying with time, 78
an irreversible process
in Tajik society, 77
of migrants, 98
Rahmon's declared policy, 154
resulting in the spread of
religious radicalism, 226

J

Jogorku Kengesh (Parliament), 76
Jund al-Khilafah terrorist group, 106
Jundullah (Allah's warriors)
organization, 83
Justice and Development Party,
Turkey's moderate Islamist, 90
Justice Social Democratic Party
of Uzbekistan "Adolat," 194

K

Kabiri, Muhiddin, 100, 153–154
Kadyrov, Ramzan, 25, 154, 183
Karimov, Islam, 36, 51, 56,
76, 139, 140, 212
accustoming Moscow to
turns in his policies, 209
actively promoting religion
and religious activities, 77

adopting a wait-and-see
attitude, 206
as America's key Central Asian
partner in the war on terrorism, 206
brutal show of force to
suppress an uprising, 21
on Collective Security Treaty
Organization (CSTO), 208
concluded that Moscow
would not and could not
come to the rescue, 211
distributed personal benefits
to foreign companies, 204
eliminated any potential
opposition, 194
leading Uzbekistan after, 193
memorials to victims of the
"Russian colonial regime," 27
merged nationalism and Islam
into an official ideology, 201
opposed Muslim xenophobia, 201
on Russian and Belarusian
plans to form a union, 10
strict control over Islam, 78
Kazakh language, gradually
acquiring status, 108
Kazakh elite, never completely
abandoned religious identity, 80
Kazakh Islamists, established
"working contacts" with
Muslim Russian citizens, 106
Kazakh ruling class, Eurasianism
providing a foundation for, 17
Kazakh soldiers, in Kyrgyzstan, 139
Kazakh territory, gas transiting, 113
Kazakhgate, 247n36
Kazakhstan
Baikonur space launch center in, 58

challenge to Russia, 218–224
challenges of canceling
out Chinese, 222
China as other major player, 222
closer ties with Uzbekistan,
206–209
CSTO as an obstacle, 56
in a dialogue with Islamists, 85
failure to sow seeds of
democracy, 221
filling void resulting from
Russia's waning influence, 6
former Soviet Air Force
base and, 192
GDP of, 229
greater rapprochement with, 205
increasing financial aid to the
Tajik government, 160
Kyrgyzstan and, 141–142
military bases challenging Russia's
authority and prestige, 224
military presence irritating
Moscow, 61
most important foreign
investor in Kazakhstan, 51
Muslim countries presenting
a challenge to, 225
no clear position on the CEA, 52
not setting any conditions
for providing military and
technical assistance, 207
offering used military
equipment after withdrawal
from Afghanistan, 58
planning to double
military aid, 6, 166
preparing professional
diplomats, 230

presence acting as a restraining
force on Islamic radicals, 69
promising to help modernize
local economies, 219
relations with, 205–2012
remaining suspicious of
Uzbekistan, 206
satisfaction with pace of
democratization in Kyrgyzstan, 221
security in Central Asia, 223
supporting cross-border
irrigation projects, 40
supporting diversification
of energy routes, 89
Tajikistan relations with, 165–167
visions of Central Asia
as a Soviet relic, 101
United Tajik Opposition
(UTO), 33, 77, 150
urbanization, in Turkmenistan, 171
U.S. Agency for International
Development, 219
U.S. Congress, resuming arms
supplies to Uzbekistan, 207
U.S. Department of State, focused on
problems of democratization, 219
U.S. dollar, rejecting as an
international currency, 63
U.S. government, divergent
interests among different
agencies within, 219
U.S.-Afghan agreement, providing
for establishment of four additional
U.S. military bases, 87
U.S./NATO presence, in Central
Asia continuing, 87
"usurpation of power," in
Tajikistan, 155

GLOSSARY

A

Akramiya
An Islamist organization formed by Akrom Yoʻldoshev. The organization broke away from Hizb ut-Tahrir in 1996.

B

Basmachi movement
(From the Russian word "baskinji" or attacker); name of the resistance movement that fought for the liberation of Central Asia from the Bolsheviks.

BRICS
Association of five emerging economies (Brazil, Russia, India, China, and South Africa). It was originally known as BRIC before South Africa was included.

C

Common Economic Area (CEA)
An integrated economic space including Belarus, Kazakhstan, Russia, and Ukraine.

Commonwealth of Independent States (CIS)
A regional organization comprising the former republics of the Soviet Union. The nine states are Armenia, Azerbaijan, Belarus, Kazakhstan, Kyrgyzstan, Moldova, Russia, Tajikistan, and Uzbekistan.

Collective Rapid Reaction Force (CRRF)
A joint combined arms task force created in 2009 comprising independent military units from the Collective Security Treaty Organization member states.

Collective Security Treaty Organization (CSTO)
An intergovernmental military alliance established in 1992. Its members are Armenia, Belarus, Kazakhstan, Kyrgyzstan, Russia, and Tajikistan.

D

Duma
The Russian parliament.

E

Eid al-Adha (Kurban-Bayram)
An Islamic holiday marking the end of the *hajj*, which is celebrated approximately seventy days after the month of Ramadan. It commemorates Abraham's willingness to sacrifice his son as an act of obedience to God.

Eurasian Economic Community (EurAsEc)
Customs union established in 1996. Its members are Belarus, Kazakhstan, Kyrgyzstan, Russia, Tajikistan, and Uzbekistan (suspended). Armenia, Moldova, and Ukraine have observer status.

F

fatwa
A legal opinion based on sharia law, offered by an Islamic religious leader.

fiqh
Islamic jusprudence.

G

GUAM Organization for Democracy and Economic Development
A regional organization of four post-Soviet states: Georgia, Ukraine, Azerbaijan, and Moldova, which later became GUUAM after Uzbekistan joined.

H

hadith(s)
(Meaning "news" or "story"); stories about the words and deeds of Prophet Muhammad that relate the different religious-legal sides of Muslim life. The hadiths are considered the second source of the Islamic law after the Quran.

hajj
Pilgrimage to Mecca.

Hanafi school of Islam
The oldest of the four *mazhabs* (schools of law) in jurisprudence within Sunni Islam. It was founded by Imam Abu Hanifa (d. 767).

hatib
Islamic preacher who delivers the sermon at Friday prayer. A *hatib* is usually, but not always, the imam. As the prayer leader, he must be a male who has reached puberty.

hijab
A veil that Muslim woman wear outside of their homes.

Hizb ut-Tahrir (HTI)
Islamist political party whose goal is to reestablish the caliphate within the Muslim world.

I

imam
(Derived from the word *amma*, to stand ahead of or lead); the head of a Muslim community, leads prayers in a mosque.

Islamic Movement of Uzbekistan (IMU)
A militant Islamist group formed in 1991 by Tohir Yo'ldosh with the goal of creating an Islamic state under sharia.

J

Jogorku Kengesh
The Parliament of Kyrgyzstan.

jüz
A traditional territorial association (Kazakhstan).

K

kishlak
Village

M

madrasa
A Muslim religious school.

mahalla
A neighborhood community within a city.

Majlis
Parliament of Kazakhstan.

mazhab(s)
A school of jurisprudence.

mufti
A religious leader who issues fatwas; expert on Sharia who provides detailed explanation of its basic provisions and resolves disputes on its principles and precedents.

mullah
An Islamic cleric.

murid
A Sufi disciple or student.

O

Oliy Majlis
The Uzbek parliament.

Q

Quran
Holy Book of Islam.

R

"Ruhnama" (The Book of the Soul)
A book written by Saparmurat
Niyazov, late president of
Turkmenistan. It was considered
mandatory reading in the country
during Niyazov's rule.

S

Salaf
The practice of formal worship in
Islam and one of the five pillars of
Islam.

Salafi(s)
(based on the Arabic word salaf for
"ancestors"/"predecessors"); a follower
of the Salafi movement of Islam. This
movement calls for the return to the
use of the Quran and the Sunna as the
only sources for religious rulings. Its
core objectives were to restore Islam to
its pristine form.

**Shanghai Cooperation
Organization (SCO)**
Eurasian security organization
founded in 2001 in Shanghai by
the leaders of China, Kazakhstan,
Kyrgyzstan, Russia, Tajikistan, and
Uzbekistan.

sharia
The religious law of Islam.

T

TAPI (Trans-Afghanistan) pipeline
A proposed natural gas pipeline
linking Turkmenistan, Afghanistan,
Pakistan, and India.

Tulip Revolution
First Kyrgyz revolution that overthrew
President Askar Akayev and his
government in 2005.

U

ulama
The plural of "alim," meaning
"scholar"; local class of clerics.

umma
The Muslim community.

W

Wahhabism
A more conservative form of Islam
practiced in Saudi Arabia, and a
popular term used for Islamists and
extremists in much of the press. The
movement derives its name from
its founder Muhammad ibn Abd
al-Wahhab Tamimi (1703–1792).

ABOUT THE AUTHOR

ALEXEY MALASHENKO is the co-chair of the Carnegie Moscow Center's Religion, Society, and Security Program.

Malashenko also taught at the Higher School of Economics from 2007 to 2008 and was a professor at the Moscow State Institute of International Relations from 2000 to 2006. From 1976 to 1982 and again from 1986 to 2001, Malashenko worked at the Institute of Oriental Studies at the Russian Academy of Sciences as a research fellow, head of the Islamic Department, and finally as senior associate. In 1990, he was also a visiting professor at Colgate University in New York. From 1982 to 1986, he was editor of the journal *Problems of Peace and Socialism*.

Malashenko is a professor of political science as well as a member of the RIA Novosti advisory council. He serves on the editorial boards of the journals *Central Asia and the Caucasus* and *Acta Eurasica* and the newsletter *Russia and the Muslim World* and is a board member of the International Federation for Peace and Conciliation.

Malashenko is the author and editor of about twenty books in Russian, English, French, and Arabic, including: *Islam in Central Asia* (Garnet Publishing, 1994), *Russia's Restless Frontier* (with Dmitri Trenin; Carnegie Endowment for International Peace, 2004), *The Islamic Alternative and the Islamist Project* (Carnegie Moscow Center and Ves Mir, 2006), *Russia and Islam* (Carnegie Moscow Center and ROSSPEN, 2007), and *My Islam* (ROSSPEN, 2010).

CARNEGIE ENDOWMENT FOR INTERNATIONAL PEACE

The Carnegie Endowment for International Peace is a unique global network of policy research centers in Russia, China, Europe, the Middle East, and the United States. Our mission, dating back more than a century, is to advance the cause of peace through analysis and development of fresh policy ideas and direct engagement and collaboration with decisionmakers in government, business, and civil society. Working together, our centers bring the inestimable benefit of multiple national viewpoints to bilateral, regional, and global issues.